THE HUMANITY OF MEDICINE:
THE STORY OF MARK E. ELLIS, MD

A Journey from Boyhood to Manhood and Cancer Patient to Cancer Doctor.

LYNN HAMILTON ELLIS

BIOGRAPHY

Lynn Hamilton Ellis grew up in New Jersey and graduated from Wake Forest University in 1975 with a Bachelor of Arts degree in English. She spent most of her professional career as an administrative director in cancer care, retiring in 2009 to embark on a new career as a writer. The *Humanity of Medicine* is her first book, inspired by her late husband of thirty-five years with whom she worked beginning in 1993. Sharing his vision of the integration of complementary therapies such as music therapy, massage therapy, pet therapy, nutritional counseling, guided imagery, social family services, hospice, and patient/family education, with traditional state of the art cancer care therapies, she helped her husband create his patient-centered dream practice as an oncologist, integrating all services under one roof. With the backing of the health system, she helped to establish an endowment fund to continue to integrate the complementary services for each cancer patient at no charge to the patient or to the patient's insurance company. Following her husband's death, the endowment fund was renamed in Mark's honor to be called the Mark E. Ellis, MD Cancer Care Endowment Fund. All of the proceeds from this book will be donated to regional cancer care programs who practice cancer care in accordance with Mark's vision. These programs include, but are not limited to, the Mark E. Ellis, MD Cancer Care Endowment Fund, Hospice House and Support Care of Williamsburg, and Wake Forest University Medical School. For more information regarding the programs, please see below:

Mark E. Ellis, MD Cancer Care Endowment Fund
Riverside Health System Foundation
701 Town Center Dr. Ste 1000
Newport News, VA 23606
757-534-7070
www.riversideonline.com/Foundation

Hospice House and Support Care of Williamsburg
www.williamsburghospice.org

Wake Forest University Medical School
www.wakehealth.edu

For Lisa, Mark Jr. and Robert

To the memory of their father, Mark Edward Ellis, MD.

And to all of his patients.

THE HUMANITY OF MEDICINE

Lynn Hamilton Ellis

CONTENTS

    "It was an epiphany. It was cancer. It was 'Hey Jude.'"*
                                        'Hey Jude,' The Beatles

    "Little League, Swim-team, and Christmas"

    "Sons of the Rising Sound"

    "I'm sorry man. I swear to God I thought you had a horsefly
    on your back."

* Used by permission. See copyright acknowledgments.

Note to Reader

The following story was written when Mark was robustly healthy and very much alive; hence the verb tenses and references to "present day" life. I invite you to figuratively don the socks and shoes of the boy who became Mark E. Ellis, MD, and experience his remarkable life just as it evolved for him. . .and consequently, for me.

INTRODUCTION

In all journeys, there is a beginning and an ending. You begin at point A and go to point B. During a future conversation with any random person, you are undoubtedly asked a simple question about one of your past journeys such as, "Where did you grow up?" or "Why did you want to be a teacher?" You might answer something like, "I grew up in New Jersey," or "I decided to become a teacher because I always loved kids." The simple statement sounds like a direct route: point A to point B. But nobody's life is that direct or that simple. There is so much living that goes on between point A and point B.

I have known Mark for a long time, and in all the time that I have known him, he has been committed to being a doctor or becoming a doctor. I met him when he was twenty-two; I was nineteen and waiting for some answers about where life would or should lead me. I was twenty and still waiting when I asked him a simple question during a dinner conversation on our first date. "Why do you want to be a doctor?" In response, he told me his story, and since that night, I have always wanted to write it down.

Of course, his story was inspirational enough way back then, when it just went from point A to point B. It doesn't stop at point B anymore. Both the story and his ability to inspire continued as the years went by. Point A led to point B, and then C led to D; I led to We, and We led to. . .Z, wherever Z turns out to be.

CHAPTER 1

THE DECISION

Mark has always maintained that his decision to become a doctor was an easy one. Furthermore, he can pinpoint the exact date on which it was made: September 21, 1968. He was eighteen years old and lying in a hospital bed at Baptist Hospital in Winston-Salem, North Carolina. As a patient, he found himself surrounded by medical personnel, and he both observed and reaped the benefits of their compassion, their intelligence, their dedication, and their spirit of cooperation.

Attending him were Dr. David Kelly, the neurosurgeon, and Dr. Richard Janeway, the neurologist. In addition, there were the nurses and the nursing assistants and the techs and the volunteers and the medical students and the residents, and he was struck, as he put it, by the humanity of medicine.

Actually, the first two things that I remember upon waking up in the intensive care unit with my head all bandaged are very specific: the urinary catheter and the absence of a TV. I wanted the catheter out because it hurt, and I wanted a TV so I could watch the game.

Wake Forest's second football game of the season was scheduled to be at home against Clemson, and it was going to be the first Wake Forest University football game ever televised. Groves Stadium was brand new and had just opened the week before with the Demon Deacons of Wake Forest losing to the Wolfpack of North Carolina State.

Fluctuating between begging and demanding, the young patient managed to gain Dr. Kelly's consent to remove the catheter and admit him to a regular room where he knew he would find a television. Because the TV in his new room didn't work, his father "went out somewhere in Winston-Salem" and rented one so that his critically ill son could watch the game. While Mark was waiting, his younger brother, looking for some subtle way to find out if his older sibling could still think clearly, asked him if he had heard the new Beatles song. Mark was a Beatles fanatic; the Beatles were (and still are) his happy music. He told him "no," and asked to have his radio brought to the hospital.

The radio was one of those little handheld black transistor radios that were popular in the sixties, and he kept it under his pillow, attached to his ear with an earpiece, so that he would not miss an opportunity to hear the new release. But it wasn't until later that week, after everyone had gone, that he heard it. In the wee hours of the morning, when his room was dark and silent, he was feeling very much alone, when from the radio came Paul McCartney's voice singing *Hey Jude.*

He was forever changed. For the remainder of his hospital stay, he kept the radio on every second so that he could hear the song over and over again, as often as the radio station played it. Not only did he immediately love the song, but the idea of taking a sad situation and making it better, would become the theme of his life. He had just survived an operation to have a cancerous tumor the size of an orange removed from his brain. The tumor was malignant melanoma, and his prognosis was terminal. For some reason the prognosis never sank in; in Mark's words, "That was probably a good thing."

As far as his decision to become a doctor, the inspiration was strong. "It was an epiphany. It was cancer. It was *Hey Jude.*"

I didn't know then just how important my decision to go to Wake Forest University in Winston-Salem, North Carolina,

had been, how important being at that particular geograph-
ical location at that particular time in my life was.

He didn't know that he had a fifty percent chance of surviving the operation itself. He didn't know he had a zero percent chance of long-term survival due to the type of brain tumor he had. He didn't know that people with such poor statistics were not usually surgical candidates.

All the doctors knew. It was at the neurology grand rounds preceding the September 20 operation, where two young bucks, undaunted by the statistics, fought their peers to earn the decision to operate on an eighteen-year-old, brand new, Wake Forest freshman kid named Mark Ellis, hospital number 4759976.

Dr. Janeway and Dr. Kelly, with both their passion and their
expertise, saved my life at Baptist Hospital in Winston-Salem,
North Carolina. Had I been anywhere else in the world under
anyone else's care, different decisions would have been made,
and the outcome could have been very different.

To this day, Mark still doesn't really know why he chose to go to Wake Forest in the first place, and he certainly didn't know then. He had been accepted to several schools, among them Brown, Gettysburg, Maryland, Western Maryland, and Wake Forest. He lost his application to Cornell and ended up not applying. He toured Brown when it was raining (an automatic "death blow" in his mind). Maryland was too close to home. He had a partial football scholarship at Western Maryland, but his girlfriend's brother went to Gettysburg and really seemed to like it, and he thought he would probably go there. He had never even laid eyes on Wake Forest, but during a visit to his relatives in Greensboro in April of 1968, he had a conversation with his Uncle Howard that went something like:

"So, you got into Wake Forest and you're not going
to go?"
"No, I think I'm going to go to Gettysburg."

"You know, Wake Forest is a pretty good school."
"Yeah."
"Ever been to the campus?"
"No."
"It's right down the road, 'bout 20 minutes or so."
Silence.
"So, you mean you're going to turn Wake Forest down without ever seeing it?"

He and his father looked at each other, and without a word climbed into the car and headed for Winston-Salem. The unintended drive seemed the lesser of two evils.

Much to his surprise, he fell in love with the campus immediately. It was a beautiful warm spring day. Classes were in session, and students were lying on the grass reading or sunning or throwing Frisbees.

> *Everywhere we went, students said hi. We walked up to the quad, and we must have looked a little lost, because a student came up to us and asked if he could help us. We explained that we were just looking around, asked him where the gym was located, had a nice conversation, and said goodbye.*

A short time later, they stopped in at the gym to investigate Mark's possibility for being a walk-on to Wake's football team. The football coach was not available, but they did meet the swim team coach who told them that football practice was getting ready to start in the field next to the gym, and they would be welcome to watch.

> *The first person I recognized on the field was the guy who had stopped to help us on the quad. He turned out to be the quarterback. I thought, what an amazing place. People are so open and friendly. If the quarterback of the football team can take the time to speak to a prospective freshman walking around the campus with his old man, this place must be pretty special.*

It just felt right.

Thanks, Howard.

On September 27, seven days after his operation, Mark went home to recuperate, home to his girlfriend, home to DC, home to familiarity. His unusual freshman orientation over, he left Wake Forest and the freshman football team and the weird looks from new suite mates, and he was happy..... . .happy to have a legitimate reason to leave.

He had no idea that he would face medical decisions concerning chemotherapy, which was experimental at the time. He had no idea that he had "mets"–metastases–from the cancer in his lung and chest wall near his heart. He had no idea that he would choose to return to Wake Forest where he would beat the odds, accomplish his goal, and where he had yet to meet his future wife.

The one thing about which he was absolutely certain, was that his life had direction and purpose because he now knew without a doubt what he wanted to be. The decision to become a doctor had been made. He didn't know how long and winding that road would be or where it would lead, but he knew that his feet had been set upon that path in Baptist Hospital on that September day.

CHAPTER 2

Growing Up

Mark's childhood is lovingly documented in a typical manner, with snapshots, a partially kept baby book, and an eight-millimeter movie camera. Artistically recorded is another piece of documentation: a framed shadow box containing his baby spoon and the hospital bill for his birth. (He cost $146.50.) According to the living testimony recorded for posterity on movie film, his family who consisted of his mother Jeanne, his father Charlie, his younger brother Stevie, and their dog Greta lived wonderfully middle class lives to an observer such as myself, who did not know the family back then. As was pretty standard for families laying down tape to be enjoyed years down the road, three main activities repeatedly light up the screen each year from the late fifties through the mid-sixties: Little League, swim-team, and Christmas.

Charlie, dark-haired, active, and robust, is seen coaching the boys' Little League teams year after year, and their uniforms get a little bigger each year as Mark and Stevie grow. Attractive, blond, and stylish, Jeanne, who is "Jeannie" to Mark's dad, is always pictured at Christmas time waving to the camera, as the two boys open presents in their pajamas. Greta, the Doberman, in her beautiful auburn tuxedo, is always romping. They all warmly remember Greta as having been funny, friendly, and athletic, and true to their description, the films show her in the midst of all the neighborhood kids as she navigates several deep winter snows in tireless deer-like leaps.

Then there are the multiple seasons of swim-team, where freckle-faced Mark, sporting sandy-colored, curly hair, and olive-skinned Stevie, with light brown, sun-bleached hair, perform for the camera in teeny-weeny bathing suits, which do not seem to grow, regardless of the boys' growth. Not only is the competitive swimming caught on film, but several antics are also frozen in time. The diving board is a platform for more than one stuck-out tongue or waggling posterior as a precursor to a spectacular jump into the water where the young stars are then lost from view. Their yearly march to manhood is more than well preserved in those silent flicks.

During the high school years, an attempt was made to capture on film their football careers, a major part of their high school lives. Mark's number was twenty-two, and since Steve is three years his junior, by the time he entered the three-year high school, the number twenty-two was available again. His number was also twenty-two in high school. Although they are seen several times zig-zagging their way down the field, their boasts of athleticism borne out, both boys complain that it is the football itself that is actually filmed during every play. The pigskin is literally followed into the air by the camera lens where its fate is lost forever, the flight, as captured by the cameraman, sometimes causing that eye-to-stomach sensation known as nausea. The half-time performance of the marching band is also immortalized at every game, without the audio of course, since all home movies were silent in those days. The band never played to a more appreciative audience than to the man behind the camera, Charlie Ellis.

Mark characterizes his life as "pretty normal" growing up. The Ellis Family lived in Oxon Hill, Maryland, a suburb of Washington, DC. Charlie worked for the Navy at the Pentagon, and Jeanne was a secretary in the guidance department at the Oxon Hill Junior High. They had met in Greensboro, North Carolina, Jeanne's hometown, in 1945, at a dance at the army base that served as an overseas replacement depot during World War II. Charlie was in the Army and preparing to ship out where he would serve in the Pacific Theatre, on Okinawa and Japan, during the Allied Occupation.

He was originally from Watertown, Massachusetts, just outside of Boston, and had attended Dean Academy (now Dean Junior College) in Franklin, Massachusetts, and the University of Maine, where he was a member of the ROTC. As it did for many, the war interrupted his college education, and during his first semester, he was called into service. After marrying Jeanne in 1946, they returned to Maine, where Jeanne worked in the alumni office and Charlie played drums in the Maine Bears Dance Band until he graduated in February of 1950 with a degree in mathematics.

Expecting their first child, Charlie took Jeanne home to Boston where they briefly lived with his parents, while he worked as a salesman for Edison Voice Writers (dictating machines). Mark Edward Ellis was born in Mt. Auburn Hospital in Cambridge on August 7, 1950, and shortly thereafter, the family of three relocated to the Washington, DC, area, where his father accepted a civilian job as a systems' analyst for the Department of Defense at the Pentagon. Three years later, Mark had a new little brother named Stephen, and Stevie, as he was affectionately called, eventually grew into Steve.

Mark and his family have many stories about growing up which have been told and retold. Some of them have shaped his character, like the "Girl Scout thin mint" story (he ate the whole box), and the "chipping of the cement steps with a hammer" story (he was bored). Some of them are just stomach-cramping-funny stories (to us, anyway), told mostly at his dad's expense, since they are usually based on a misunderstanding due to his razor-sharp Bostonian dialect that has survived fifty years of living in the south. One of those stories would be the "Rap the Statta" story referring to a car that won't start, in which sixteen-year-old Mark confuses phone instructions from his dad to "rap" the "statta" and "wraps" the starter. . . ....with rags. And then there is the Oxon Hill legend, "Goatman," who is some kind of terrible half-man, half-goat creature who terrorizes Oxon Hill. I believe the top half is a man with two human arms situated on a two-legged goat. This guy evidently struck fear into the hearts of those who grew up in Oxon Hill, but having grown up myself in Jersey Devil country, Goatman was always hilarious to me.

I could truly write an entire book on Ellis stories alone, since there are so many, but I will tell just one in its entirety here. This story from the Ellis repertoire is from Mark's and Stevie's elementary school days and would fall into the category of character shaping.

Mark and Stevie walked to and from Oxon Hill Elementary School along Indian Head Highway each day, rain or shine. It was a rather monotonous trip to and from school, and due to that fact, various and sundry things that might otherwise have gone unnoticed piqued their interest: "like the time we found a dead chicken with a rope around its neck on the side of the road. Stevie picked up the rope, slung it over his shoulder, and dragged it all the way home." Mighty hunters they were, their fantasies fed by the passersby who yelled out of their car windows, "Caught you your dinner, did you?" and "Your mom's gonna be real proud of you hunters!" She wasn't.

One particularly wet morning when the boys were in the fifth and second grades, respectively, Mark had his hands punched down into the pockets of his yellow slicker as far as they would go. Unfortunately, only the top of his lunch bag, which was clenched in his hand, was safely traveling in the dry pocket. By the time he got to school, he had, of course, only the stub of a paper bag in his hand, having lost his lunch somewhere along the road, due to the soaking rain and his young lack of foresight. "I was really looking forward to that lunch too, because I knew it had fresh orange sections in it."

On their way home that day, the weather had cleared and—lo and behold—they found those orange sections right in front of the Oxon Hill Junior High School, which they passed everyday and where his mother worked. It just so happened that the second story windows in the junior high were open.

Stevie's excuse might have been youthful misguidance from his older brother, who was, after all, suffering from hunger, having had no lunch. But for whatever reason, the two boys thought it would be a great competition to try to toss those orange sections into the second story window from their position on the side of the road. "I'd say we had total success and won the game, if only some nosey driver hadn't seen and recognized us and called the principal of our school."

Together, both brothers were summoned by their principal the next day to his office, whereupon they admitted their competition from the previous day and were tasked with writing a letter to their parents informing them of their misdeeds. They were expected to return to the principal's office the next morning before the start of the school day with the letter signed by a parent.

Knowing that their mother worked at the school where the transgression had occurred, and knowing that the recent "kicking the can incident" (which had also occurred on Indian Head Highway on their way home from school) was still fresh in her mind (again, due to an informant), they embarked on a strategic plan never before conceived by man. "We decided to forge her signature."

It took a great deal of planning, and there were many obstacles to be overcome. First, there was the signature itself. What did it look like? How could they get her to sign her name on anything to see if they could reproduce it? There were those old letters and things on top of the refrigerator, but not being able to think of any believable reason to ask to examine them, the boys decided to wait until she was out of the room. Were they ever in luck! It was bowling night, Mark's night to baby sit Stevie.

Once they were alone, they got all the letters down, found a likely signature candidate, and set about practicing the signing of her name. "But, no matter how hard we tried, none of the forgeries looked real. Then, the thought that would save our behinds struck like a bolt of lightning—carbon paper!"

Having successfully traced her signature onto the letter of explanation in that shade of purple that only the carbon paper of the late fifties could create, the two young deceivers returned to the principal's office the following morning before the start of school to deliver the goods. The very nice secretary asked if she could help them.

When we told her why we were there, instead of accepting the letter on behalf of the principal as we had hoped, she asked us to have a seat while she went to get him. The wait damn near killed us. Finally, the principal arrived, stood behind his counter, which was eye-level to little Stevie's big brown eyes, and asked us to produce the signed letter, which we did. After scrutinizing the letter for an excruciating few seconds, he asked us if this was our mother's signature. We said, "Yes, sir." He said, "Have you boys learned your lesson?" We echoed, "Yes, sir." He said, "Very well, you may go to your classrooms now." I very nearly wet my pants.

Years later, Mark realized that the very serious expression worn by the principal the day they got away with their clandestine operation was probably an expression he had frozen onto his face to keep from laughing. Whether it was Stevie's big browns, or Mark's pale countenance, or just out of respect for their mother, the principal never told on them.

Southlawn in Oxon Hill was the first neighborhood in the DC area where the Ellis Family lived, and Mark remembers it as a friendly, close-knit community of small, neat homes that were all similar, with chain link fences in the back yards and no garages.

I remember being reluctant to leave it. Our family lived directly across the street from the Self family. Mary Ann Self and my mother became the best of friends, and our families did everything together, from shopping and movies with mothers and kids, to Little League and Redskins games with the fathers and sons. We spent many holidays together, including Christmas night at the Self house, and we even went on vacations together. Johnny Self was my best friend, and he, his brothers Dan and Mike, his sister Jo Ellen, and Steve and I, all being pretty close in age, hung around together a lot during our elementary school years. Mary Ann remained my mother's best friend even after we moved, and my mother was shattered when Mary Ann died from lymphoma in 1972.

Mark was in junior high when they moved to Riverbend. His parents had built a rancher with a carport on a nice piece of property from which you could see the Potomac. The river couldn't really be seen from the house, but if you walked to the end of the yard, you could just barely see it as a small silver ribbon off in the distance. Their piece of land sat much higher than the river and actually bordered the land that bordered the river.

> *I remember distinctly how large that one acre of land was because it was my duty as well as my brother's to rake rocks. We must have raked twenty million rocks. It was probably to help establish a lawn, but at the time, it was for no apparent reason.*

Despite the rock raking, Riverbend turned out to be a great neighborhood. Jeanne and Charlie were gregarious, and once again, the family who lived directly across the street from them produced a best friend for Mark.

> *Jimmy Spain and I went to junior high together. We went to high school together. We played football together in and out of school. We went to Redskins games together. One year, when I was in the eighth grade and Jimmy was in the seventh, we collected returnable bottles that had been discarded at construction sites and took them back to the stores to collect the deposits (as was the custom with glass soda and beer bottles in the sixties). Earning two cents for every twelve-ounce bottle, and a nickel for every quart bottle, we saved enough money to buy Redskins season tickets, $49 in 1964. We were the envy of Oxon Hill Junior High that year.*

A few years later, they would both be diagnosed with cancer, Jimmy with leukemia, and Mark with malignant melanoma. They would battle their illnesses at the same time. Jimmy had acute lymphocytic leukemia, which in the late sixties was nearly always fatal. Had Jimmy had his illness in the nineties, he would have had a greater than fifty percent chance of being cured. He was nineteen when he died.

Mark at age two. 1952

Mark and "Stevie" with parents Charley and Jeanne. 1953

Mark and "Stevie" with Greta. 1957

CHAPTER 3

The Band

The band is such an important part of Mark's past that it deserves its own chapter. Pursuit of a career in rock and roll music ranked pretty high on his list of ambitions prior to his decision to become a doctor, and the band is responsible for many of his greatest teenage memories. He never tired of telling old band stories, and one day a few years ago when we were on one of our typical jaunts to Winston-Salem to go to a Wake game, I asked him to start at the point when he first became interested in music and tell me the whole story of how the band came about in chronological order. He was only too happy to oblige, and it was a four to five-hour trip.

I first took up the guitar at the urging of my mother in 1956 when I was six years old. She thought Elvis was faaabulous, and she thought the guitar was going to become a very important instrument in popular music. I thought Elvis was ok, but I wasn't enthralled like she was. I was only six, after all.

My dad still played drums in a swing band, and a guy by the name of Brian Vance played the sax in the same band. He agreed to give me guitar lessons once a week at a small music store located near DC's Anacostia section. After three years of taking lessons, Mr. Vance told me he couldn't take me any further on the guitar, and I would need to have a new teacher. I really liked music, and I liked my teacher more than the guitar, so I asked if he could teach me to play a different instrument. He suggested the clarinet over the sax, so I put the guitar away and took up the clarinet. I even played in the junior high band.

But, *everything changed on February 9, 1964, when I saw the Beatles on the Ed Sullivan Show. Within twenty-four hours I had resurrected my old guitar and began seeking out friends who wanted to play music together. The first friend to play guitars with me was Joe Case. We mostly played from sheet music, and nobody sang. But, Joe had an older brother, and one day at his house, his older brother, who looked really cool because he had long hair like the Beatles, brought over his "band." They had electric guitars. Although they looked the part, I thought, "Yeah, right, like they're gonna sound like a real band." But, they did. They played "Tell Her No" by the Zombies, and my first thought was, "They are awesome!" My second thought was, "I can do that."*

I went out and bought an old Kay guitar and a Silvertone amp at Sears and started playing guitars with another friend, Jerry Smith. He usually played rhythm, and I played lead, and after a while, I bought a Shure microphone and began to sing. We really needed a drummer, and upon finding some of my father's old drums in the basement and setting them up on two stacks of old tires, we drafted my brother.

With a few pointers from my dad, and some demonstrations of what we were looking for, Steve essentially taught himself how to play, and soon we were ready for our first public outing. I was in the tenth grade by this time, and Steve was in the seventh.

Our first gig was a talent show being held at a local country club. We adopted Jerry's naming suggestion and competed as the Tri-Knights. We even had a go-go dancer, complete with the fringed mini-skirt and boots, who was in my brother's class. Even though we lost to a band who were younger than we were, but who had all the fancy equipment and clothes (and a bass player), we got our first paying gig from a man named Jack who had seen us perform. He booked us for two upcoming parties.

In the meantime, my mother got us our next job—the opening of a mini-golf course. The job was harmless, but the evening was not. . ....

Mark was in the eleventh grade by this time, which meant that many of his friends had driver's licenses. Several of the band's friends had come out to the new mini-golf place to hear them play, and while they putted around the eighteen holes, the Tri-Knights covered songs like "House of the Rising Sun" by the Animals and "Satisfaction" by the Rolling Stones." To celebrate the event of their second paying band job, they used the money they got paid to take everybody out for pizza.

My girlfriend, Elaine, along with a couple of her friends, my buddy Robert, a couple of other guys named Sammy and Paul, and my brother and I, all drove to a pizza place in a strip mall. As we were walking into the restaurant, a carload of guys drove by with their windows down and the radio blasting "The Lion Sleeps Tonight" by the Nylons. Sammy pointed to the car and remarked, "I really like that song." The guys whipped their car around, jumped out, and confronted Sammy, demanding, "What did you say?" Sammy repeated what he had said when the first group of guys was suddenly joined by a second group.

Now, Sammy was a pretty big guy, as were Robert and Paul. But the two groups outnumbered the band group by about three or four guys. Realizing that a gang was jumping us, we told the girls to run into the restaurant. Swinging to defend ourselves, we moved toward the restaurant where the people inside were horrified. The last one through the door was Sammy. Robert and I had a hold of him around his waist while the hoods outside had a firm grip on both of his arms, each arm being pulled in a different direction, leaving his face terribly vulnerable. Before we could pry Sammy all the way inside, one of the gang members just hauled off and kicked him in the face, breaking his jaw.

He was taken to the hospital while the gang drove off. Fortunately, a jeweler, who had stayed in his store after closing to work, saw the entire incident, wrote down the license plate numbers, and called the police. The individuals involved in the gang were tracked down, prosecuted, and forced to pay medical expenses. Sammy spent the next several weeks with his jaw wired. Meanwhile, the Tri-Knights played the first of Jack's two parties.

Jack was purportedly a lobbyist and held parties at his penthouse apartment in Arlington, VA, from time to time. The first party was pretty benign. The crowd was fairly small and we had a great time playing and got paid fifty dollars.

Between the parties, the Tri-Knights recruited a bass player, Art Weston, which meant they were going to need a new name since there were now four band members. Ideas come to creative people from the darndest places. In this case, the idea for the new name of the band came to Steve from the *Prince Valiant** comic strip. At the end of each edition of *Prince Valiant*, the newspaper would run a small blurb about the upcoming installment. One of the upcoming installments used the words "midnight sun," and Steve took his naming idea to the other band members who readily adopted it.

The second of Jack's parties wasn't as small, and it got pretty rowdy. It ended with our new bass player, Art Weston, who was only fourteen, drunk, and the party being raided by the police and Jack getting hauled away. I remember being jammed into the elevator with a bunch of people, including the cops and Jack, with my guitar. When we reached the ground level, Jack yelled, "Wait, wait, I gotta pay my band." He pulled out a wad of bills and peeled off a couple hundreds and gave them to me. Art wasn't allowed to play with the band anymore, but we kept the new spelling he had come up with, The Mydnight Sonn.

The girls said we needed a keyboard player and suggested a guy by the name of Alan Creveling. He was the boyfriend of my girlfriend's best friend, Jessica. I was skeptical at first. Jerry, Steve, and I wanted someone who could play stuff like "Light My Fire," by the Doors, and we weren't sure Alan, whom we didn't know, would fit the bill. But he did. He turned out to be great. He also had a friend named Ricky Seal who just liked to hang around while we practiced. In a fairly short period of time, he taught himself how to play the bass and finally filled the hole left open by Art.

We now had five band members: Steve on drums, Ricky on bass, Alan on keyboards, Jerry on rhythm guitar, and me on lead. Ricky became our manager/ promotional agent and came up with our logo. We were the Mydnight Sonn, "Sons of the Rising Sound."

We began to get bookings for dances at junior highs, high schools, college fraternities, weddings, and the like, and by the time I was halfway through my junior year in high school, we were making some real money and had developed a pretty nice repertoire of pop songs by groups like the Beatles, Rolling Stones, and Bee Gees. However, I remember that we never seemed to have enough slow songs to suit the couples who wanted to cling to each other on the dance floor. "Unchained Melody" by the Righteous Brothers became our default slow song.

Years later, it would be the default song for the band who played at our wedding in 1976. We had chosen "In My Life" by the Beatles to be "our" song, but the singer couldn't sing it, and the band couldn't play it. As we stood on the dance floor in front of three hundred guests ready for the traditional first dance, the only song that came to our minds was "Unchained Melody." Many married years later, when the song renewed its popularity again after being the theme song for the movie *Ghost*, Mark got himself into trouble when I sweetly asked him, "What does that song remind you of?" and he replied, "Alan Creveling."

We eventually lost Jerry from the band because we felt that he no longer considered it a priority, and by the time I was a senior in high school, the other band members, excepting my brother, had finally entered high school. I guess I'm responsible for breaking up the band because I graduated from high school first and chose to go to a college several hours away.

I could fill volumes with band stories, like the time the football players at a local university crashed a fraternity party where we were playing and began to throw around stuff, like furniture and beer bottles, and we had to hide under tables for a while until they burned themselves out and left. Or, the time someone had the nerve to dance with Alan's girlfriend while we were playing a slow song. We had to do without the organ for a few songs while Alan "straightened the guy out." Or, the time my brother yelled, "Fuck you!" into the microphone just as it became live. It seems it was in response to something I had said under my breath (too bad his response wasn't under his; we were playing a job at a junior high).

I did actually write down one band story in a journal that I used to keep. I'm not sure why I picked that particular story, but. . .

The entry follows:

We were performing at a Jay-Cees party in Beltsville, Maryland. Steve had just bought a new set of black pearl Ludwig drums for about $600. So, when Alan and I had our turn at watching the equipment during a break, the drums were a primary concern. About five minutes after the break began, some drunk son of a bitch went up to admire the equipment, and before we knew what was happening, the goddamn slob fell into the new drums, and everything went crashing. Like a flash, Alan was up and running toward the guy.

"You stupid fucker, what in hell do you think you're doing?" he bellowed. A second later he was beating on the

guy, failing to realize that the drunk was about six feet three and probably weighed two hundred twenty pounds.

"Christ, Creveling, you're gonna get killed!" But he didn't pay any attention to me, or to anybody else, for that matter. At five feet ten and one hundred forty pounds, Al was flailing away, and all of a sudden we had a full-scale brawl going on.

By this time, Steve, who was with Ricky, checking out the girls at the party, realized what was going on, and he, too, jumped into what had already become a five or six man shoving, pushing, and pulling match.

When I saw that my own brother was getting his two cents worth in, I screamed "Steve, get the hell out of there!" All he could do was look sheepishly at me and say, "I can't!" He was right. The drunken son of a bitch had him by the collar and was holding him a foot off the damn ground.

I do remember that things did get back to normal with apologies abounding, and we finished the evening without further incident. But that wasn't the only time a fight was started during a band job. Nor was it the only time the band was involved. Most jobs were fairly docile. We went; we played; we looked at girls; we got paid; we left. It was fair money and a lot of fun.

My wife (to whom he is speaking right now, pretending that I am a journalist he does not know) *would never let me tell any band stories to our kids while they were growing up. She thought they were too violent. I don't know what she was thinking. At any rate, she had all the stories memorized, and I needed a new audience, so I kind of let a few slip out.* (That probably explains a few things.)

Music is still a very important part of Mark's being. He associates every instant of his life with a particular song that was popular at the time, and not just major events. A certain song might remind him of when he was driving down some specific road, or going to a sporting event, or chasing me, or eating a turkey sandwich.

Playing music has remained a hobby for him as well, and regardless of what he says, he's still pretty good. After becoming a doctor, one of his goals was to have a music room in his house. Indeed, we do, complete with several guitars, keyboards, drums, amplifiers, microphones, and thanks to one of our sons, a home recording studio. On Thanksgiving, each and every one of our twenty-five or so visiting family members is a musician. Steve can still flawlessly perform "Wipe Out" on the drums just like the Surfaris, and Charlie can still keep that swing beat. Last Thanksgiving, at the young age of eighty, he even sang. It was an old scat song called "A Good Man Is Hard To Find," and I gotta say, he was pretty awesome.

THE MYDNIGHT SONN
"SONS OF THE RISING SOUND"

Mark, singer and lead guitar. Steve, drums. Jerry Smith, rhythm guitar. Alan Creveling, keyboard. Rick Seal, bass guitar. The jackets were hunter green, the ascots black, the shirts white, and the trousers black. Photo composite pictures taken and arranged by Rick's dad, Rodger Seal. 1966

"I'M SORRY, MAN. I SWEAR TO GOD, I THOUGHT YOU HAD A HORSEFLY ON YOUR BACK."

CHAPTER 4

THE ILLNESS

As Mark has previously confessed, he used to keep a journal in his younger years. The following is an entry made by a much younger man a long time ago, when he was chronologically and psychologically much closer to his teenage years and the beginning of his illness:

It's hard to remember, now, exactly when I noticed it. The mole, that is. I seem to remember summertime at the pool and all the kids telling me I had a giant horsefly on my back. My best buddy Robert would use that as an excuse to slap me on the back, while I informed him that no, it wasn't a horsefly, just a big mole. Anyway, that's when I first began to wonder why in hell a stupid mole was causing such a commotion.

Then, in school that year, in the eleventh grade, I remember being constantly aggravated because I had difficulty trying to sit comfortably in the chairs. It felt like the mole was being rubbed off by the constant friction between it and the back of my seat as I slouched. So, I figured, what the hell, maybe I should get the damn thing taken off. It wasn't supposed to be such a bad experience – just a few hours in the hospital – no real problem. Plus, someone said that sometimes those moles can cause you real trouble if you don't watch them carefully. Well, I watched it carefully as hell for a few more months, and finally decided to get it taken off in March of my junior year at Oxon Hill Senior High.

The mole was expertly placed on the upper right side of my back, just so I could not touch it to feel how much it had grown recently. It was about three quarters of an inch in length and one quarter of an inch across; it stood off my back by about one quarter of an inch. But when our family doctor, Dr. York, referred me to a fellow named Simmons, a surgeon, I still didn't think anything was wrong – I mean, why should I?

So, Simmons got his blades and chisels together and met me at a hospital in Washington, about five miles from my house. And, before I knew it, I was removed from my mole. Simmons, a fiftyish graying, self-confident, bull of a guy, said he thought he "got it all", which is what all surgeons say when they are supposed to get it all. But, I didn't really care, because I had too many more important things to worry about.

Although I was a sprinter on the track team, I had other things on my mind that spring, besides track . . .such as girls; there is something about springtime and short skirts that has always distracted me. But, when summer came, it wasn't any different than any other Washington summer for me – hot, muggy and full of hard work. We did make it to the beach a couple of times though.

I think my dad had big ideas about my brother and me going to college. College was a place where we were expected to go after high school. Actually, it never really entered my mind that I might not go to college somewhere, because that is what everybody did, at least everybody who wanted to be "a success in life." At that point, having just finished the eleventh grade, I was not even interested in what being "a success in life" meant. I knew lots of kids, friends of mine, who either didn't have the money to go to college or just didn't want to go; but for some unexplainable cosmic reasoning, those things didn't apply to me, and I simply didn't even think of them. It was expected that I would go to college, period.

It's strange to think about it now, but I can't help wondering what would have happened to me if I hadn't gone to college to become "a success in life." Somehow, I feel robbed that I couldn't have made the decision about those four years of my life. But, just the same, the expectation that I would go to college made my life a lot easier. It kept me protected from the HARD, CRUEL, WORLD for a few more years.

So, on the assumption that I would go to college in a year, I began to look around for a place which would turn me into a "success in life," and that summer, between my junior and senior years in high school, my father and I took off and traveled all over the east coast looking at colleges. I was really impressed with Cornell University in Ithaca, NY, but later lost my application, and never applied. I also liked Villanova, Tufts, and Gettysburg, especially Gettysburg. Ultimately, the most important thing that happened on that trip emerged on the New Jersey Turnpike, leaving New York. I found a lump in my right armpit.

Before I could bat an eyelash, Dr. Simmons had his tool kit out again. I was beginning to like him, and going to the hospital for a week, I thought, wasn't so bad. Hell, the operation was a breeze, and I got all the attention I could have wanted. Everybody came, it seemed. People I didn't even know came. It was a real zoo. Only one thing kept the stay in the hospital that summer from being totally enjoyable; it was late August, which was synonymous with the words: FOOTBALL PRACTICE.

My previous two years on the football field for Oxon Hill had been anything but spectacular, but this was my

senior year, and I felt that I had a crack at the starting team, at least on defense. While the doctor insisted
that I forget about playing football, I began to plan my
comeback from surgery, fully intending to make football a
part of my senior year. After the first week of practice, me
standing on the sidelines watching my buddies win their
positions, I had to do something. Although I had only
been out of the hospital for about ten days, and was having great difficulty moving my right arm and shoulder,
I decided the least I could do was run around the track.
Still, people were starting to get to know each other; the
team was beginning to feel its way out of the dark, and I
was running furiously around the track like a damn idiot.
It was frustrating as hell.

After that week, I decided, to hell with the doctor, to hell
with the armpit. I had to start practicing or they were
going to leave me behind. On the day school started for
everybody else, and the fifteenth day of football practice, I
got my equipment and was assigned to the "green team,"
the third string. I stayed on the green team for that whole
week. Jimmy Spain, a good friend of mine who lived across
the street, and was a junior that year, was the quarterback
for the green team; so, I didn't feel too bad. The upcoming Saturday, however, we had a scrimmage, and if I was
going to make a serious bid for a starting position, I would
have to make a good showing in that scrimmage, providing they would even let me play.

Saturday came, and we scrimmaged Annapolis Senior
High School at Oxon Hill. Every year I went to Oxon Hill,
we scrimmaged Annapolis, and every year they humiliated us. That day was no exception; some guy named
Bailey ran all over us. But, I scored our only touchdown
and felt fairly sure that I was close to first string. I guess
it's a shitty thing to say, but I was very happy that day,

with the way things turned out. Only, I had one helluva blister on my foot, so I went over to Elaine's house, and she fixed it up and fed me a meal.

Actually, I had met Elaine the night before the scrimmage with Annapolis. She was a sophomore at Oxon Hill that year, and I had asked my good friend Alan Creveling to set me up with her. Alan and I, along with my brother Steve, Ricky, and Jerry had formed a band called the Mydnight Sonn. It was mainly a local rock band, not too good, but good enough to make a little money every weekend. Alan told me that he had talked to Elaine and that she seemed interested. So, the night before the Annapolis scrimmage, I went over to her house. She wasn't at all what I had expected. In fact, I found her astoundingly naïve (like myself), and incredibly attractive, like a magnet. Elaine was about five feet four inches tall and weighed a well-proportioned one hundred ten pounds, with short blond hair in a "pixie" and pretty blue eyes. Some model friend later told her that her best facial feature was her mouth, and I agree that she had a fine mouth, but it was her eyes that grabbed me. They looked at me like I was a king, but also like she knew something I didn't know.

That first night I was with her was after a bad band practice. Alan and his girlfriend, Jessica, came along for moral support, and the four of us ended up in Elaine's basement. Alan and Jessica got right down to business on the couch, and Elaine and I walked nervously around the floor, mostly sizing each other up. Before I could help myself, I kissed her, mostly for the hell of it, just to see what would happen. Everything happened.

Later, we all went to McDonald's, but Alan was the only one who ate anything; I was too excited about Elaine and the game the next day. Somehow, Elaine was something

I really needed then, even more than the satisfaction of making the first string on the football team.

Sometime during the bliss of that fall, which consisted of football games on Saturdays, school during the week, and goofing around with Elaine every spare moment, I learned a new word, "malignant." Although I knew that cancer could be benign or malignant, I couldn't see the connection of the term "malignant" to my own case. I began to think that I must have something like cancer, but certainly not the same thing. Only old people got cancer; the word sounded like it was for old, decrepit people, not young people.

I eventually realized that the mole removed from my back, biopsied as malignant melanoma, was a type of cancer. It was cancer of the melanin (pigment) producing cells (melanocytes). I also learned that the axillary (armpit) nodes removed a month or so earlier had simply been a metastasis of the primary melanoma. Even though I learned that melanoma was highly invasive, I didn't realize the urgency of that news.

To be frank, I had no idea whatsoever of the nature or prognosis of a malignant melanoma diagnosis. And what's more, I didn't care to know. It was enough at that stage to be able to say, "Hey, I've got cancer," and watch all the funny looks people would give me. It was a gas. Never during my senior year in high school did I have any idea of the seriousness of my disease, even though I had two more recurrences on my back, which were surgically excised, one during football season, and one during track season. Life was too simple to be confused by such things as cancer. I was happy in my situation, and the thought that my very life was in grave danger was no problem. I simply didn't realize it.

Since that time, I have looked back many times and have been thankful that I did not understand what "malignant melanoma" meant. If I had really known, I would have probably gone through a terrible crisis, not only in realizing and accepting the fact that I had what most doctors considered terminal cancer, but also in trying to find a way to cope with the fact that I might be dead soon. There must have been periods when I pondered death as a possibility, but those thoughts didn't affect me seriously. I was too involved with the things and people around me to have to worry about a subject which could only bring pain.

Probably, my inability to comprehend fully my medical situation was helped along by my own refusal to accept the inevitable truth. But, whatever the reason, my unknowing naivete concerning my recent medical history was a blessing, and kept me from going over the deep end before I could handle, emotionally and intellectually, the real truth.

On June 12, 1968, the senior class president of Oxon Hill Senior High sat on the stage at Cole Field House at the University of Maryland and rehearsed the words he would use to address his graduating class. He felt healthy, confident, accomplished, "As seniors, we have come so far. . ...." He knew his life was about to change; after all, he stood on the brink of adulthood. Today he would graduate from high school; he would turn eighteen on August 7; he would enter college at Wake Forest University at the end of the summer. He was ready. He felt well prepared to face the challenges that lie ahead. He would never have guessed that there was a dragon that lay sleeping but ever growing within him, who would awaken soon, very soon, a Goliath he would have to slay, or be slain himself.

Mark at the age of eighteen on duty as lifeguard. 1968

CHAPTER 5

FRESHMAN ORIENTATION

After graduating from high school and spending the summer as a janitor at the junior high, the end of August rolled around, and once again it was time for football practice, except this time it was college football. Mark headed down to Wake Forest to vie for a position on the freshman football team as a walk-on.

My dad had stuck me on a bus at midnight in DC with all of my college luggage, and I arrived in Winston-Salem at 8 a.m. and took a cab to the campus.

The first thing I had to do was have my head shaved; it was a freshman football tradition, and it was pretty traumatic. In 1968, very few kids on the college campuses still had short hair. The good thing was we did everything together. We got our heads shaved together, we ate together, we studied the plays together, we worked out together, and in general, we were pretty busy. But the walk-ons were not in the same league as the scholarship recruits, and we did not live with the rest of the jocks.

Nobody except football players had arrived at school yet. I had been assigned to Davis Dorm, and it seemed big and empty. The rest of the freshmen were due to arrive in about two weeks, with the upper classmen following the next week. Other than being hot, practice went well enough, although the players seemed a lot bigger and hit a lot harder than the ones in high school. I had been selected as an "All County" and an "All Suburban DC" football player in my senior year at Oxon Hill, and I had even set a new school record for the longest kick-off return; I had run a kick back for ninety-six yards. I knew I was fast, and I felt that I had some good experience, but I felt pretty small, physically.

After practicing for about four days, I took a pretty hard hit to my head during a practice session, and I noticed that my head was ringing. It was still ringing after practice was over. That had never happened to me before, and I really began to wonder if I was cut out for college football. I decided to talk to the coach about it the next day, and I went to see him after practice. I told him that something was wrong. He asked, "What do you mean?" I told him about my head ringing, and I told him that I had serious questions about whether or not I should play. I also told him that I was having trouble concentrating on the playbooks and concentrating in general. He was a nice guy and tried to pump me up. He said it was probably because everything was new and that he had "big plans" for me. He said I was at I-back position right now, but that he also wanted me to be a kick-return receiver due to my speed.

I think he could tell that I had pretty much made my mind up already, and he gave me an out. He told me to go back to my room and think it over, and if I decided to leave, I didn't need to tell him. If I didn't show up for practice, he would know I had left, and if I did come to practice, we didn't need to talk about it anymore. Most of the other walk-ons had already left.

The next day I boarded a bus and headed for home without even notifying my parents or my girlfriend. My short hair earmarked me as either a soldier or a freshman football player, and I was neither. I had two or three more weeks before I had to start school as a regular student, and I had no better way to spend my time than with my girlfriend back home.

The bus station was in DC. I was embarrassed at being a quitter, and I didn't want to have to call anybody for a ride. I didn't have much to carry since I had left most of my things at school in my dorm room, and I decided that it wasn't really that far to walk home to Oxon Hill. That lapse in judgment was an indication that my brain wasn't working just right, and although I knew that much, I had emotional reasons to explain it away.

I began walking. I remember walking past the Washington Post and the Washington Times building. I crossed the river and wound up in Anacostia at a Little Taverns hamburger place before I finally realized that it was too far to walk. So, I called my parents and told them I was in Anacostia, and they said, "What in the hell are you doing there?" I told them I had quit football; I felt real bad about it, but I just couldn't do it, and I needed a ride home.

From that point on, for the rest of the summer, the relationship between my father and me was strained. My father didn't seem especially pleased that I had quit football, or maybe it was the loafing around I got to do for about two weeks. He always seemed to be "on my ass." I remember being irritated by his repeated remarks to me to "wipe that smirk off your face." I didn't know what he was talking about, and I chalked it up to his displeasure at my circumstances. I was comfortable with my decision, and I was happy to have the extra time with Elaine.

The only physical problem I knew that I had was a habit I had seemed to develop whereby I felt the need to suck in the side of my mouth every so often because it felt like I was over-salivating or almost drooling. It made a slurping sound, similar to sniffing when you have a cold, and I kept resolving to quit doing it. But, it seemed that I would forget about it and then catch myself doing it again.

The weeks passed very quickly and without further incident, and on September 12, I headed back to Winston-Salem to surrender myself to Wake's freshmen orientation week, again with my short hair. "Oh, you must be a football player." "No, I quit."

I remember walking back into my room at 208 Davis and seeing a set of golf clubs and golf shoes there, and I realized that my roommate must already be at school. I had taken the bottom bunk earlier when I was there for football, and he had made up the top bunk for himself. Nobody was around, but soon he appeared with a bunch of other freshmen, who he appeared to already know. They said they were going off campus to get something to eat and invited me to go. I made the fatal mistake of declining, saying I had some stuff to do. I rarely saw him after that first day, and I was never invited to do anything with him again.

I met the other suitemates, who were all really nice guys, and we went up to the Tavern on the Green, which is an I Hop now on University Parkway. We all walked up the back way going down Faculty Drive, and I remember thinking, "This is pretty cool. I'm in college now."

There was a lot of dull orientation stuff going on, and I remember having to meet in the chapel for something. I had arrived early, and I was sitting on the aisle on the right hand side of the large main gathering area. That was the first time that I really felt like my brain wasn't working right. Having nothing else to occupy my mind while I was waiting for the rest of the students to arrive, I devised a mental counting game. I kept trying to count the rows of pews in Wait Chapel, but I kept losing count. I would count up to five or six and then get lost and think, "Was that row number five or six?" So, I would start over again. I remember thinking something is not right. Then, the program started, and I tried to put it out of my mind.

The haunting thought that something was wrong with my thinking recurred and really began to piss me off. So, sometime during the program, I took my comb out of my pocket and tried to count the teeth, just to prove to myself that nothing was wrong. I couldn't do that either. I rationalized that maybe I was tired; maybe I missed my girlfriend; and I put the comb away.

I remember leaving the program and going back to my dorm room and looking in the mirror. My face didn't look exactly right to me. I brushed my teeth, but my mouth didn't seem to work the way it had before. I was unable to prevent myself from drooling. I tried to smile in the mirror, but I was unable to get my mouth to form a smile. I also realized that I was having trouble getting my words to sound normal. My mouth was unable to form them properly. My speech sounded like I had been chewing on ice cubes, leaving my mouth too cold to form the words.

I was too scared and embarrassed to admit to anyone what was happening because I could not determine the cause. I just knew that I was "screwed up." I went to a meeting at my adviser's apartment on the edge of campus, where I didn't say a word to anyone for fear of not being able to talk right. There were other social events beginning to happen in those first few days of orientation week, like "smokers" hosted by the fraternities. I went to one smoker, and it was clear to me that those guys thought I was a loser. I mean, here I was a dork with very short hair and no football excuse, who didn't talk right and didn't smile. What were they supposed to think?

Finally, about three days into the week, there was a big cookout planned out at Lake Catherine in Reynolda Gardens. The Royal Guardsmen of "Snoopy and the Red Baron" fame were going to be there to perform, and I resolved to go to the barbecue and be friendly. I was going to beat this ridiculous situation, whatever the cause, and be myself. I would be gregarious. I would be Charlie Ellis if that's what it took. But I was not going to be this unfamiliar demented person I had suddenly become.

I walked over to the gardens with a couple of my suitem-ates; my roommate was with his other buddies. I ate some barbecue, listened to the band, talked to a few people, but I could not overcome my speech and smile difficulties. I went back to my room early.

It was Saturday night, the fourteenth of September.

On Sunday, I had my first seizure. I had been talking to Elaine on one of the phones located in Reyolda Hall at about 9 p.m. There were no phones located in the dorm rooms in those days, so access was limited. We tried to have a nice conversation, but she could tell something was wrong with the way I was talking, and she kept asking me, "What's wrong?" I came up with a list like, "I don't know. I miss you. Nobody likes me here. I wonder if this was a bad decision to come to school here. I don't like it. I'm not having any fun." Evidently, the class president, football star of Oxon Hill, lead singer in the band, was having a little trouble making friends at college. I was humiliated and depressed.

I walked back to my dorm, and I was climbing the steps that border the brick wall, next to the KA house, that lead into Davis when I first noticed that something was begin-ning to happen to my body. Just as I entered the door to my suite, I started shaking, and I remember thinking, "This is really fucking weird. I hope to God my roommate is not in the room." I fell into my bed shaking, and I don't remember exactly what happened, but I don't think I really lost con-sciousness. I know that my right arm started shaking, and eventually, the rest of my body followed suit.

I did not know that I had had a seizure, but I knew that I had had some type of episode that meant that something was undeniably wrong, and I knew it was bad. I got up and immediately went downstairs to the phone booth that was located at the bottom of the stairs, outside the dorm, in the corner of the courtyard. I placed a collect call to my father, but I couldn't communicate with the operator. She kept asking, "What are you trying to say?" and I was still trying to tell her who I was when my father answered his phone at the other end of the call. He could hear the conversation transpiring between the operator and me, and although he could not understand what I was saying, he recognized my voice. Realizing who I was and that something must be wrong, he told the operator that he would accept the charges.

He asked, "What's wrong?" and I said "Dah dah dah dah dah." He said, "Where are you?" to which I again replied something unintelligible. He said, "Go to the infirmary." I tried to say that I didn't want to, and he said, "I can't help you from here. Go to the infirmary."

I knew where the infirmary was because that's where I had gone for my football physical. I walked across the quad and down the steps to the infirmary and knocked on the door, thinking "I am either dying, or I am having a nervous breakdown." Nobody came. I tried the door. It was locked. I didn't know there was another door that was unlocked for after-hours problems, so I left. I walked back taking a route that led behind Reynolda Hall, passed by the Pit (cafeteria), and turned right.

As I was walking through the parking lot next to the administrative offices in Reynolda towards Davis, my peripheral vision picked up a beam of light reflecting off of a WFU window sticker on one of the parked cars. That beam of light attracted my eyes like a magnet, and I could not stop looking at it. I didn't know what in the world was happening. It was like I was being taken over by the aliens or something. Then, I started twitching, and I thought, "Oh no, this is going to be a repeat of whatever it was that happened to me twenty minutes or a half an hour ago."

I noticed that there were a few people walking around. It was probably about 10 p.m., and I thought, "Maybe I can get into my room unnoticed." As I headed for the steps, my head began to shake more violently, and I thought that maybe I could use the brick wall to steady my head so no one would notice. There were people ahead of me on the steps, and I started up behind them and leaned into the brick. By the time I got to the top, my head was being battered against the brick, and I was rapidly losing my vision.

Fearing that I would be noticed, I scrambled back down the steps and rolled under a large bush to hide myself from view. My head continued to jerk and finally began to slow into rhythmic jerking episodes that got slower and slower until it eventually stopped, and I remember resting my face against the cool ground. Once again, I did not lose consciousness.

I learned years later that my seizure would have been representative of a Jacksonian type of seizure, something called a Jacksonian March, where one part of the body begins to shake and the rest of the body follows. I wasn't stiff at the end of the seizure, and I never really passed out, so it wasn't a Grand Mal seizure. At the time, I knew nothing about seizures, much less that I had had two; I just lay there thinking, "What a pathetic individual you are," and I was thankful that no one had seen me.

When I was confident that the episode had passed, I got up and went back to my room. I was pretty scared by that time, and I realized that I needed help. My roommate was not there, so I knocked on the door of A Suite (I lived in D Suite), which was right across the hall from me. The guy came to the door and said, "Hey. How you doin?" I said, "Dah dah dah dah dah." Surprised, he asked, "What's wrong with you?" I said, "Dah dah dah." He immediately pulled me into his room and told me to sit down. He ordered me to, "Sit right there, and don't go anywhere." He ran out and got the RA. They tried to make me lie down, but I was resistant, and I still could not talk. I knew what I was trying to say, but I couldn't make the words come out. Recognizing that something was clearly wrong, they got somebody's car and drove me to the infirmary. Fortunately, they knew where the after-hours door was located and helped me inside.

By the time I got inside, my speech had improved somewhat. I still could not speak clearly, but I could make myself understood. There was a nurse on duty, and all of a sudden my father was on the telephone. He had called there after he had talked to me the first time, and I was just now showing up, probably about thirty minutes later. My speech was rapidly getting better, and the nurse put me on the phone to him. He asked me why I had not gone to the infirmary when he had told me to go, and I told him I had gone, but had found the door locked. He said, "Well, never mind, we'll figure that out later. What's wrong? What happened?" and I answered, "I don't know. I don't know what happened." Somehow it was determined that I would spend the night there. The nurse plugged me into an IV (I don't know why), and I slept on a stretcher all night in the infirmary, without any more episodes.

The next morning the doctor came in and talked to me, looked me over a little, and said he thought I was just a little anxious. He gave me some sedatives to take and told me to take it easy and to get some rest, and try not to get stressed. I was happy. I thought, well if that's all it is, I can get over it. My mouth still wasn't normal, but I thought maybe those symptoms would continue to improve too. He told me he wanted me to take the sedatives right away, but I told him it was registration day, and I needed to register. He insisted, so I took the medication, somehow registered, and then, the rest of Monday is lost to me. The medication was Nembutal, and it zonked me.

On Tuesday, I had to go get my books in preparation for starting classes on Wednesday. I waited in line, got my books, and on my way back to my room, I remember thinking, "I'm doing better now. I think I'm going to be all right." One of the classes I had registered for was an English class in which we were going to study John Milton. I had bought my copy of Paradise Lost, *and I decided to scan it. I opened the book and tried to read and realized that I could not keep my place. It was frustratingly similar to the counting problem I had experienced in the chapel. (I learned later that the letters I was writing to my girlfriend during this time period contained lots of uncharacteristic misspellings and partial sentences.)*

As I sat there trying to force myself to concentrate, the hall phone rang. The nurse from the infirmary was the caller, and she asked how I was doing. When I told her I was fine, she said that the doctor had set up an appointment for me to see a neurologist, whereupon I asked her, "Why?" She said he thought it was a good idea, and that the appointment was on Wednesday at Baptist Hospital. I said, "I can't do that. Classes start on Wednesday." She said that the doctor thought it was pretty important to keep that appointment and hung up.

There was no way I was going to Baptist Hospital to see anybody. I had had enough of this nonsense, and I was anxious to get started on some sort of normal routine. I walked over to the infirmary and confronted the nurse. She said she would give me a note for my professor, but that I had to keep the appointment. I left with the note in my pocket and with no intention of keeping that appointment.

That night as I lay in bed, I was thinking, "That stupid doctor's appointment is tomorrow morning, and I will have to leave right in the middle of my first class, to get to the hospital on time. I've never had economics before, and I don't want to miss my first class. I am doing better, even though my mouth is still not quite right. I'm not going to that appointment." That's when the twitching began all over again.

Fortunately, I was in bed with the lights out, and my roommate couldn't see my seizure, but I knew that I was going to have to keep that neurology appointment with a Dr. Janeway at Baptist Hospital.

The next morning, I got up and brushed my teeth, which was a big deal because I was still trying to look in the mirror and get my mouth to work right. My mouth still didn't want to behave. I went to class early so I could tell my professor that I had a doctor's appointment and had to leave. He said that was fine and to just get up and leave whenever it was time.

After depositing my books in my room, I called a cab and went outside to wait on the curb. I remember that it was a chilly gray day with a fine mist coming down, and I remember waiting for the cab wondering, "How can this be happening? Everything I have tried to do down here has gotten off on the wrong foot. I can't even manage to go to my first college class properly. How is it possible that I am having this much trouble?"

It was Wednesday, the eighteenth of September, and I had been a college student for seven days, not including the four days in August when I was a freshman football player.

I remember walking into Baptist Hospital like it was yesterday. The waiting area was in the location that would become the residents' lounge in a few years, and I would remember today every time I walked into that lounge years later. On this day in 1968, however, it was the waiting room for neurology.

I had to fill out forms at a desk, and although I was having a little difficulty writing, I managed to accomplish the task. A very nice nurse called me back into a room and began to ask me questions and write down information. She asked all the right questions.

"Are you having any twitching?"
"Yeah."
"Are you having any difficulty with speech?"
"Yeah."
"Are you having any difficulty thinking?"
"Yeah."

Whether from relief or fear, I broke down and started to cry. "Maybe," I thought, "maybe these people can help me figure out what's wrong with me." She was very comforting. She put her arm around me and walked me into another room to see the doctor. Dr. Janeway appeared. Robust and handsome, he was the kind of guy that put you at ease right away. He began to ask me to perform various movements of coordination.

"Do you play the piano?"
"No, I play guitar."
"OK. Well, put your hands out in front of you like you are going to play the piano."
Done.
"Now wiggle your fingers."

He pointed out that my right hand wasn't following my commands like my left hand. That was the first time I noticed that my right hand really had not been working very well, just like the right side of my mouth, and the right side of my face in general. He asked me to attempt a few more coordination feats, and then told me, "Stay right there. Don't go anywhere."

He left the room and called my parents. When he returned, he broke the news to me that he thought I had a "mass" on my brain. I asked him if that's why I was having all of the weird symptoms, and he said yes. I was relieved to know that there was a tangible reason, and the term, "mass" to me, meant water or something. He never used the words "tumor," or "melanoma," or "malignant," and I never made any associations with my past medical history. He told me I needed to stay in the hospital for a few days. I told him that I didn't want to miss the whole first week of school. He said, "Trust me." I stayed.

Unbeknownst to me, my father had placed a call to my family doctor, Dr. York, on Tuesday. Dr. York had placed a call to the doctor at the Wake Forest infirmary that same day, informing him of my medical history and conveying the possibility that I might have a malignant melanoma on my brain. The infirmary doctor had called Dr. Janeway at Baptist Hospital, and he had worked me in as an emergency on Wednesday.

I remember that my cousins Gail and Joan came over that afternoon from Greensboro. They were a sight for sore eyes because they were the first familiar faces I had seen in a week, and it had been a very long week. They told funny stories and cheered me up, and my parents arrived that night. They had taken Steve out of school for the trip down. He didn't know how sick I was, and he was happy to get out of school.

I remember that the arteriogram was gruesome. I thought my head was exploding. I remember that on Thursday, the doctors confirmed to me that I had a mass on my brain and that they were going to take it out on Friday. I thought, "Good." I remember talking on the phone to Elaine on Thursday night when a very large man came into my room to shave my head, and I thought, "Damn, it was just starting to grow out." I remember when he said he was going to insert a catheter into my penis, but that it would be no problem to continue talking on the phone to my girlfriend. It was a problem.

That damn catheter killed me all night, but the next morning, prior to the surgery, a doctor appeared and gave me something to relax me. I remember that the catheter stopped hurting.

I remember being wheeled down the hall.

Dr. Janeway had had breakfast with my parents the previous morning in the restaurant at the Howard Johnson's on Stratford Road where they were staying. He had shared the bad news that I had a fifty percent chance of surviving the brain operation, but as I have already mentioned, he had that way about him that could put people at ease. Even under such a stressful time as this must have been for my parents, they have fond memories of that breakfast. Among other topics, Dr. Janeway regaled them with stories of his boyhood days in Hollywood when he was a child actor. He appeared in several movies, among them, The Little Rascals.* To the best of my knowledge, he is one of the neighborhood kids who appear in scenes when the main characters are interacting with other kids. My parents were very grateful for that breakfast.

I never did join a fraternity, but I'm pretty sure that was Hell Week.

Mark was one happy son-of-a-gun on Friday, the twenty-seventh when he got out of that hospital. For some reason, the medical recommendation was that he fly home to DC rather than ride in a car, and Elaine had flown down so she could accompany him back on the plane. The first thing a guy needs as soon as he walks out of a hospital is real food, so they decided that they would go to the Tavern on the Green for pizza as soon as he had retrieved the rest of the stuff from his dorm room.

As usual, my roommate was not there. A few of the guys from the suite were there, and were awed by my bandage and the brain operation. We said our good lucks and good byes, and my semester was over.

I was on top of the world when we walked into that pizza place. I did not even care that my head was bandaged in

---

* Our Gang, Little Rascals, Hal Roach Studios 1927-1928 sold to MGM 1938 *a big white turban. Everything was working right again, my mouth, my speech, my right hand, and my brain. I was ecstatic that there had been a real reason for my previous symptoms. The frustration was over. School, which had not been a very happy place so far, was over, and I was going home where I had a damn good excuse to relax and spend time with my girlfriend. I was looking forward to familiar surroundings and old friends.*

The airport was in Greensboro, which was where his cousin Gail lived, and they stopped at her house for dinner while they waited for the flight time to arrive. Gail's husband, Shug, (pronounced like the first syllable of "sugar") told some funny story about the castration of bulls that had to do with the size of the testicles and whatnot. That called to Mark's mind one little question he had failed to get answered at the hospital.

Prior to his operation, his medical history had been taken by a resident. (A resident is a member of the hospital staff who is a doctor, but who is still in training within a specific area of medicine.) During the history, he had asked Mark if he was having any trouble with various things:

"Speech?"
"Yes"
"Walking?"
"No"
"Ejaculation?"
"What?"

Thinking that his young patient did not understand the word, he said, "Oh, never mind," and continued down his list. Mark understood the word; he was wondering if he had heard him correctly and, at the same time, thinking, "What? You mean that can be affected too!?" But, he was too embarrassed to ask, and the open question remained open and, actually, forgotten as the rest of that week got under way.

What with the dinner conversation, and his girlfriend present, he began to feel some familiar sensations, and he remembered the open question. He became consumed with a physical need, as well as a mental need, to know the answer to that question. A short after-dinner stroll around the property produced the answer for which he was longing, and a very happy young man with a large white bandage on his head boarded the plane for the flight from Greensboro to DC.

CHAPTER 6

DR. GOLD'S GOLD

Mark's medical instructions from Baptist Hospital were, "Stay on Dilantin, don't drive, and see a cancer specialist." A cancer specialist in those days was an internist who specialized in cancer care. Oncology was not yet its own boarded subspecialty. In 1968, malignant moles were biopsied, excised, and diagnosed, and the patient was watched for evidence of recurrence, regardless of the degree of invasiveness already achieved by the cancerous mole.

Today, the degree of invasiveness is determined by a staging process and treated with radiation or chemotherapy or both, depending on the stage. At that time, there was no known treatment. Therefore, a malignant melanoma that had metastasized to lymph nodes, like many other cancers, had a very poor prognosis, because it was only a matter of time before it made its presence known, via the lymph system, in other vital areas of the body, eventually causing death.

The slick trick about malignant melanoma is that if the mole has not penetrated too far beneath the surface of the skin, and it is removed at that stage, it is one hundred percent curable without further treatment. If the mole has grown under the surface of the skin far enough, it has already invaded the lymph system and is nearly one hundred percent fatal without treatment. Even with today's treatment options, the prognosis is very poor. There is only about a thirty percent response rate to chemotherapy, with a lesser percent achieving five-year survival or actual cure.

Regardless of the fact that Mark is in the statistical group of people who are most prone to skin cancers, fair skin that freckles and does not tan, as well as childhood summers spent highly exposed to the sun without sunscreen (there was no sunscreen in the fifties; there was suntan lotion—to enhance the rays of the sun), sixteen is incredibly young for an invasive malignant melanoma.

He was an enigma when his case was presented to Dr. Gold. He was too young to have the advanced stage of cancer that he had and too young to die. Dr. Mark Ellis now knows just how Dr. Gold must have felt when he reviewed the case of a young man, eighteen years old, referred to him by Dr. York, the family doctor.

As an oncologist, I want all of my patients to do well, and I know that some of them will not. The young patients, especially, are very hard to lose, because you want so much for them to have a chance at life.

He has seen many times the myriad emotions on the faces of their parents that Dr. Gold must have seen on the faces of Jeanne and Charlie Ellis in 1968.

Reprints of Mark's actual medical records follow:

September 27, 1968

Re: ELLIS, Mark Edward
No. 4759976

Dear

Dr. H has called you about this young man, and I just wanted to bring you up-to-date from our standpoint. You will find enclosed for your records a copy of our transfer note, date September 18, 1968.

At operation, Dr. Kelly removed a discrete mass in the left frontal lobe. This presented on the surface and was removed without significant disturbance of the adjacent relatively normal brain. The pathological diagnosis is metastatic melanoma. His postoperative course has been quite good with only minimal weakness of the right face and, for the first day or two, slight hesitancy with speech. All of these things seem to have recovered, and his wound is well healed. He is being discharged on anticonvulsant medication with instruction to gradually resume his normal activities except for driving a car, or working around open dangerous machinery, or in high places where he might harm himself should he have a seizure.

It is Dr. H's feeling that he should have local radiation to the brain and treatment with BCNU and Vincristine, and I believe that Dr. H has discussed with you the advisability of consultation at the NCI for this treatment.

We would appreciate your keeping in touch with us about this young man's further course, and if we can supply other information, please let me know.

Sincerely,

cc:
Enc

NAME ELLIS, Mark Edward   HISTORY NO. 4759976

DATE
SIGNATURE

TIME   SERVICE   NS/P
TRANSFER NOTE
Transferred: 9-18-68

CHIEF COMPLAINT: This 18 year old white male was admitted to the Baptist Hospital on the Neurology service and transferred to Dr. Kelly because of a diagnosis of metastatic melanoma.

PRESENT ILLNESS: The patient had a malignant melanoma excised from his back in March 1967, and a metastasis removed in October of 1967, from the right axilla. He did well following this surgery and had no evidence of recurrence until about the 12th of September, when the patient noted that his speech was thick and that he was weak on the right side of his face. He then noticed episodes of drifting of his head to the right, which lasted three to four minutes accompanied by complete aphasia. The patient had several of these episodes although he never had any episodes of unconsciousness and was seen by the Health Service at Wake Forest where he is a student, and referred to Dr. Janeway, who noted that this young fellow had signs of a left cerebral hemisphere lesion including right and left disorientation, dysphasia, dysgraphia, weakness of the right side, etc. He obtained a brain scan, which showed a marked uptake in the left posterior frontal lobe, and an arteriogram showed a tumor stain corresponding to the brain scan. With the history of melanoma, a tentative diagnosis of metastatic melanoma was made and the patient was referred for surgery.

PAST MEDICAL HISTORY; REVIEW OF SYSTEMS See old chart. Allergies; none.

PHYSICAL EXAMINATION: A well-developed, well-nourished white male who is just after his arteriogram when seen and appears rather acutely ill. Blood pressure is 130/80 bilaterally and pulse rate is 70. The head was of normal size and shape without bruits or tenderness. Eyes; conjunctiva, schlera, and visual fields appear normal. The patient occasionally seems to have an exotropia of the left eye and the pupils were unequal with the left about 2 millimeters greater than the right and slightly sluggish in reaction. The fundi showed blurring of both nasal margins and paleness, which represents probable early papilledema. The ears were normal. The mouth and pharynx were normal. The neck was supple but was tender secondary to the recent arteriogram. Chest; heart had a regular rhythm and the size and sounds were normal and there were no murmurs. The abdomen was soft and flat. Lungs clear to P&A. Liver, kidneys, and spleen were not palpable and there were no masses. The extremities were normal with good pulses out to the periphery. The back showed scars of surgery and the right axilla had scars of surgery and was slightly nodular.

ELLIS, Mark Edward 4759976

Admissions note 9-18-68 cont.

NERUOLOGICAL EXAMINATION: The patient was alert and oriented but stumbled on his words, had slow object naming. He read with much stumbling and displayed good comprehension. He wrote fairly well a dictated sentence but said that his handwriting was not as it normally is. Cranial nerves 1 and 2 were normal, 3, 4, and 6; there was a question of mild 3rd nerve palsy. The 5th cranial nerve was normal, 7th revealed a moderate right central facial weakness worse on expression than on voluntary grimace. Motor examination revealed a slight drift of the right arm on Barre testing. The legs did not drift. Sensory examination failed to reveal any gross deficit. Reflexes; deep tendon reflexes were brisk throughout, being slightly brisker all up and down the right side with the exception of the ankle jerks which were equal. Abdominal reflexes were not elicitable. There was a right Babinski and a left normal plantar response.

IMPRESSION: Left frontal brain tumor, probably a metastasis, from previously known melanoma.

Asst. Resident in Neurosurgery

ELLIS, Mark

OPERATIVE NOTE   Hospital Number: 4759976
Date: 9-20-6   Room: 375

OPERATION: Left frontal craniotomy with removal of metastatic tumor, malignant melanoma.
Surgeon:
Assistant:
Anesthesia: General

CLINICAL SUMMARY: This 18 year old boy has a known history of malignant melanoma first diagnosed with removal of a skin lesion. He now has a known recurrence in his lung. His present problem began several days ago with numbness and weakness of his right face and hand and some difficulty with speech. He was admitted to Dr. Richard Janeway for evaluation of this problem.

A left carotid arteriogram was carried out which revealed evidence of tumor in the posterior frontal area on the left, just above Broca's area. Carotid arteriogram on the right did not show any definite lesions. Also, there were no definite lesions anywhere else on the left side.

Because of the location of the tumor and his obvious very poor prognosis it was decided to remove this lesion.

OPERATIVE PROCEDURE: After satisfactory general endotracheal anesthesia the patient was turned with the left side up on the table with an LP needle in place and Mannitol running. A left frontal craniotomy was then carried out exposing the posterior frontal area on the left. The bone flap was placed directly over the tumor, which could be identified just beneath the arachnoid. An opening was made in the arachnoid and the center portion of the tumor was removed initially. With the removal of this there was some collapse of the capsule, which was grasped and as far as we can tell the entire tumor was removed. Care was taken not to remove any brain in this area because of the close location to the Rolandic area and also to the speech area of the brain. Following the removal of the tumor a cotton ball was put in place. Hemostasis was obtained with cautery, gelfoam and tie. At the completion of this, there was considerable dryness of the wound; the dura was closed in the routine fashion with 0000silk sutures. Bone flap was sutured in place and the galea closed with 00 catgut and 0000silk was used in the skin. The patient received no blood and tolerated the procedure well.

Preoperative Diagnosis: Metastatic left frontal malignant melanoma.
Operative Procedure: Frontal craniotomy with removal of metastatic malignant melanoma.
Postoperative Diagnosis: Same

SURGICAL PATHOLOGY
DEPARTMENT OF PATHOLOGY

NAME: Mark Edward Ellis.

LOCATION: HOSPITAL NUMBER: 4759976.

PHYSICIAN: ACCESSION:
DATE RECEIVED: 09-20-68
STATUS: Private. SERVICE: Neuro*   DATE COMPLETED: 09-23-68

SEX: Male. BORN: 08-07-50. RACE: White.

TISSUE SUBMITTED: "Brain Tumor".

CLINICAL SUMMARY:
An 18-year-old patient had a melanoma removed from right axilla last year. Has had seizures for 2 weeks. Arteriogram showed a vascular lesion of left posterior frontal area. Specimen submitted as brain tumor, probably melanoma.

GROSS ANATOMIC FINDINGS:
A moderately soft, irregular, gray-tan and gray-brown piece of tissue is up to 2.0cm* across. Additional fragments of soft, gray-tan and pink-tan tissue up to 0.4 cm* across, are received. The entire specimen is processed as received.
MICROSCOPIC FINDINGS AND INTERPRETATION:
MALIGNANT MELANOMA (BRAIN METASTASIS).

Even though there was no specific treatment for malignant melanoma at the time, there were treatments that had been developed for other types of cancers, and research and experimental therapies were ongoing, as they still are today. Mark had several treatment suggestions from various sources, as did Dr. Gold, but the good doctor had his own ideas.

The first recommendation for treatment came from a cancer specialist at Baptist Hospital, and it involved local radiation to the brain to be followed by a regimen of chemotherapy that included BCNU and Vincristine. BCNU is a specific drug that was and is still used for brain tumors. Vincristine is a chemotherapy drug that is now used mostly for Hodgkin's Disease.

Mark didn't like the idea of having to go to the hospital every day for six weeks to get radiation therapy, "And I didn't like the side effect of losing my hair. . .again. I also didn't like the term 'radiation.' I decided against that mode of therapy." Chemotherapy didn't sound like much fun either, having side effects that included nausea and fatigue, but doctors were adamant that he begin treatment, and within two weeks of his homecoming, he was in Dr.

Gold's office on Georgia Avenue in DC preparing to receive his first dose of chemotherapy.

Dr. Gold was involved in a clinical trial through NIH with a new drug regimen called ICDT. He was convinced that ICDT (Imidazole Carboxamide) was the only treatment that suited Mark's situation, and he was determined to find some way to get the drug for him. Due to its experimental nature, it was not available for use in patients unless they were on study. The problem with the study was that it was a randomized study, meaning that there was no way to select which patients received that particular regimen, and Dr. Gold was firmly convinced that his young patient needed ICDT. Somehow, and in very short order, he was successful in procuring the chemotherapy drug, and Mark was started on a regimen of 130mg per day for ten consecutive days every month. Due to the experimental nature of the regimen, there were no conclusive results or statistics that could be used to define an end to the therapy or to establish a prognosis for any beneficial effect. There were, however, some unavoidable detrimental effects.

> *As Dr. Gold explained, there were known side effects to ICDT that included nausea and fatigue, but there was the additional probability that I would also become sterile. At the time, sexual performance was more important to me than having children. I didn't know if I would ever want to have children anyway. (Freezing sperm was unheard of at that time.) As long as my sexual potency was not affected, I was not very concerned. I think my parents were probably more concerned than anybody about the possibility of not being able to father children, but they understood much more so than I did that my situation was dire, and the cancer was their primary concern. I really don't know if the sterility was much of an issue to Dr. Gold, but being well aware of the mortality rate of my illness, he knew that if I did not have a miraculous response to his drug, I wasn't destined to live long enough to have children.*

We covered one other important aspect of my illness, my draft status. I still had a bandage on my head when the letter from the federal government came that stated that I had been reclassified from a 2S (Student Deferment) to a 1A (First Call to Active Duty). I showed it to Dr. Gold, and he laughed. He said, "You're no 1A, son. You are a 4F (Medically Unfit to Serve). The Army doesn't want you; you're damaged goods to them. I'll take care of it."

My life began to revolve around my "shots," and who was taking me to get my shots, and how I reacted to the shots. The drugs were mixed and given as a "push" directly into a vein in my arm. There was no IV drip running. There were no anti-emetics given. The shot was given by the doctor rather than the nurse, and it took about ten to fifteen minutes to inject, as the contents were pushed slowly into the vein depending on patient tolerance and venous strength. Great care was taken to make sure the vein did not rupture during administration of the drug.

The effects of the drug were felt immediately in the form of an aching in my arm surrounding the injection site. Within about nine or ten seconds, I could taste it. It was a strong metallic type of taste that would seep into my tongue and my palate, overtaking my sense of smell, and eventually permeating my pores by the time I was done receiving the shot.

The ride to Dr. Gold's office took about forty minutes each way, and friends and neighbors took turns driving me, since I was not allowed to drive. It was always a game to see if I could get home before I started vomiting. Day one and day two were the most difficult days of the treatment cycles because I always got sick on those days. Days three through eight became merely nausea days from greater to milder as the cycle progressed. By day nine and ten, I had no ill effects.

Vomiting doesn't really seem an adequate word to describe my stomach's reaction to chemotherapy. From about forty minutes after receiving the shot until about eight to nine hours later, I would heave about every twenty to thirty minutes. Even after my stomach had emptied its contents, I would retch over and over again. Eventually, I became an expert at vomiting. I got good at not allowing it to go up my nose from the back of my throat as it was leaving my stomach. I also learned how to flush the toilet just as I started throwing up so that the unappetizing appearance and smell was being swept away as soon as it hit the toilet water.

On day two of my first cycle, some of my old friends were scheduled to come over to my house to pay me a visit. I had not seen them since I had left for school, and I was looking forward to their visit. But I was so worn out by the nausea and vomiting that I really needed to lie down, and I was determined not to receive them in my bed. My parents rigged up a lounge chair from the patio, one of those aluminum jobs with the woven mesh slats, with blankets and a pillow in the family room. There I sat, partially reclined, with my head still bandaged and desperately hoped that I wouldn't get sick while they were there. After they left, I thought about how pathetic I must have looked, and I wondered if I could do this chemo stuff. "Was I going to get this sick every time? How could I possibly do this for ten days every month?"

Between my first and second cycle of chemotherapy, I had a chest x-ray to track any shrinkage of the tumors in my lung. When I showed up for my second cycle, Dr. Gold was astounded. He said, "They're gone!" I said, "What do you mean?" He said, "They're gone. They're not there. They're totally gone!" After one cycle of chemotherapy, I had no more evidence of cancer. I wasn't sure why I had to keep taking the treatments, but Dr. Gold said we couldn't quit yet.

The chemotherapy became a predictable cycle, and I learned to base my activities around it. I knew that I would feel okay after the eighth or ninth hour on the first two days of my cycle, because as suddenly as the nausea would appear, it would disappear eight or nine hours later. About two months into my treatment, I regained control over my life.

I decided to disregard the order not to drive. I had never taken the Dilantin to prevent further seizures, and I had not had any seizures after my surgery. I saw no reason to make other people cart me around. I began to drive myself to get my shots; at least I was in control of whether or not I would throw up in the car on the way home. (I never did.)

I also began to substitute teach. It was during my substitute teaching career that I decided to go back to Wake Forest. While I was essentially babysitting the junior high and high school classes, I was also pouring over both the University of Maryland and the Wake Forest catalogues and comparing pre-med programs. Wake Forest won the toss due to practical reasons, because they had a three-year premed program, whereas Maryland's program was the typical four- year one. I got excited because I realized I could make up for the time I was presently losing if I went back to Wake.

I already knew what type of doctor I wanted to be, and I had already counted up the years of study. The road to become a neurosurgeon was fifteen years: four for college, four for medical school, five for general surgery residency, and two for neurosurgery fellowship. Shaving off a year of college would be very helpful.

James Ralph Scales, the President of Wake Forest University, had written me a letter in early October stating that he had heard of my illness and that he wished me a speedy recovery. The letter also said that I was welcome to come back in January for the spring semester, if I was ready. My parents really wanted me to stay closer to home, and I wasn't sure if I really wanted to start in the middle of the year, but more importantly, I wasn't sure if I could think well enough to take on a rigorous academic challenge. The frustrations of my earlier freshman orientation were not forgotten, and even though all of my mental faculties seemed to have made a full recovery, my concentration and academic abilities were still untried. I decided to put in a semester at Prince Georges Community College and, providing that went well, return to Wake Forest in the fall.

After a week at PGCC, I knew my thinking skills were fine. I was taking three courses that I knew would transfer, and better still, I knew I could ace them. I looked for something else in addition to my classes to fill my time, and happened on an assistant coaching job in track for Oxon Hill. Spring was pretty nice that year. I was working with the track team at my old school, seeing my old friends, hanging out with my girlfriend, and taking classes. Chemotherapy was a major pain in my neck two days out of every thirty and an inconvenience of varying degrees for the other eight days.

I really liked Dr. Gold. He was tall and confident like Dr. Kelly, but I got to know him better because I saw him so often. I liked the way he ran his office, and I liked the dynamic between him and his staff. He was funny, and he cussed. He would say, "Ah, shit. Where is that damn chart?" I thought it was the funniest thing to watch this very intelligent man of stature in his starched white coat gesturing and spouting common language. He was obviously well liked and respected by his staff. When I would ask him, "How long do I have to take this chemotherapy?" he would say, "Eh, I dunno, whadda I look like?"

August finally rolled around and found Dr. Gold on vacation. I saw a colleague from a different practice for my usual cycle, and while he administered the push, we talked. I asked him how he thought the Redskins looked in preseason and how he thought they would do in the upcoming regular season. One year later, I would see the same colleague again, get the usual treatment, and have the same conversation about the Redskins, but in mid-August of 1970, his answer to the Redskins question was different. He said, "Well, the team looks pretty good now, but they're not going to have their coach very much longer." I was shocked and said, "What? Why not?" He said, "Well, he's sick. He has colon cancer, and he's probably not going to live longer than about two more weeks." I said, "Really? How do you know?" He said, "I know his cancer doctor." Two weeks later Vince Lombardi passed away.

CHAPTER 7

WFU, THE THIRD TIME

By now, Mark was nineteen and had been on chemotherapy for a year. "I couldn't wait to go back to Wake Forest and start on my road. I had a much different attitude about college this time." The social aspect of college life was no longer important to him, and without the necessity of social acceptance, he felt no anxiety or pressure. He had one reason to be at college, and that was to achieve his goal. "I would not be deterred. I would study whatever I had to study and work as hard as I had to work to get into medical school."

His medical case had been transferred to Dr. Charles Spurr, a cancer specialist at Baptist Hospital, so that he could continue with the treatment cycles. By that time, ICDT had been used in clinical trials long enough to document early response rates. The initials had been rearranged to read DTIC, but the drug was the same. Dr. Spurr was a quieter, more serious man than Dr. Gold, but his answer to the big question, "How much longer am I going to have to take this chemotherapy?" was essentially the same. "I don't know. We don't know enough about it yet."

I had to take a taxi over to Baptist Hospital, which was about fifteen minutes from campus, because I did not have my own car. I would wait, wasting precious study time, in the waiting room for about an hour, and then I would go into a very small nursing station with one chair in it to get my shot. A very nice nurse by the name of Cherry would draw up the dose while I watched. First, I would focus on the vial of medicine itself, and I would start to salivate, anticipating the familiar disgusting taste. Then, as I received the medicine, I would focus on her. She was young and pretty, and her touch was immensely comforting to me. I don't know how I would have survived those chemotherapy years without her.

Having a nurse instead of a doctor administer the chemotherapy was a major change in Mark's treatment. Not only was oncology becoming a specialized field in medicine for physicians, but it was also becoming a specialized field in nursing. The chemotherapy nurses who work with Mark in his present oncology practice are outstanding, and when his patients and their families tell him how great his nurses are, or how they couldn't have survived their ordeal without them, he knows exactly what they mean. Oncology nurses are angels on earth. There is no way to overestimate the value of their service to mankind.

My freshman fall was a good one. My hall in the Effird dorm was good, and my roommate and I got along great. I was the only freshman on the hall that fall due to my re-admit status. Since I had already completed freshman orientation the previous year, I was not assigned to a freshman dorm, and the arrangement worked out well. My roommate was not a big party-guy, and I was a serious student. My life revolved around studying, corresponding with my girlfriend, going to football games, and chemotherapy. All the guys on the hall got to recognize day one and day two of my cycle, and they generally cleared the bathroom.

In November of that fall, Elaine and I broke up. We had had our ups and down during the summer from July fourth on, but had ended up back together when I left for school. In October, she had come down for homecoming, and we had a nice weekend, but we were growing apart, and when I went home for Thanksgiving, we didn't even call each other.

When I went home for Christmas, I had a long talk with my close friend, Jimmy Spain. Since he was one year younger, and since I had lost a year of school, we were both college freshmen at the same time at different schools, and I looked forward to seeing him. However, I never expected to have the conversation that took place. In a bizarre twist of fate, Jimmy's college career had had a similar start to mine; he had been diagnosed with Leukemia. We found ourselves sitting on the floor at his house listening to music, discussing our chemotherapy, and wondering, why us? I don't recall the possibility of dying ever creeping into the conversation.

January of 1970 found Mark back at school, a single man. He had never had a date at Wake Forest that wasn't with his girlfriend from home. Basketball season had started, and he was looking for a young lady to accompany him to a game. Discussing his plight at a chemotherapy session with Cherry, she offered to set him up with a nursing student she knew and liked. He thought that was a good idea, and he made a date with the student nurse for an upcoming game. The only problem was that game night was on day two of his chemo cycle. So he asked Dr. Spurr if he could skip the shot that day, so he didn't have to worry about vomiting on his date that night. He agreed, and Mark had his date. "There was no kiss goodnight, and we never went out again, but we did beat Carolina."

The skipped dose in his treatment made him start thinking, "Maybe I'll just stop taking chemo." He had been on the drug for eighteen months, and there was still no defined end-time. The open-ended treatment plan, combined with the inconvenience of that particular life style had begun to frustrate him. "It was in my way." The next day when he showed up for his shot, he asked to talk to Dr. Spurr. "I told him about my frustrations, and when he still could not give me an end time, I told him I had come to a decision. I was going to quit chemotherapy."

He said, "I don't think that's a good idea." When I asked, "Why not?" he said, "You don't realize how lucky you are." I asked, "What do you mean?" and he replied, "Only thirty percent of the patients who take this drug have a response."

I said, "Well, what happens to the other seventy percent?"
He said, "They die."

I took the shot, and I left the hospital, and for the first time
in my entire illness, I thought, "You mean, I could actually
die from this?"

With each successive chemotherapy session, Mark began to employ a new visualization trick. "As the medication began its journey through my body, I imagined thousands of little army DTIC guys seeking and destroying all of the cancer cells." Today, this kind of visualization is a well-known positive thinking technique, recommended by many cancer-care professionals, called "guided imagery." At the time, it was just a private mental game he had made up to keep from focusing on the vile taste of the medicine and its dreaded side effects he knew would come.

One good thing about that spring semester was that he had gotten a car for Christmas, which meant he didn't have to take a taxi to and from the hospital. Since he obviously wasn't going to be able to stop the treatment any time soon, he developed a new plan of attack. The nausea and vomiting was the worst part of every cycle, and he was constantly trying new ways to combat the two. He decided that if his stomach was full, maybe the bouts of vomiting would hurt less.

There was a Hardees between campus and the hospital,
and as soon as I had my shot, I would drive to Hardees
and eat a hamburger and a shake and make it back to my
dorm room before I started heaving. The plan worked to
the extent that I had less "dry heaves," but I still threw up
for the requisite eight or nine hours. I stuck with that plan
for several months before I came up with a new one, and
I have to say that just the sight of Hardees still nauseates
me today.

Somehow, he ran track that semester, and one day, on his way to a meet at Duke, he stopped at the hospital to get his shot. The guys he ran with knew he took chemotherapy, and they were all riding together.

Fortunately, it was not a "vomit" day. I got my shot, went on to the meet, and clocked the fastest time I had ever run in the one hundred-yard dash, nine point nine seconds. My teammates joked that they might like to try some of that miracle drug. Anytime, man, anytime.

When the National Guard opened fire at Kent State and killed four students that spring, the Wake students held a candlelight vigil up on the quad that turned into a demonstration against the war in Vietnam.

We all left the quad about 10:00 p.m. and marched up the street to the president's home and demanded that he come out. Someone stepped out onto his porch in his robe, and asked what we wanted. We told him we wanted an end to the war, and he said he understood how we felt, and what did we want him to do? We didn't have an answer to that question, and we all turned around and walked back.

During spring break, a few friends from home, who were students at the University of Delaware, came down to visit. Bud and his friend Vince were pole-vaulters on Delaware's track team and had a scheduled meet in Gainesville with the University of Florida that just happened to coincide with Wake's spring break. Mark's friend Seth had come along for the ride. Three guys had made the trip from Wilmington, Delaware, down to Winston-Salem, North Carolina, in a Volkswagen Bug with two vaulting poles attached to either side of the roof. That should have been a sign.

The plan was to spend the night in Mark's room in Effird and then pack everything in Mark's car, which was an old station wagon, and all head to Ft. Lauderdale for a fun-in-the-sun week before the track meet, which they would catch on the return trip. They unpacked a few unexpected items in the dorm room, and in short order, there was a strange odor coming from the quiet, serious kid's room which caused other students who lived across the hall and in adjoining rooms to bang on the door and demand access. They were not looking to "turn in" but rather to "turn on." That was the first time Mark had ever been around hash or marijuana. He wasn't crazy about having it in his room. That should have been another sign.

The next morning the station wagon looked like a larger version of the weird horned animal the Bug had resembled, and four guys and two vaulting poles headed for sunny Florida. Florida is a long state. They stopped in northern Florida not too far from the Georgia border and got a room at a truck stop motel that had a restaurant next to it. After at least some members of their little four-man party had indulged in hors d'oeuvres of the smoke variety, the fearless vacationers put in an appearance at the restaurant, where they simpered their way through dinner, finding everything hilarious, including the looks from "rednecks" who didn't like "hippies." It was quite fortunate for them that they looked like drunken athletes instead of "wrecked long-hairs." They passed the night without further incident.

In the morning, they headed south to Ft. Lauderdale, where they found throngs of cars and people, college kids everywhere, girls in bikinis hanging out of car windows, street and beach venders, and not one single hotel room. Why did they need a room? After all, they had the beach, and it was free! They had a great day in the sun, drinking beer, eating hot dogs, watching and talking to girls, burning up. Long after the sun went down, when the beach was deserted, they stretched out on their towels to sleep, stomach side down, with hands above their heads partially on the sand. Around 5:00 a.m. they were awakened by the feeling that something was nibbling at their fingertips. Something was. Rats.

Realizing that two in their party (Mark and Seth) were too burned to be out in the sun another day, they began a diligent search for a room to rent. They finally found one room that could only accommodate two people. They finished out their vacation sleeping in shifts of four hours, two guys in the car and two guys in the air-conditioned room. Lauderdale was great.

When they arrived in Gainesville for the track meet, they found that it had been cancelled. Having had enough of sunny Florida, they decided to blitz on through to Winston-Salem and make it back in one day. They had four drivers. Why not?. . . Because if one driver gets caught speeding, they all might have to pay????. . .On the side of the road???. . .Their last penny???. . .To a cop in South Carolina??? . . . Who might threaten them with jail?. . .It is too bad that Bruce didn't write "Darlington County" in 1970; those boys might have been a little more careful.

Mark was asleep in the back of the car when they got stopped doing ninety-five, but as the policeman from South Carolina pointed out, "It's your car, son. You go to jail too. How much money y'all got anyway?" It could have been worse. He could have searched the car.

On the academic side of things, Mark was taking the second semester of introductory biology. It was held in a large (by Wake Forest standards) lecture room, which seated about one hundred students. There was a redheaded guy who always sat in the very front and had the annoying habit of raising his hand and commenting or questioning. "One day for a reason unknown to me, he brought a chicken to class, and I remember that stupid chicken running around the front of the room while the professor lectured." Mark never would have guessed that that chicken-toting redhead would be his roommate in a few years, "or that we would become close friends while we went through medical school together, or that his brother's girlfriend would recommend me to my future wife."

His freshman year ended successfully, and he went home to DC, where he worked on an asphalt crew for the summer.

I laid asphalt by day and caroused by night. Even though Elaine and I remained broken up as a couple, we were friends, and I drove her to Towson State near Baltimore to start her freshman year of college. By the time I got back to school in the fall, Wake Forest was home.

As Mark started his sophomore year, he had been cancer-free and on chemotherapy for two years, and there was still no end date for the treatment. He was on the same hall in Effird that he had been the previous year with the same roommate, Lawson, who was a senior. Lawson had a girlfriend at school named Nell, and he remained a serious student; later, Mark would be best man in their wedding. But a new player had been added to the hall, a guy by the name of Tom Prybylo.

I remembered him from football, because the announcers never said his name correctly. They always said "Prib bi lo rather than "Per bill lo," and he was as funny as his name. He definitely changed the hall atmosphere, and we had a blast. We spent the year drinking beer, eating pizza, chasing women, and studying, not necessarily in that order. Somehow, I managed to maintain my grades. I also developed a new plan of attack for my "vomit" days. . .beer. It didn't work very well. I still got just as sick, and the toilet was a more difficult target drunk.

It is with good reason that he classes his sophomore year as his "screw-off" year. One of their antics, "which I'm not very proud of now, but which seemed like a good idea at the time," was the sign fiasco.

Schlitz had a brewery across town from campus, and fraternities as well as other groups held social functions there. At the entrance to the brewery was a very substantial wooden Schlitz sign. The fraternities used to steal it as a prank, and several Greek groups already had their initials on the back of the sign to indicate their success. One night, Mark and his best buddy Tom were enjoying themselves at the brewery. "On our way home, as we were about to pass the sign, we impulsively thought, 'Wouldn't it be a great idea to steal that sign?'" They jumped out of the car, uprooted the sign, and threw it into the trunk. Back at school, they decided it would be an added attraction to Tom's room. It probably did look stunning, or cool, or whatever the dorm vernacular was at the time, until the RA saw it and reported them to the honor council.

Since the sign was worth more than $100, they were told, they were lucky to not be charged with a felony. The honor council hearing was to decide whether or not they would be expelled from school. (Medical schools don't generally consider candidates who have only three semesters and an expulsion under their belts, and it is doubtful that they are too crazy about felons.) Fortunately, it was decided that the jokesters would return the sign, pay restorative damages to Schlitz, and be on disciplinary probation for a period of time.

In the midst of all of the merry-making in Winston-Salem, Jimmy Spain died in Oxon Hill.

I went home for his funeral and found the whole ordeal incomprehensible, probably on a variety of levels. When I think of him now, I remember all the things we did as kids in junior high, and I'm glad that, during my one-year hiatus from Wake Forest, I got to watch Jimmy's glory days in his senior year as the quarterback of the Oxon Hill football team.

At the end of his sophomore year, he decided not to go home to DC for the summer. He wanted a summer job that would involve some type of medical work, and he found one with National Health Labs at Baptist Hospital. He worked as an accessioner in the lab, and his job was to collect the tubes of blood samples and log them into the record book.

Mark had decided to move off campus for his junior year, and he moved into a house at Greenway with Sam Leaf, one of the guys from his hall in Effird, as soon as school ended for the semester in May. While Mark worked at the lab, Sam worked at Salem Tavern as a waiter.

Salem Tavern was and still is a German restaurant in the section of town called Old Salem, which is a restoration of an old Moravian settlement. The people who work in Old Salem are historical interpreters and dress the part, much the same as they do in Colonial Williamsburg, Virginia. Sam's costume was a ruffled shirt, knickers, stockings, and large-buckled shoes.

In 1971, that costume didn't go over very well in certain areas of town, like, for example, the city jail, and more specifically, the drunk-tank. Mark has firsthand knowledge of this fact because he happened to find himself in the drunk-tank one hapless day . . . and not for being intoxicated. "I had gotten a speeding ticket, which I didn't think I deserved, and I decided to appear in court, unrepresented by an attorney."

> *When my case was announced, the judge read the speeding charge, slammed his gavel, and said, "That will be sixty-five dollars. The bailiff will escort you to the payment window." I was shocked. I had not even been allowed to utter a word. The bailiff, having witnessed the decision, said, "So, don't you think you got a fair trial?" I said, "No. I didn't get a chance to speak." He asked, "Do you want to talk to the judge?" I said, "Yeah. Can I?" He said, "Sure."*

> *He took me back into the courtroom and told the judge that I had requested a chance to be heard. The judge said, "You don't think you got a fair trial?" I said, "No, your honor. You didn't give me a chance to speak." He said, "Speak." I said, "I'm not guilty. I wasn't speeding." He said, "The fine is now raised to seventy-five dollars. Please see the bailiff." The bailiff, seeing my consternation, said, "Do you want to talk to the judge again? He didn't really listen to you, did he?" I said, "I want to talk to the judge again."*

> *Upon returning to the courtroom, the judge said, "Are you back again?" I said, "Your honor, you didn't give me a chance to defend myself." He said, "You have taken up enough of this court's time. The fine is now eighty-five*

dollars." I said, "Wait a minute. I don't have eighty-five dollars. I only brought enough to cover the ticket." He said, "If you can't pay, you go to jail, and if I see you in this courtroom again, the fine will be higher."

The bailiff led me away and locked me in the drunk-tank. I had one phone call, and it went to my roommate, who was getting ready to go to work. I said, "Please bring money." When he showed up in his ruffles and stockings to spring me, the inmates went wild with catcalls and whistles.

One would have to wonder if the experience had the intended repercussion. He was served with speeding tickets every once in awhile over the next few years; he paid them via United States mail.

Life with Sam was pretty free and easy. They had found an abandoned empty wooden spool, about three or four feet wide and on which industrial telephone cable had once been wrapped, that they used as a coffee table, and Sam would throw his tips that were coins into the middle of it. He also grew a few plants, for his own consumption. "I tried those plants out as yet another method of combating the violent nausea that accompanied my cycles, but without success. I hated the smoke, and brownies and nausea just didn't go very well together."

It was during those lazy days that Mark began to research his illness, and it was during those lazy days that he finally allowed himself to read about the real prognosis for a malignant melanoma that had metastasized to the lymph nodes, and the lung, and the brain.

His junior year began in the fall. "I was back to being a very serious student. I found it much easier to study living off campus than in the close quarters of the dorm." Early fall was the time to apply to medical school, and November was the acceptance/rejection time. "My whole life was focused on that expected letter, and I was shattered when I got rejected."

On a chemotherapy visit, Mark talked to Dr. Spurr about the rejection. The wise doctor advised his disappointed patient to switch his major from biology to microbiology, and reapply the following year. Microbiology was not a major offered at Wake at that time, but Dr. Spurr thought it was possible to take the required courses at Bowman Gray, Wake's medical school. His opinion was that a major in a field like that was unusual enough to make a student stand out from the rest of the applicants. Mark liked the idea, and he switched. The spring semester found him driving across town everyday to the medical school to take the required courses. He was on a mission. "I had the same goal with which I had entered college; it was just going to take me a year longer."

Midway through the spring semester, a book at the campus bookstore caught Mark's attention. It was *Brian Piccolo, A Short Season*, by Jeannie Morris. He didn't have a lot of time for extracurricular reading, but the story of the former Wake Forest football player's battle with cancer, so warmly told, gave him the feeling that he had a very real bond with Brian. When he heard that the author as well as Brian's wife, Joy, were going to be at the bookstore to sign books, he decided to take the opportunity to meet her and perhaps get a chance to talk to her. The store was mobbed that day, and realizing that he would not get an appropriate chance to talk to her, he wrote her a note as he stood in line waiting to get his book signed. During the signing, he slipped her the note.

He was pleasantly surprised about two weeks later when he received a hand-written letter on pale blue stationery from Joy Piccolo, postmarked May 19, 1972, from Deerfield, Illinois, with her return address on the back of the envelope. She had taken the time to read his note and respond with words of inspiration for not only his own battle with cancer and his aspiration of becoming a doctor, but also for some cancer research he was about to embark upon at Bowman Gray. He still has the letter; he keeps it inside the pages of his signed book.

The research he had non-specifically mentioned in his note to Joy had to do with the effects of electroconvulsive therapy (ECT), otherwise known as shock therapy, on cancerous tumors. The project had been proposed and funded by a grant based on an idea that there might be a connection between some type of shock, whether physical or emotional, and the body's own immune system in cancer cases where a spontaneous regression or remission had occurred.

The ECT portion of the study was scheduled to begin in the summer of 1972 and was brought to Mark's attention by Dr. Spurr. Needing a summer job, and jumping at the chance to do some cancer research, he eagerly accepted the challenge. He was given all of the background information and was relegated the duty of setting up the experiment, including the ordering of the laboratory rats on which the experiment would be performed. Although he found the thought of performing experiments on live animals distasteful, he knew that medical research involved live specimens, and he plunged into the task of setting up the experiment.

He had a set of specific directions and guidelines from the research doctor who had designed the project, and he also had a designated supervisor at Bowman Gray, whom Mark has described as a "pure scientist." The short title for the experiment was *Effect of Electroconvulsive Therapy on the Growth of a Specific Rat Tumor*. It basically involved injecting rats with tumors, administering shocks to the heads of the rats through some specially designed headgear (shock therapy), and monitoring the tumor growth or shrinkage. When he realized that he actually had to shock the entire rat as opposed to only the tumor on the rodent, his empathy for the plight of the laboratory rats took over, and he paid a visit to his supervisor. After explaining that he was philosophically opposed to performing this experiment on the poor little rats, he was admonished by the "pure scientist," who told him he was going to have to grow a backbone if he was ever going to accomplish anything in medicine.

He spent the summer shocking rats, keeping very careful records, and writing up his results. Near the end of his experiment, he was invited by the originator of the experiment to dinner at her beautiful mansion home in Winston-Salem, which she and her husband had built in the early sixties. He remembers rich dark wood and elaborate furnishings in a dining room with a very long table set only for a few, that looked out over the back of the small estate, and he remembers having a conversation about the ongoing research in which he had to tell a very hopeful woman that the tumors were not shrinking. He later presented his results to a conference at Bowman Gray. ECT had had no measurable effect on the cancers induced in the rats.

Relief is the term he uses to describe how he felt when his summer of cancer research was over, and he looked forward to the more ordinary grind of his senior year and the second application process to medical school that it would bring. Since the people who were applying to medical school were all taking the same classes, they knew each other in some manner, and they knew who had been accepted or rejected. Fred Beyer, the redheaded guy from introductory biology had gotten into Bowman Gray on the three-year plan. When his roommate fell through late in the summer, Mark moved across town to share an apartment closer to the medical school with him.

> *Although we didn't know each other very well, the arrangement worked out better than I could have imagined. Not only was the apartment more convenient for my microbiology courses at Bowman Gray, but I got a good look at what the first year of medical school was like. Fred was a very regimented guy, and I adopted his way of life. We studied hard during the week, drank beer and ate pizza on one weekend night, and studied the rest of the weekend.*

If you ask Fred what he remembers most about that year in the apartment, he'll start singing, *"I can see clearly now."* The two girls who lived across the hall from them in the apartment complex were obsessed with Johnny Nash's new song and played it constantly. The walls were not thick. Once again, Mark applied to medical school, and once again, he waited.

I will never forget the range of feelings I felt when I opened the letter that said I had been accepted to Bowman Gray School of Medicine. I remember I was sitting on the floor of the apartment, and I just stared at the letter for a long time. I was thinking that in my hand I held a thin piece of paper that had just changed my entire life, and it would never be the same again. I was numb. I was philosophical. I was ecstatic.

By now, it was November of 1972, and Mark had been on chemotherapy for more than four years. He had also remained cancer-free. It was finally time to lessen the frequency of his chemotherapy cycles. Dr. Spurr still could not give him an end date, because there was no data that documented such a complete and sustained response as his patient had enjoyed, but he agreed to the experiment of changing the cycles from ten days every month to ten days every four months. That news was absolutely celebratory!

By the spring semester, Mark was sailing. It was 1973, and his life was pointed in the right direction, except for one minor thing. He had one more divisional requirement to take for his undergraduate degree that was not offered at Bowman Gray and had to be taken on the Wake Forest campus. . .religion.

I had put it off until the last semester of my senior year. So I signed up for a New Testament course that was to be taught in a classroom in Wait Chapel by Dr. Fred Horton, and I was not particularly looking forward to it. That's where I saw her. She had long blond hair, a pretty face, big green eyes, a short skirt, and nice legs, and she sat in the front row. I resolved to meet her.

Mark always makes me tell the story of how we actually met because there is a tiny but critical piece of the tale that he strongly dislikes.

I prefer to have my wife tell the story of how we met, because although she acknowledges being in that same exact religion class in the spring of 1973, she claims that she does not remember me being in the class. That's how memorable I was to her.

I know this sounds bad, but I have a very reasonable defense and a comment: Let me just respond by saying that if Mark was truly watching me so intently, he will surely remember that I was late to every single religion class. Through no fault of mine, just prior to religion I had a psychology class in Wingate, which is located at the farthest corner of the campus from Wait Chapel. I also had a long-winded professor, who made it very difficult to get up and leave at the sound of the chapel bell that signified the end to classes.

I would literally run across campus and up the two flights of stairs in the chapel to the religion classroom. At the entrance to the class, I would pause to catch my breath so that nobody would hear my labored breathing. I would also pray that the professor had not yet begun to lecture, but my prayers were never answered. The door was in the front of the classroom and faced the students, and I was mortified to have to make a grand entrance every day.

While Dr. Horton stopped talking in mid sentence, which he did during each and every one of my late entrances, I would avert my eyes and grab the closest seat that I could find, too embarrassed to meet anybody's stare, and whisper, "I'm sorry." Since the closest seat was in the front row, everybody else was behind me. I still don't know who else was in that class with me.

I do remember that after class, as I walked towards the post office, there was a guy who would occasionally catch up to me as I approached the front of the chapel from the exit door near the rear, where the classrooms were located. I don't really know why I thought his name was John, but I did. My husband maintains that this person's name was not John. It was Mark. Perhaps, he assumed I knew who he was from class and didn't introduce himself? I don't know. I really, really don't know.

At any rate this John/Mark person appeared at my dormitory door in May at the end of the semester, as I was packing to depart for the summer. I had a plane to catch in Greensboro, and I had no time to spare. I remember that John/Mark seemed to need assistance from my doorframe in order to remain standing, and I remember the smell of beer. I believe he mentioned that he and his brother had just been celebrating the fact that they had spent all of their money purchasing furniture for their new off-campus condo that afternoon. He extended an invitation to accompany him to Simo's for some beer, and although I shared his fondness for the frozen mugs at Simo's, I had that plane to catch, and he had obviously already partaken of a few brews.

With a smile, a thanks for the invitation, and a goodbye to John, and without any exchange of contact information, I departed for the summer. After all, I did have a hometown boyfriend, and although we had an open dating arrangement during the school year, I wasn't particularly in the market for a replacement.

CHAPTER 8

Medical School Preamble

The summer preceding medical school for Mark was once again spent in a lab at Bowman Gray, where he worked on four major projects. The first was entitled A *Preliminary Study on the Effect of Various Allogeneic Gynecologic Tumor Antigens and Fetal Antigens on Lymphocytes of Patients with Specific Gynecologic Cancers.* The second project was called *How to Buy a Hot New Sports Car When I am a Lowly Student,* and the third was *How to Get the Attention of a Girl from Last Semester's Religion Class Named Lynn Hamilton.* The name of the fourth project was *How to Fund Medical School.*

The first three projects involved the collaboration of a new acquaintance by the name of Nick Iannuzzi. He was a graduate student working on a few projects of his own within the same lab room, namely a master's degree and a spot in the following year's class in the medical school as a first-year student. He was kind enough to help Mark learn some of the lab techniques that were necessary for the research project. The gynecologic tumor research being done by Mark was made possible by his receipt of a summer fellowship from one of the health foundations of America and funded by a pharmaceutical company.

The research was one of the preliminary projects across the country involved in trying to understand the possible relationship of the immunology of the tumor-host system, and that of the mother-fetus relationship. In other words, could the harboring of a tumor in a patient be immunologically analogous to the harboring of a fetus by a mother?

That hypothesis may sound almost as far-fetched to the non-medical, non-scientific crowd as shocking the rats was to most people, but as it turns out, there are certain proteins called antigens on cells of embryonic tissue that are also present on human cancer cells, e.g., the carcino embryonic antigen (CEA) found in gastrointestinal tract tumors, especially colon cancer, and the alpha feto protein found in hepatocellular (liver) cancers. Today, we know that these specific proteins are present in the blood of patients with these types of cancers, and they can be used as markers (tumor markers) of disease activity by measuring their levels in the blood. The levels are monitored through periodic blood tests to follow the effects of treatment on patients who are being treated for colon and liver cancers. It certainly took a few years to get to that level of understanding and more years to develop the standard of care described in following these tumors, but they were on the right track back in 1973 with the research projects similar to the one in which Mark was fortunate enough to play his small role.

In addition to the academic studies in the lab, Nick and Mark also studied sports car magazines and discussed women. They discovered that they had briefly dated the same young lady (not me) with a slight crossover in timing. Evidently, that sort of situation fosters male bonding. During their off-hours, they test drove cars. Mark had his eye on a French blue Triumph TR6 and the little blond (purportedly me) from his religion class when he finally opted to send a "Snoopy"* card to the young lady.

My first memory of Mark Ellis is that "Snoopy" card. The card's sentiments were *"I thought about you at lunch today, and I got so excited, I tied my peanut butter sandwich in a knot."* The personal note he had penned in blue ink was warm and funny and very well written. He filled me in as to what he was doing over the summer, and he expressed a desire to have me write back to him and do the same. He refreshed my memory that he had been in my religion class, and he wrote that if he didn't hear from me in the summer, that he would give me a call after school started again. He signed the card, Mark Ellis. I was tickled. I was intrigued. I was at a loss. I didn't know anybody in my religion class named Mark.

---

* Snoopy, *Peanuts* by Charles Schulz

But I wanted to know him. I knew from the way he wrote that I liked him. I called a couple of my friends from school to find out if they knew who Mark Ellis was, to see if they could jog my memory. I didn't really want to write back to somebody I didn't know. I didn't even know how he had gotten my home address in New Jersey. When nobody could help me, I resigned myself to waiting until school started to solve the mystery. I kept the card.

With his plan of action initiated on the first three summer projects, he began an intensive investigation into the fourth one, how to fund medical school. His parents had funded the largest part of his undergraduate expenses, but they had made it clear that he was on his own for any post-graduate education. Upon hearing of his acceptance into Bowman Gray, his father had said "Congratulations. How do you plan to pay for it?"

The living arrangements had already been solved, and his parents had played a substantial role in that scheme. "Scheme" is the word of choice here because the Ellis brothers once again had put their heads together and cooked up a plan that appealed to their father. Steve, having spent one semester at Miami, had transferred to Wake Forest beginning with the second semester of his freshman year. He was a sophomore when his brother was accepted to medical school, meaning he would spend at least two more years at Wake, while Mark would spend at least four more. During the winter break between semesters, Mark and Steve discussed their situations (Mark's roommate, Fred, planned to get married during the upcoming summer, and Steve was tired of living on campus). They came up with a plan whereby Charlie and Jeanne would invest in a condo in Winston-Salem in preparation for retiring from their jobs in DC in a few years. In lieu of rent, Mark and Steve would furnish the condo. The boys would have a decent place to live for the next few years, and their parents would have a nice place to visit them and later, perhaps, to which they could retire. If they chose to retire elsewhere, they could always sell the condo, which would, hopefully, appreciate in value.

The condo was in a brand-new development called Stonebridge, located off of Country-Club Road, about fifteen minutes from both the medical school and the main campus. It was not your typical college housing by any stretch. Exuding old-world charm, the development was warm and inviting with stone and wood exteriors and gas lamps lining the one street that encircled the neighborhood. Townhouse-styled condos were situated in groups of four on both sides of the street, which was appropriately named Lamplighter Circle. The terrain was hilly and wooded, and the entrance itself was marked with a rock-surrounded duck pond over which a stone bridge carried the cars into the neighborhood. The interiors of the condos were spacious and beautifully decorated with touches of wallpaper and deep shag carpeting. The boys had worked with a decorator and put together a beautiful product.

(It would have been helpful to me to have known the background of this particular condo deal in greater detail than "I live off campus; my brother and I have a condo." Steve was not home when I saw it for the first time on my first date with Mark, and 136 Lamplighter Circle was so gorgeous, I wondered who this Steve character really was. Perhaps he was a very successful interior designer. It was just so well done. Both of these guys could not be college guys; one of them had to have money, and from the looks of Mark's car, it wasn't him.)

The condo was three floors with the ground floor consisting of an unseen laundry room, a spare unfinished room, and a striking foyer entrance. Light from a large window to the right of the front door flooded the gray flagstone vinyl floor. A winding set of steps carpeted in thick bright red shag with a curving black wrought iron hand rail was set against walls that were papered in large black swirling patterns on a white background. A little wrought iron bench with a gold velvet cushion sat just inside the door against the left wall opposite the staircase to complete the picture.

The steps wound up to the second level, where full length mirrors on either side of the coat closet's bi-fold doors directly faced the top of the stairs, greeting everyone with a likeness of themselves as they completed their ascent. To the right, an L-shaped living room and dining room carpeted in the same red shag flowed towards two sets of sliding doors draped with pleated gold fabric that led to the backyard patio. Inside the "L" was the kitchen, featuring white counter tops, walnut cabinets, gold appliances, and walls that were papered in a red and gold print with touches of black and white. To the left, was a guestroom, again carpeted in red, and a full bath that opened both into the guestroom and into the living room.

In the farthest corner of the living room, there was an angled fireplace trimmed in black, over which was hung a haunting contemporary piece of art that consisted of several raised bronzed faces that faded into one another, with each eye in every pair of eyes belonging to two different female faces. Between the fireplace and the sliding door was a tropical fish tank supported by a wrought iron stand, its lower shelf storing a couple of large stuffed pillows. The dining room showed off a beautiful contemporary globed chandelier with smoked glass above a polished walnut dining room table.

The living room furniture was made up of a comfortable-looking, matching black-and-white zebra-striped sofa and chair, a black leather recliner, and heavy walnut coffee and end tables on which were large chrome, wood, and smoked glass lamps. Complementing the wood in the tables was a bookshelf/cabinet style entertainment center, which sat against the wall that screened the kitchen from the living room and contained a TV, a stereo, and a large collection of record albums, among them *all* the Beatles albums. The stereo speakers sat on the floor on either side of the entertainment center, and each one was topped with a piece of art. On one speaker sat a wooden world globe; on the other sat a wooden sculptured couple entwined in an intimate embrace. A large rectangular painting, framed in dark wood and centered above the striped sofa, depicted an aged solitary cottage and stream surrounded by lush green forest, and hung in calming contrast to the otherwise modern boldness of the décor.

Another set of curving red-carpeted steps wound up to the third floor in front of an almost floor-to-ceiling glass window from which you could see Pilot Mountain as the back drop to a farm some thirty miles in the distance. The third floor was the location of both of the brothers' bedrooms and two more full bathrooms, one in the hall outside of Steve's room, and one in the master bedroom, which was Mark's room. Steve's room was trimmed in black, carpeted in sunny gold shag and had an inset that housed the chimney tiled in shiny black ceramic tiles. Mark's room was larger and contained a walk-in closet and full bath, all carpeted in rich chocolate brown shag. His walls were blue, but only because the pale green he had chosen looked blue on the walls. He had intended to paint his walls green and the ceiling blue to go with his "Thoreau" theme, so he could escape from the anticipated daily grind of medical school to Walden Pond.

(I had never known any college guys who didn't have unidentifiable greenish-black gunck stuck to the spoons, that were stuck to the glasses, that were stuck to their kitchen counters, let alone two college brothers who actually owned and/or used a dishwasher, had a gleamingly clean kitchen, and lived in a palatial, by comparison, college abode.)

Mark and Steve moved into the condo in early summer, and while Mark worked at the lab with Nick, Steve worked for Stonebridge as part of a cleaning crew. He actually did the final clean-up detail to the unit they would inhabit before they moved in.

Living arrangements were definitely under control, but tuition and books were a different matter. Since his acceptance to Bowman Gray, Mark had received a number of unsolicited printed advertisements for loans and grants seeking to help him fund school. It was the military pamphlets, however, that caught his eye because they advertised that they paid for everything, including tuition, books, and a small monthly stipend. It was a program called the Health Profession Scholarship Program (HPSP), and all he had to do was sign on for a tour of duty to be fulfilled after medical school at the rate of four years of school for four years of active duty.

The year was 1973, however, and Vietnam had tarnished the idea of the military as a popular choice for most young men and women. In the summer of '73, the war was not yet over. In addition, there was still that nagging cancer problem and the resulting 4-F military classification. But there had to be a way around that; after all, he had survived nearly five years, and chemotherapy was winding down. As far as Vietnam was concerned, who knew what would be the state of the union or of the world by the time he had finished school and was ready for active duty? He at least knew in what capacity he would serve; he would be a doctor.

He opted for the Navy. He filled out the paperwork and reported to Raleigh for the required physical and found himself walking from station to station in his skivvies with about thirty other young men who were being inducted for various reasons. There was nothing that set him apart due to his application for HPSP, and he passed all the aspects of the physical and was feeling confident until the very end, when a Navy doctor called him into his office.

"We're going to have to reject you, son."
"Why?"
"Well, because of your medical history."
"But, you knew that before I came."
"Nevertheless, the fact remains, that we can't take you."
"Why? I'm alive. I'm physically fit. I passed all the other aspects of the physical."
"We can't have you out on some ship somewhere and chance your getting sick. I'm sorry."

The drive home from Raleigh was a long one. "Now what am I going to do?"

A day or two later, a three-by-five card, the kind that looks like a *Do you want to renew your subscription to our magazine?* card, came in the mail. It was from the Air Force and advertised their HPSP program. It made the claim that all you had to do was fill out the card to sign up. He was still fingering the card when the phone rang. The caller was his old friend Jerry Smith from The Band. He had become a test pilot for the air force and was home on leave and happened to be calling from Mark's parents' home in Oxon Hill. He told him what a great time he was having in the air force and that if Mark was considering the military, he should definitely "Go air force. They treat their officers better than the navy."

Shortly, a three-by-five card signed by Mark E. Ellis was winging its way through the United States postal system to another branch of the United States military. About two weeks later, a letter arrived stating that Mark had been accepted into the program and would be inducted as a Second Lieutenant into the United States Air Force. He just needed to report to Charlotte for the induction physical. "Here we go again."

In Charlotte, Mark once again trekked from station to station in his skivvies and passed the physical. This time, he was not called into anyone's office. He was just told that he had passed. Knowing from experience that this was too easy, he confronted the air force physician with his medical history.

"That doesn't matter to the air force, if you are going to be a doctor."
"Why not? It mattered to the navy."
"If you were blind, or you were missing a leg or an arm, it would be different. But, as long as you've got both legs and both arms, we'll take you. We need doctors."

A few days later, papers confirming Mark's commission as a Second Lieutenant in the United States Air Force arrived in the mail. So did a check for four hundred dollars. It was the first of four years of monthly stipends yet to arrive, and it suddenly became very clear as to how he was going to fund that little sports car, in French blue.

Chronologically speaking, this was about the time that I was returning to Wake Forest after summer break to begin my junior year, and I was looking forward to living with a group of Fideles on

3B Babcock. (Wake did not permit national sororities at that time. Instead they had groups of women called "societies," which were designated with meaningful names as opposed to Greek letters. I was a sister in the Fideles Society.)

On the day that I arrived back on campus, I was still moving into my room when the hall phone rang. It was Mark Ellis wishing to speak to Lynn Hamilton. I thought, "Uh oh, the mystery author of the card." We talked without me admitting that I did not know who he was. He suggested we get together for dinner, and I told him I had a boyfriend. He said it didn't have to be a date, and "You have to eat, don't you? Friends eat together all the time." I was still hesitant, but I relented and agreed to meet him in the parlor (lobby) downstairs in a few hours. In 1973, men were not allowed beyond the parlor in the women's dorms during the first week of school. After the first week, they were allowed on the halls between certain hours, but they were never permitted in the rooms.

My first priority was to figure out who he was, preferably before the dinner. I went to Mary Simpson. She had been on my freshman hall in Bostwick Dorm, had pledged Fideles when I did, and was a close and trusted friend. When I asked her if she knew a guy by the name of Mark Ellis, she said yes, she knew him well. Mary dated a guy by the name of Dick Beyer, whom I also knew, and as it turned out, Dick had a brother named Fred who had been Mark's roommate the previous year. She also said she had to confess that she had given him my home address over the summer because he had asked her if she knew me. She told me he had been talking about this girl in his religion class, and she finally realized the girl was me.

I said, "I'm going to dinner with him in about an hour. What is he like?" She said, "He's going to be one very happy guy, and Lynn, the best description I can give of Mark Ellis is that he is worth getting to know." I was stunned. I thought that high praise indeed. It had been my experience that usual descriptions of people included physical attributes, height, eye color, build, good looks, average looks, etc., or achievements, football player, fraternity guy, sports car owner. It was the best recommendation I had ever had, and I began looking forward to having dinner with this Mark Ellis, who was worth getting to know.

Of course, there were several gentlemen in the dorm lobby that evening waiting for their dates, and none of them had a sign that said "worth knowing" on it. I didn't know which one he was, or if he was even there yet. And I did not want him to know that I didn't recognize him. He knew. He walked up to me and said, "Hi, I'm Mark Ellis. I guess you don't remember me from religion class." Gesturing to the guys at the other end of the lobby, he asked, "Were you hoping Mark was one of them?" I know that I looked utterly confused, and he had no way of knowing that I actually did recognize him from religion class . . .... as the guy named John! Feeling that there was no longer a graceful way out of my compounded blunder, I just confessed all, adding that I was just hoping for the real Mark Ellis, because he had come highly recommended.

We went to a restaurant called Mr. Steak on Stratford Road, and just as we sat down, in walked Dr. Fred Horton, our religion professor from the previous spring. We both said together, "It's a sign." Nobody said of what. There were other signs. He had no pretense, and he had all the confidence in the world without a trace of arrogance. He was easy to talk to, quick to laugh, and genuine in his words and his demeanor. We talked and laughed for hours, first at the restaurant and then back at his shockingly beautiful condo. We covered a broad spectrum of topics, and when the evening was finally over, I knew him, and he knew me, and I suspected something else: I had just met my soul mate.

He was open about his cancer, without seeking sympathy, and I felt like the war he had waged with his illness had taught him more about life in his young twenty-three years than most people learned in a whole lifetime. I liked the fact that he was grounded in reality and still optimistic. I liked his perspective, his philosophy. He saw himself as a simple, uncomplicated guy, and it humbled me.

As I lay in my dorm room bed that night, I thought, "He is more than worth knowing. He is worth loving, even marrying." Then I chastised myself, thinking, "Why did the word marriage even cross through your brain? Or love? You just met him. You can't possibly know whether or not you love him." But, as I fell asleep, I did know. I still know.

The following week found him standing in my doorframe on 3B Babcock.

"I joined the air force."
"Really? Why?"
"They're going to pay my way through med. school."
"Cool."
"What do you really think of that?"
"I really think it's cool. How much time will you owe?"
"A year for a year."
"Sounds like a pretty good deal."
"Really? I was sort of afraid to tell you."
"Why?
"Well, it's not a very popular thing to do right now. Most guys are trying to get out of the military. I'm going in. Most people think I'm crazy for doing this."
"You seem pretty sane to me. Don't you have to cut your hair?"
"Not until I go on active duty."
"Oh."

He asked me if I wanted to go for a ride, and I accepted. When we went out to where his nondescript, gray jalopy should have been parked, there was a shiny bright red TR-6 with black leather interior in its place. He claimed ownership of the unfamiliar car, and I thought he was teasing me. But, he wasn't. He had the keys to prove it, and we climbed into the two-seater and drove off, top down, with all of his long kinky-curly hair blowing in the breeze and all of my long blond hair becoming a hopelessly tangled mess.

"This is gorgeous! I love it! I can't believe you really did it! Wait a minute; I thought you wanted a blue one."

"You said red is your favorite color, right?"
"Yeah."
"I got it for you, babe."

I just looked at him; I could think of no verbal response that made any sense. My thoughts were rapidly fluctuating from, "Surely, he's kidding," to "What if he's not?"

With summer project numbers one, two, and four just about wrapped up, medical school was scheduled to start in a few days. Project number three was destined to take on more meaning, become somewhat complicated, and take almost as long as medical school to complete.

Mark in 1973, the year we met, in a Redskins jersey, of course.

CHAPTER 9

ANATOMY

The first thing I remember about med school is that we all met in the main auditorium, and it seemed so easy because we didn't have any work to do. We were all getting to know each other, "Hi. Mark Ellis. Where are you from?" That kind of thing was easy, and then we started class, and all of a sudden, it became very hard. All of a sudden there was all this stuff to do, and it was washing over me. I thought, "I'm organized. I can do this," because I knew what Fred had gone through.

And I did have some idea. I knew the names of the courses, for example, before they told me. I knew there was something called cellular basis of medicine, CBM, and I knew that we had anatomy, and I knew that we had some other classes. So it wasn't that unfamiliar. I had been in the classroom. The building was not unfamiliar. I knew where to park. So it wasn't that bad. But, the load of work was incredible, particularly anatomy. The minutia you had to know was just laughable. But everybody had to know it. If you looked around the room, you could tell immediately who the strong people in the class were and who the weak people were. I felt like I was somewhere in the middle. I thought I could work hard and do it. That's how I approached it.

The first-year class numbered one hundred eight students, and they were divided into modules. A module was a windowless room that contained lockers and big desks with compartments to hold textbooks and other supplies. Each module was a home base for twelve to sixteen students where they could study between or after classes, where some labs were done, and where lunch was eaten.

That particular group of students was usually the group of people who got to know each other the best because they did everything together.

A separate building housed the classroom, which was institutionally colorless, and classes and labs were scheduled all day for eight hours. All the lectures were held in the same room, which, like the modules, was without windows. During a block of back-to-back lectures, any number of students would get up and take a break and then return with candy bars or drinks. Many used tape recorders to tape the lectures. There were multiple textbooks and additional handouts as well as lectures from which to attempt to learn everything there was to know about medicine.

The curriculum in medical school was organized differently than it was in college. Rather than being run on a semester basis, Bowman Gray's schedule was organized by units. The first year consisted of two units and ran closely along the lines of a two-semester college year, with a summer break of about three months. The second year was organized into slightly more than two units with a ten-day summer break, during which time part one of the National Boards was taken. The third year had no summer break, and the fourth year consisted of a final unit and finished in time for a May graduation.

Another difference in the medical curriculum compared to the college curriculum was the organization of the courses themselves. Unit one consisted of only three courses, the cellular basis of medicine (CBM), gross anatomy, and behavioral sciences. However, CBM was an "integrated course" which meant it presented a variety of subjects from a multidisciplinary or interdepartmental approach. According to the 1973-74 Admissions Bulletin, CBM was designed to:

> *Provide the incoming medical student with a common body of fundamental bio-medical concepts pertaining to the correlation of morphology and function at the subcellular,*

*cellular, and tissue level in order that he may possess an
overall concept of the dynamics of cellular processes.*

CBM was scheduled for the first four hours of the day, five days
per week. Behavioral sciences was a course designed around lectures and some patient interviews to begin to develop the doctor-
patient relationship. It was interspersed between certain subjects
covered in CBM and gross anatomy when there was "time."

Individual student evaluations (grades) were given at the end
of a unit or sub-unit by a promotions committee and were both
objective and subjective. The grading terminology was "pass with
honors," "pass," "marginal pass," and "fail." A relative class standing would be established from this grading system and would be
important four years down the road when internship and residency applications were being considered.

Although the amount of in-class time and workload was greatly
increased compared to that of college, the individual subjects
within CBM involved lecture, lab, and periodic tests, most of which
were multiple choice, much like the sciences in college.

Anatomy was different. It separated the college students from
the medical students, the men from the boys, the women from
the girls. It determined your success or failure in medical school.
Anatomy was held every afternoon and would begin with a one-
hour lecture given by Walter Bo, PhD, in the classroom, immediately followed by a three to four-hour stint in the anatomy lab,
which actually had windows and real daylight. It also had corpses,
known academically as cadavers, about twenty-seven of them, one
for every four students.

The cadavers were bodies that had been donated to medical science by the people who had inhabited them during their
lifetime, for the purposes of research and educational studies. As
such, they were treated with respect. Dr. Bo was very specific in
his orientation of the anatomy lab about the reverence due these
bodies of former men and women who had been selfless enough

to allow themselves to be used in this manner for the benefit of generations they would never know.

Cadavers were assigned to each group of students rather than being chosen. Before the first approach to the lab, the atmosphere surrounding the students was somewhat analogous to parents waiting for the birth of a baby, in so much as they did not know what gender or characteristics with which their "baby" would be endowed. Some hoped for a male, and some hoped for a female. A great deal of the student's first semester time would be entirely devoted to that cadaver, because it was the only way to tackle the enormous task of truly exploring the physical make-up of the human species.

Along with the excitement of expectation also came some trepidation, because the sight of twenty-seven gray, semi-transparent, plastic, sheet-draped, motionless human forms lying on tables was not without some emotional impact. Even though Fred had introduced him to the anatomy lab the previous year, Mark remembers his first walk to the anatomy lab as a medical student accompanied by the other first year students, as a somewhat somber affair.

He describes the smell of the lab as quite strong, and he distinctly remembers the round hand-washing sink. Looking more like a fountain, the sink was endowed with several spigots installed around a central cylinder providing a place for several people to attempt to scrub off the smell of formaldehyde at one time. Not even their former experience dissecting fetal pigs and cats in undergraduate biology labs rendered them immune to the odor. In fact, even though the elevator doors were at the farthest distance down the hall from the lab, as soon as the elevator door opened on the fourth level of the medical school, one could readily tell that the anatomy lab was also housed on that same floor. The smell of the preservative permeated the entire fourth floor.

As Mark and his group approached their assigned table, he found himself hoping for a male. When the sheet was pealed back for the first time, the group discovered they had been granted a female. They named their cadaver Mary.

The sixth edition of *Grant's Atlas of Anatomy*, written by J. C. Boileau Grant and published by Williams and Wilkins Co. in 1972, was just one of the textbooks used by the first year students in 1973. Depicted on its cover is a black and white reproduction of the famous painting by Rembrandt entitled *The Anatomy Lesson of Dr. Nicolaes Tulp*. The table of contents alone is daunting, and identifies seven regions of the body, with the last region being the head and neck. Each region of the body has hundreds of meticulously detailed drawings and photographs grouped in order of dissection. The incredible amount of detail, knowledge, and work that went into this atlas is almost indescribable, making the ingestion of its information in one semester a formidable challenge. Every vein, every artery, every nerve, every muscle, every organ, every system, every region has a name and a function and a location. My guess is that it is just a bit more difficult for a first-year student to locate everything described in the atlas inside a real human body.

Welcome to medical school. There is no time for emotional adjustments to cadavers. There is no time for a social life. There is no time to eat. There is no time to sleep. And there is no time for chemotherapy.

It was at this point that Mark went back to see Dr. Spurr, where he enlightened him on his previous summer jaunt to another medical university to be considered in their experimental immunotherapy program as per Dr. Spurr's recommendations. Mark described the visit as a wasted day.

> *They didn't seem to know why I was there. It was very confusing. Nobody knew who I should even talk to. I spent a lot of time waiting to do nothing, really. After several hours I had had enough, and I got back in my car and drove home.*

They didn't have a program tailored for someone with his statistics. Nobody did. He was unique. He wasn't sick anymore. He

THE HUMANITY OF MEDICINE

had been on chemotherapy for five years with no evidence of cancer after the first cycle, but no doctor and no institution had any answers for what might happen if and when he stopped taking chemotherapy.

In one of Dr. Spurr's last follow-up notes in 1973 to Dr. Gold in DC, he wrote:

> *As you know, we have continued to give ICDT therapy at a dose of 130 mgm per day for ten days every fourth month. We are now in a dilemma as to whether to continue this program or chance discontinuance.*
>
> *A few months ago I had Mark go over to_____. He plans to return for a four-day study in their Clinical Research Unit in early summer, and possibly we will find some immunologic excuse to discontinue ICDT for a period of observation.*

What Dr. Spurr already knew and what Mark had recently discovered, was that he could not pass anatomy and take chemotherapy at the same time. Together, they made the decision to stop the chemo. Dr. Spurr said it was for a period of observation. Mark knew it was forever. A six-month follow-up appointment was scheduled, and a very happy future doctor walked out of the oncology clinic a free man. He had an important phone call to make.

> *"Hi, Lynn?"*
> "Yeah?"
> *"Let's go drink some beer."*
> "It's the middle of the week."
> *"I've got something to celebrate."*
> "I have a paper to write."
> *"I just saw Dr. Spurr. I'm off chemotherapy for good."*

The first test in medical school was an anatomy test, and Mark remembers exiting the classroom with other students who thought the test they had just taken was pretty easy, which was just the opposite thought in his own mind.

I thought it was terrible, and I did terrible. I think I got a fifty-eight or something. That was the first time I thought I might be in over my head. That's when I realized that studying a couple hours per night and reviewing my notes was not going to cut it. I was going to have to really start digging out information and memorizing. The art of note taking was going to have to be further honed.

My brother, who planned to apply to law school, and I came up with a study plan. After dinner, we would go upstairs to our separate rooms and study for an hour and then come downstairs and goof off for ten minutes. Then we would go back upstairs and start studying again. I studied for four or five hours per night during the week, and then on the weekends, I studied my ass off and caught up on my sleep.

He began to realize how valuable the dissection of the cadavers was. He realized that if he saw "it" in a real human body, he would remember "it." Everybody's cadavers became important, because the insides of people, like the outsides of people, are both similar and individual. The students began to walk around the lab and look at cadavers other than their own. "What does your vagus nerve look like? The vagus nerve on their guy doesn't look like the one on my guy."

"Gestapo sessions" were another reason to be diligent in anatomy. Dr. Bo would walk through the lab and select two students, "You and you." The selectees would accompany him to a nearby room that could only have ever been a broom closet in its former life. Barely large enough to accommodate the small desk behind which he sat, two chairs in which the students sat, one light bulb, and no windows, the room had none of the comforts of the lab. Dr. Bo would proceed to fire a command at one of the two captives. "Trace the course of the brachio-radialis muscle."

If you knew it, you were fine. If you didn't know it, you were dead. He didn't yell at you or anything if you didn't know it, but you would feel embarrassed and stupid. He would turn to the other student and ask him or her. "Do you know?"

You were not only up against him; you were up against the other student. With one hundred eight students in the class, and unable to hold the session with more than two students at a time, there were, thankfully, only a few times any one of us was chosen.

Although the "Gestapo sessions" were feared, they were actually a pretty good indicator of how much information one student had learned or memorized compared to another, a barometer of weakness verses strength.

There was one anatomy class that was very different from all the rest, and according to Mark, nobody ever forgets that class. One day it was announced that the anatomy class was going to get to do something clinical, and they would not be working on their cadavers that day. "Great!" Everyone was excited to be doing something with living people for a change. The challenge they were to undertake was learning how to put in a nasal-gastric tube, and they were instructed to pair off. "Uh-oh."

The purpose of the exercise was to show us that we were going to have to learn how to do things we had never done before, and we were going to have to be able to react appropriately and have some degree of willingness to perform them. The reality of being a medical student meant that in the not-too-distant future, there would be times when we would be called upon to do something clinical on a real person who didn't know that we had never done that particular procedure before; that living person was going to experience our ineptitude. Not only did they want to teach us what it was like to perform as a novice on someone who was going to experience our ineptitude, they wanted us to feel what our own ineptitude felt like. I think it was one of the most important classes in medical school that we ever had.

Mark remembers about half of the class successfully installing their nasal-gastric tubes in each other. He thinks he remembers being successful on the installation side of his partner, but he knows without a doubt that his partner was unable to return the favor.

"It's all downhill after the head and neck." That was the saying that rolled through the anatomy class just before the Christmas break. It was a bit of medical school humor, since the head and neck was the last and most difficult region of the body to be tackled. The first semester was not over until late January, which meant final exams for the other courses as well as the last few weeks of anatomy occurred after the break as opposed to before it.

One night before the semester break, I returned from the library to find a six-pack of beer in the hall beneath a note that had been scribbled on the erasable message board that hung on my dorm room door. The author had instructed me to call 768-7738, and it was signed "The Beer Fairy." I put the beer, which was no longer cold, into the little mini-fridge and dialed Mark's number. He said he was sick of studying and wanted some conversation and beer. In about fifteen minutes he appeared, and we climbed into the TR-6 with the six-pack, and drove around the "New Dorm" (which has since been named Luter) onto Faculty Drive. We turned left and drove an equivalent distance of about three or four city blocks to the end of Faculty Drive, which dead-ended in a wooded area where no houses yet existed, and parked the car. We popped the tops off of a couple of beers and began to talk. It was the historic occasion when Mark told me I was the reason he was flunking anatomy.

"How can I be the reason you are flunking anatomy? We hardly ever even see each other."

"That's what I mean. You turn me down every time I ask you out. I'm spending all my time trying to come up with some creative thing to do or way to ask you to spend some time with me. You make me ask you one hundred and fifty times before you agree to do anything. You're gonna have to help me out here."

The "Beer Fairy" was creative, and I admit that I had never parked or drunk beer on Faculty Drive, mostly due to the uncomfortable fact that the Wake Forest faculty resided there; however, a simple truth remained. I was having trouble getting my mind around this kinky-haired medical student who was a living contradiction. On one hand he was so laid back, yet he was a med student. He was confident about his future, yet he was allegedly flunking anatomy. He was alive, yet he was supposed to be dead. Who was this person who had been through more, and philosophically come to terms with more in his young life, than I could imagine myself doing if I was granted the privilege of living a very long life? How could I possibly be so important to him? I certainly didn't have the credentials to rival his; I was just a little steel town girl from New Jersey who loved art and literature and who credited James Taylor and Carole King for getting me through college.

Mark and I did share the Wake Forest phenomenon. I had picked Wake Forest out of the college handbook because it just "sounded" like the right place for me, and its southern location offered me the opportunity to live in a different area of the United States from that which I knew. I, like Mark, never saw Wake Forest until after I had been accepted, and like many prospective students, I fell instantly in love with the campus when I visited during my spring break; there was no question in my mind about where I would spend my college years. *But. . .*who was this guy who changed the color of his dream car to impress or please a girl he barely knew and then told her? Who does that?

Christmas break came and went. The end of January and the end of the first unit in medical school approached. Despite what Mark perceived as my continued resistance to his overtures, he did pass anatomy. He also passed his six-month period of observation free from chemotherapy. During his medical check-up, which involved scans head to toe, he was found to be cancer free.

The second half of the first year of medical school went more smoothly than the first half, due in large part to experience. Structured much like the first unit, except that anatomy lab was over, new classroom courses took the place of the first unit courses. The bulletin states:

> *The second half of the first year is a continuation of the study of the normal structure and function of the human body and is organized on the basis of the major systems of the body. This material is presented in an interdisciplinary course termed "Organology."*

In addition to organology was medical microbiology, which filled the course slot which anatomy had occupied in unit one. (Medical microbiology was one of the courses necessary for the undergraduate degree in microbiology. Knowing that he would have to take it in medical school anyway, Mark did not take it as an undergraduate student and earned his bachelor of science in microbiology after he completed this course in medical school. His official year of graduation from WFU is listed as '74 rather than '73 for that reason.) Medical microbiology was presented in a progression of six blocks: *(1) basic biology of microorganisms including microbial genetics, (2) immunology, (3) medical bacteriology, (4) mycology, (5) virology, and (6) medical parasitology.* Behavioral sciences continued in much the same way as they had in unit one, advancing the student to more in-depth patient interviews.

Springtime at Wake was beautiful that year as it is every year, and a happy, healthy, well-organized, young medical student found himself with a little more time to pursue some leisure activities. He remembered me on Valentine's Day with dinner and a dazzling necklace that surprised and took my breath away. The heart-shaped charm that hung on a silver chain was created from nine sapphire chips with a diamond chip at the center; he told me it was his heart. Later, he could be found zipping over to the field that used to be next to Reynolds Gym in his TR-6 with his shades on and the radio blasting Doobie Brothers tunes to watch softball games. I played center field for the Fideles. In late April, I asked him to accompany me to the first ever "Wine and Roses" formal held by the Fideles, and on my birthday, May 2, he gave me a necklace, again in the shape of a heart, and told me he loved me. It wasn't the first time he had said it, but it was the first time that I believed him.

Much like college, there was a three-month summer break between the first and second years of medical school. According to the Air Force HPSP rules, Mark was supposed to do six weeks of active duty during his break from school. There were two great things about the active duty stint. Stipends doubled, and almost anything counted as active duty or deferred active duty. . .even hernia repairs. While I spent the summer in New Jersey with my family, Mark had a hernia operation in Winston-Salem. He checked out of the hospital both hernia and cancer-free, with his summer active duty instructions to recuperate. He had been off of chemotherapy for a year.

"THANK GOD FOR UNIT III, FOR OTHERWISE
WE WOULD HAVE EXPERIENCED LIFE."

*GRAY MATTER, 1975**

CHAPTER 10

MEDICAL SCHOOL CONTINUES?

The second year of medical school began in early September with unit three, which presented another interdisciplinary course called "Introduction to Clinical Medicine" that dealt primarily with pathology, physiology, and pharmacology. It would be the last course in medical school taught in a true classroom setting. Once again, mornings were spent in lecture or lab with the afternoons devoted either to various laboratory procedures or to "community medicine."

"Community medicine" involved not only the taking of medical histories, but also the performing of mental status and physical examinations on living patients. For this reason and for the additional second year fee of two hundred seventy dollars, the future doctors received their short white coats and black bags as well as their diagnostic equipment such as otoscopes, blood pressure kits, and stethoscopes. The first living patients the students got to practice on were, of course, each other.

Many of the labs and laboratory procedures also involved living patients, but the patients were not people. They were, I am sorry to say, animals. Procedures to attempt anesthesia and bowel resection at that time in history were performed on stray dogs that had been scheduled for demise by the city pound. Students who already knew that they wanted to become surgeons or who had been especially good technically at cadaver dissection usually did most of the cutting, while other students administered anesthesia or performed assistant tasks. Mark hated working with the dogs,

---

* Gray Matter was the Bowman Gray yearbook.

but he had no choice in the matter if he was to complete medical school.

In the middle of unit three, Mark took me home to Oxon Hill to spend the weekend with his parents and to go to The Game. Mark was a Redskins fanatic raised in the DC area by a family who held two hard-to-come-by Redskin season tickets, while I was an Eagles fan raised in the Philadelphia area by a family who followed the Eagles, but never went to the games. Having watched a few Redskins games on Sundays at the condo with Mark and his brother, who kept Redskins jerseys on the bench inside the front door as required attire to enter the premises on game days, I did realize the difference in our fan status. I never rolled around on the floor in front of the TV clutching my heart or tearing out my hair or yelling anatomically impossible threats in the direction of the TV at decibels approaching the sound barrier. My mistake was that I thought this behavior was peculiar to the Ellis brothers and, perhaps, to a few of their friends, and I was good at being stubborn. I refused to don another team's jersey, so Mark had an Eagles jersey made up for me with his old high school football number on it as a compromise so that I could "legally" enter the hallowed Redskin ground at 136 Lamplighter Circle on Sunday game days.

My flawed thinking revolved around the assumption that if it was good enough for game day at the condo with the Ellis fanatics, it was good enough for the live game at RFK in Washington, DC. Having spent the previous day at Fort Washington enjoying delightful weather, and the previous night on a rare dress-up date at the Washington National Theater seeing the play *All Over Town* (where we had sneaked our McDonald's cheeseburgers into our balcony seats), I presented myself at breakfast the next morning dressed for the game. I had on green slacks and Mark's gifted Eagles jersey with number twenty-two emblazoned across my back. Mark said, "You can't wear that to the game!"

The blond asked, "Why not? You're playing the Eagles, right?" Mark's dad nearly burned himself with his coffee.

We parked on a side street several blocks from the stadium, and walked to RFK hand in hand, Mark sporting burgundy slacks and a number nine Sonny Jorgensen jersey. Mark said, "Whatever you do, don't let go of my hand." I assumed that the precaution was for my protection, but I think it might have been for his.

"Hey Redskin! Whacha doin with that Eagle on your arm?"
"Hey Redskin! You can't bring that @#$%* bird in here!"
"What kind of a Redskin are you, anyway!?"
"You're lucky you're pretty, little lady, 'cause otherwise, we'd have a problem."

The inside of the stadium was worse. RFK housed about fifty-five thousand fans with all of the idiosyncratic characteristics I had formerly attributed only to the Ellis brothers. Fortunately, for our physical safety, the Eagles went through three different quarterbacks, played pitifully, and lost the game. By half time, the fans immediately surrounding us were much less hostile; by the end of the third quarter, they were downright friendly, and by game's end, they felt sorry for me. Better pitied than dead, I guess.

Mark still has the ticket stubs from that game. They say: Redskins, Sunday 1:00 PM, November 24, 1974, Philadelphia, Robert F. Kennedy Stadium, Section 526, Row 11, Seats 9 and 10. He displays them with all the rest of his other favorite paraphernalia in his study. That first black bag, somewhat tattered now, rests nearby.

Christmas break came and with it a disagreement about where and how the holidays should be spent. The adoring medical student thought he should spend them in New Jersey. Sister Golden Hair, which he called me due to the frustrating blond girl in America's popular song, did not. What's more, despite his ongoing declarations of love for me, I had still not told him how I felt about him; so I guess I deserved the name as well as what followed.

Just after Christmas, frustrated by my refusal to allow him to visit me in my home town and meet my family, and being the recipient of yet another of my famous declinations to one of his invitations, this time to spend New Year's Eve in DC, he sent me a telegram in New Jersey. The telegram contained Jimmy Webb's words to McArthur Park, and they broke my heart as well as the last vestiges of my armor.

I returned to Wake devastated, wondering if he was lost to me forever, and knowing without a doubt that he didn't merely think he loved me; the telegram forced me to face the daunting fact that I was the love of his life whether or not I was worthy of him. Not only was my lack of faith in myself costing him the love of his life, it was also costing me the love of mine.

While I silently suffered through my inner conflicts and sought respite in a Jane Austen winter term course, unit three was drawing to a close for Mark. At the end of January, I, having always been the prey, became the hunter. I broke the silence and called Mark. We met for the first time in six weeks, and I finally was able to say the three words he had longed to hear that I had not yet spoken. On Valentine's Day I gave him a self-authored poem that I, for some reason, thought was good enough to embroider onto a piece of black velvet and frame. (I have long since regretted not writing it down in pencil on a piece of paper so it could be erased, because he won't let me throw the framed evidence into the trash.)

That night we returned to Jordan's, the restaurant in which we had dined on Valentine's Day the year before, and I remember that I could see his heart beating under his yellow shirt. He seemed nervous and distracted, and I became worried about his physical health. I kept asking him, "Are you okay?" He answered each time in the affirmative and laughed rather nervously. Later, we returned to the condo, and in the privacy of his "Walden" room, he asked me to marry him. I was shocked. He was serious. He had the diamond ring to prove it. Before I said yes, I think I blundered something stupid like, "Are you sure you want me?" He was sure.

He told me I could pick out a different diamond if I didn't like the particular one he had selected, but I did like it. A few days later, during the ring sizing, the jeweler said it was an investment and that I would be able to trade it someday for a different one. What a silly man. I will never trade the diamond that my future husband chose especially for me on a hope and a prayer that caused his beating heart to be visible to me under his yellow shirt, across the dinner table, on February 14, 1975.

By mid-February, unit four, "The Introductory Clerkship" was well underway. It was a short unit, only seven weeks long, that served as a bridge between the world of the classroom and the actual world of the hospital which would soon dominate the lives of the second-year students. Students met with faculty mentors to fine-tune their abilities at putting together a complete picture of a patient's situation from the medical history through the thorough general physical examination. By the end of unit four, the second-year student was expected to show progress toward competence in developing a diagnosis with emphasis on objectivity and persistence, as well as the ability to distinguish the primary disorder from underlying associated problems.

Clerkships, also known as rotations, made up unit five and were ten-week periods of time in which the student rotated, in no particular order, through each of four major areas: medicine, surgery/emergency room, obstetrics and gynecology/pediatrics, and neurology/psychiatry, with one week of anesthesia experience. The clerkships took place the last ten weeks of the second year and the first thirty weeks of the third year.

For a second-year student like Mark, everybody on the ward was more experienced and held a higher rank. Mark describes a phenomenon he calls the yo-yo effect, where "You are constantly fluctuating from being the smartest guy on top of the world to the dumbest ass around." For example, you are at the top of your high school class and you get into college, where you are a freshman all over again. You struggle to the top of the heap again in college and get into medical school, where you are a freshman again. You struggle through the classroom phase of medical school to get to the "clinical stuff" to feel like a real doctor, and you suddenly find yourself on the lowest rung of the ladder again.

Nobody knew what to do with their black bags at first, or how to hold them. We got released onto the wards, and there we were in our pressed white coats with our new black bags and our new equipment. I didn't know whether to wear my stethoscope or carry it in my bag. I felt like a real geek.

The pecking order on the wards is from lowest to highest: second-year student, third-year student, fourth-year student, intern, second-year resident, third-year resident, sometimes chief resident or fourth or fifth-year resident, first-year fellow, second-year fellow, third-year fellow, attending physician. Everybody listed after the fourth-year student, including the intern, has already graduated from a medical school such as Bowman Gray or from an osteopathic school and is technically a doctor who has earned the degree and the title. If one graduates from a medical school, one is a medical doctor, with the degree of MD; if an osteopathic school, one is a doctor of osteopathy, with the degree of DO. In either case, the license to practice medicine requires a passing grade on a standardized test, either the national boards or a specific state board. Part one of the national boards is taken after the second year of medical school, and part two is taken at the end of the four years.

Residency is the period of specialty training immediately following graduation from a medical or an osteopathic school and usually consists of three to five years, depending on the specialty. The first year of residency is a year of internship—hence the terms intern and resident. Interns and residents earn small salaries paid by the hospital and are responsible for covering the hospital with their presence at all times. For this reason, they are referred to as house staff, and there are always one or more interns and residents "in house" twenty-four hours a day. All hospitals do not have house staff; only teaching hospitals (meaning they are partnered with a medical school) do.

An example of a three-year residency program is an internal medicine program in which the doctor trains to be an internal medicine specialist, called an internist. Another three-year residency is family practice. In the "old days," one could go through a four-year medical school and practice medicine as a general practitioner, or a GP, without further training such as a residency. By the mid- to late seventies, most schools had created a specialty program called family practice that took the place of the GP. Physicians who are internists and family practice physicians are primary care physicians because they take care of a wide variety of patient problems and usually see the patient first before any subspecialty doctor, such as a gastroenterologist (GI) or an oncologist.

All residency programs in the United States prepare the doctor to sit for the board within that specialty, making him or her board eligible. After passing the board, the doctor is board certified by the American College of Surgeons, or the American College of Medicine, or the American College of a particular specialty or subspecialty. Specialty and subspecialty board certification began as a status symbol but has become increasingly important over the years. Many hospitals will not grant admitting privileges to non-board-certified physicians, and many insurance plans will not allow non-boarded physicians to participate within their networks.

Once a doctor has completed a residency program, he or she can elect to seek further training in order to subspecialize. These training programs are called fellowships and may be two to five years in duration. While in subspecialty training, the doctor is called a fellow. If the fellowship immediately follows residency, it is during early fellowship that the physician sits for his or her specialty board. It is critical that the doctor passes the board because without the specialty board certification, he or she is not eligible to take the subspecialty board upon completion of the fellowship.

During Mark's tenure as a student, house staff as well as attending physicians graded the medical student's performance. Many of the interns were not especially friendly toward second-year students, probably because they had the responsibility of accomplishing monumental volumes of hospital work twenty-four hours per day. Having been second-year students themselves, they realized the knowledge gap, were too tired to feel empathy, and didn't need extra students "in the way." The hands-on teaching of how to do many procedures was a large part of their job and most often involved interaction with a fourth-year student, while a second-year student stood around observing or attempting to get as much of the action as possible.

Mark's first rotation was surgery. Surgery was further divided into two sections, five weeks of general surgery and five weeks of an elective surgical subspecialty. He started off with his elective, and neurosurgery, which had already played a huge role in his life as a patient, became his introduction into the hospital world through which he would rotate for the duration of medical school.

The five-week section of neurosurgery was also subdivided, as many of the other rotations would be, into two-and-a-half weeks of the surgery subspecialty and two-and-a-half weeks of emergency room. Mark was excited to finally begin his rotations, and he remembers neurosurgery as a particularly good rotation where he actually got to assist by holding a retractor during brain surgery with Dr. Kelly, who had been his own neurosurgeon several years before. The surgeons went to work very early in the morning, and therefore the students went even earlier. The students were also on call for any cases that the intern or resident might deem interesting or necessary for them to observe, resulting in the first real taste of the unpredictable hours that came with the territory.

Neurosurgery began in mid-March, and it quickly became clear to Mark and I that if we wanted to see each other on any semblance of a regular schedule, we would have to be living under the same roof. I was doing my student teaching at West Forsyth High School, and by the end of March, I had moved out of the dorm and into the condo. Having no car of my own, I would take Mark to the hospital in the predawn hours if he wasn't already there, and then return to the condo, prepare for my day of student teaching, and then drive the TR 6 to school. After school, I was on call to pick him up whenever he was done at the hospital or to meet him there for a break if it could be arranged.

April brought an end to neurosurgery and the beginning of two-and-a-half weeks in emergency room, which was scheduled in shifts of eight hours, in stark contrast to the preceding weeks. Although the work schedule in the ER was predictable, nothing else was. The peace of mind gained from the knowledge of when he had to be there and when he could leave had to be weighed against the unpredictable nature of what might show up on the doorstep and the flurry of activity that would ensue. At that time, he made a mental note that the surgeons had no problem with blood and guts showing up in all manners of disarray in the ER. Four weeks into his first rotation, he had not yet achieved that level of comfort.

The end of the scheduled bliss of the emergency room brought the beginning of general surgery and with it, for the very first time since his epiphany in 1968, the seeds of doubt about his chosen career. What kind of a life had he chosen for himself? What kind of a life had he chosen for his future married life? Many of the surgeons seemed married to the hospital. Off time was rare and unpredictable. This aspect of medicine was not what he had expected, and his feet still had so far to travel on the path to achieve his goal. Would the end result be worth it? By the end of April, he thought he had an answer to that question. The answer was no.

The attending in Mark's general surgery rotation was a general surgeon whom Mark had heard characterized as a "wild man" due to his particular sense of humor and the reputation he had for thriving on trauma surgery and being available any time day or night for messy, complex cases. Fred, who wanted to be a surgeon, loved working with him, and he also thought he was funny. Mark agreed with the wild man characterization, but he thought his brand of humor was more along the lines of embarrassing the people around him, and he decided that he didn't really like him very much.

During this rotation, Mark would arrive home at about nine in the evening, only to be called back to the hospital a couple of hours later, around eleven or so, to observe some procedure or operation. He would then return home in the early hours of the morning to catch a few hours of sleep before returning to the operating room around six to begin his day all over again. He really saw no point to having students called back to the hospital just to observe, and he felt like a spectator watching a performance on stage. At this point in his clinical rotations, he had already decided that he did not want to be a surgeon.

On one of these occasions at home after a long day at the hospital, Mark was called back to the operating room, not to assist, not to perform any valuable function, not really to interact in any way except to observe a leg amputation, performed by his attending. The patient had been involved in a serious car accident earlier in the evening, and as he watched the surgery team saw through a bone in the leg, he listened to their conversation. They were having a discussion about another topic unrelated to the procedure at hand, and they laughed and joked amongst themselves as though they were removing a chicken wing in a restaurant rather than someone's leg. Once the leg was removed, it was laid in a pan and placed on the other side of the room, and all Mark could think of was the sadness of the fact that the limb, now severed from its owner, would never walk again. What's more, the mundane and sometimes raucous conversation, never about the patient, but around the anesthetized patient, who now had a bloody stump where his leg used to be, seemed somehow irreverent.

His realization that he did not want to become a surgeon of any kind—even a neurosurgeon, to which he had once aspired— was further impacted by the very real and pertinent practical questions concerning his future career in medicine he had begun to ask himself. He decided to quit medical school. He simply was not meant to be a doctor.

Feeling enlightened and firm in his resolve, on April 28, he went to inform the Associate Dean of Student Affairs. The dean tried to talk him out of quitting by pointing out that he was a promising future doctor in good academic standing, and offering that perhaps he was depressed or he needed a break. Mark didn't think so, but the dean finally told him that he was going to consider this period of time a leave of absence rather than an end to medical school. He also pointed out to Mark that, like the rest of the students, he would be expected to use one five-week rotation period as a vacation break anyway, and he would be willing to count this leave as his vacation period if he chose to come back to school in five weeks. If not, he could take an entire year off to make his final decision. Aside from the obvious advantage of being able to return to medical school, that option had the added advantage of maybe being less complicated in dealing with the air force scholarship.

Although he agreed to call the absence a leave, Mark walked out of the associate dean's office believing that he was not coming back and feeling good about his decision. However, since he was in the middle of a rotation, he had one more person he needed to inform, and that was his attending.

I will never forget having to talk to my attending about my decision to leave school. There we sat facing each other one on one. There was no trace of the personality I had seen in the operating room. Much to my amazement, this surgeon, whom I had found so intimidating, was genuinely kind, compassionate, and understanding.

"Why do you want to quit school?"
"Well, I just don't think I'm cut out to be a doctor."
"Why not?"
"Well, I just don't like it like you do."
"Maybe you are depressed."
"No, I don't think so. I really feel pretty good about this decision."
"Is there anything I can do for you?"
"No, thank you."
"I hope you will reconsider. You are a good student with a lot of potential."

If he had not already been so firmly convinced that quitting was the right thing to do, he might have begun to think that perhaps he had not only misjudged his attending surgeon, but that he had also misjudged more than one aspect of being a doctor as well as the road one must take to get there. He might have reconsidered his decision. He had less than two weeks to go to finish his surgery rotation. Instead, he went to the bank of pay phones located in the medical school hallway just around the corner from the student lounge, which had formerly been the neurology waiting room where he had sat as a patient seven years before. From there he called the air force to ask them what to do in his situation. They said, "We don't want you if you're not going to be a doctor." And, they said one more thing: "You are going to have to pay us back all of the money we spent on you in medical school, if you quit."

For some reason, Mark came home feeling as though a huge burden had been lifted. As far as he was concerned, he was done with school, and he would find a way to pay the air force back. He immediately began to make plans to investigate job opportunities. Within a few days, two letters came in the mail. One was from the dean documenting Mark's leave of absence. The second one was a copy of a letter dated May 5, 1975, that he had sent to the air force on Mark's behalf. It read:

Dear Captain:

Mr. Mark E. Ellis, a sophomore medical student at Bowman Gray, who has a Health Profession Scholarship with the Air Force, has asked that I write you concerning his year's leave of absence. During the past five weeks, Mark has experienced his first clinical rotation while in medical school. During that time, doubts have arisen as to his choice of medicine as a career. He has requested a year's leave of absence to determine whether his career choice was proper for him or not. As you know, Mark has been an excellent student and is a very dedicated and personable individual. We, of course, would hate to see him end his medical career but want to assist him in any way possible to make the proper choice. We, therefore, have granted an official one-year's leave of absence beginning April 28, 1975. I have informed Mark that if he makes the decision to return prior to that time, we will accommodate him. We would request that you likewise grant Mark this leave of absence.

If we can provide you any additional information, please do not hesitate to write.

May 19, 1975, was the date of my graduation, and a couple of days prior to it, my family traveled to Winston-Salem from New Jersey to witness the occasion and meet my future husband for the first time. Mark was a very likable, confident young man, and my parents were won over by his personality and demeanor right away. When I explained that he quit medical school, and that he had taken a temporary job as a lifeguard while he looked for a job with a pharmaceutical company, they must have had some questions, but they did not voice them at that time. I later explained to them that I just really wanted him to do whatever he felt was right for him. He clearly had the knack of being successful in whatever he did, and I felt that he knew himself pretty well.

My sister, who was ten at the time, had already determined that she did not like this guy who was going to be the reason her big sister didn't come back to New Jersey to live after college. She had previously asked me detailed questions about Mark and had developed a checklist of categories comparing my former boyfriend in New Jersey, whom she knew pretty well, with the unknown stranger in North Carolina. The New Jersey guy had won the battle, according to her, by one point, the hair category. According to my description of Mark's hair, the New Jersey guy definitely had better hair than Mark, and he was the one I should be marrying. The outcome of her "battle of the beaus" stood firmly rooted in her mind until Mark fixed her, my fourteen-year-old brother, and himself giant-sized bowls of ice cream, and then let his brother's cat, Madchen, lick ice cream right off of his own spoon. Hair be damned. This guy just might have some potential after all.

One of the pharmaceutical companies with whom Mark was investigating a job was based in Atlanta and had subsidiaries all over the world. A company representative speaking to Mark on the phone told him, "You know, you are really not trained to do anything except be a doctor. It's your call, but if I were you, I would go back to med school." By May 25, Mark was back in school. Just as the dean had hoped and probably suspected, his crisis had fit nicely into the five-week period of time and was used as a vacation. He rotated through obstetrics/gynecology, pediatrics, neurology, psychiatry, and anesthesia, before completing his general surgery rotation. His surgery evaluation reads as follows: (The first three evaluations are prior to his leave of absence.)

An excellent student. He came to us early in his clinical rotation but performed well. (Neurosurgery)

Works hard, good student, good attitude. (Emergency Room)

Interested mildly, quiet, solid performance, probably not interested in general surgery. (Cardio-Thoracic)

Good student, excellent worker, easy to get along with, gives compassionate patient care. (General)

Overall Grade: High Pass

I have often wondered about the part I played, at least in Mark's subconscious mind, in his decision to quit medical school. During the "chase" years, I had often remarked that I did not want to marry a doctor. My reasons had to do with the life style. I had grown up assessing the life style of my uncle, a very dedicated, revered general practitioner, and his family. Although they lived several hours away from us, and we only visited once per year, I thought I had a pretty clear idea of their daily life. My uncle brought home nameless stories about setting a bone, or delivering a baby, or particular illnesses in town, which he shared at the dinner table. Although the conversation seemed pretty standard at their house in that none of my six cousins or my mother's sister seemed to have any problems with what he said, I lost my appetite on occasion. Also, he could never be counted on to be home for dinner by a specific time; nor could his presence during the evening or even overnight be guaranteed. The phone could bring a call for help at any time, and he had to go. He always seemed willing, but he sometimes left behind him resolute but disappointed family members.

In contrast, my father had a very set schedule. He was a teacher, and we ate dinner as a family every night at five o'clock for most of my growing up years. My mother, who was trained as an RN, was a stay-at-home mother of four, who cooked our breakfast every morning, and we all began our day at the same time. My ideal daily schedule was more along those lines.

But I fell in love with Mark, and I couldn't ask him to be anything other than who he was. If anybody was ever meant to be a doctor, it was Mark. I was happy when he decided to go back to school.

Perhaps all or at least part of the contribution I would make in my adult life would be through being his life's partner. Nothing about our lives was going to exist in the nice tidy box I had once planned for myself and Mr. Right anyway. What about the children I had planned to have? Mark had shared with me very early in our relationship that he probably was not destined to be a father due to chemotherapy. And then there was that prognosis somewhere out there. Just how long did we have?

Nope. I was out of the box. We were going to be together for whatever time we were granted. If we defied the predictions and were blessed with children, fine. If not, fine. If he wasn't home on a regular schedule, fine. I had an independent facet to my personality; I would call on that. I was ready. But I still wonder if my earlier pontifications during the years when I was being so frustratingly elusive, made him question himself as to whether he was being fair to me by choosing medicine as a career. He denies that I had anything to do with his decision to quit, and I don't think about it often because it is just a blip on the screen over thirty years ago. But when I do, I still wonder.

CHAPTER 11

MEDICAL SCHOOL, THE CLINICAL YEARS

The third and fourth years of medical school brought forced exposure to all the various clinical specialties in medicine. Students gained as much hands-on experience as they could and began to discover their likes and dislikes, as well as their greater and lesser abilities. As Mark began his internal medicine rotation in January of 1976, he knew more about what he disliked than he did about what he liked. Ironically, neurosurgery, having been his goal eight years earlier, had been the first medical field to be eliminated. The romance with which he had faced that first clinical rotation, so relevant to his personal history, faded into methodology.

I went into every clinical rotation with the intention of becoming a physician within that particular specialty. I decided that I needed to try them all on for size to find out where I best fit.

He decided that he did not want to be a pediatrician early in the rotation. The pediatric hospital ward patients were heartbreakingly very sick, mostly with leukemia. Although the kids held up pretty well emotionally and were many times almost stoic during procedures such as bone marrow biopsies, their parents were usually devastated.

Mark remembers a particular six-year-old leukemia patient, whose father offered to give him a lift to the mall where I was working and where his car was parked. He remembers with defining clarity the ride to the mall with that father who could do nothing for his seriously ill six-year-old son. He remembers his own feelings of helplessness. He could neither relieve the suffering of the young father nor the suffering of the young patient. Even small events during our lives can leave their marks as niches on our individual time lines because they represent pivotal points at which decisions were reached. Somewhere between Baptist Hospital and Hanes Mall, a niche was carved into Mark's time line. He would never be a pediatrician.

The outpatient children, especially the babies seen in the free clinic, were a totally different circumstance. It was in that setting where Mark discovered the frustration of working with patients who could not tell the doctor what was wrong, or where they hurt, or why they were crying. Unlike the stoicism of the pediatric cancer ward, there was a great deal of expressive emotion, mostly in the form of crying. Mothers had the responsibility of holding the very young child or infant in position so that certain procedures or examinations could be carried out while the little patient flailed and screamed. A decision was easily reached that any practice involving pediatrics was out, which also meant that family practice was automatically ruled out.

Psychiatry proved more interesting academically than practically, so psychiatry joined the "no" list. I remember a call one Sunday afternoon during a Redskins game from a psychiatric patient who was "feeling suicidal." My husband, the young medical student, spent one and one half hours of his precious game time on the phone with the patient. I can't vouch for the advice but I distinctly remember the comment, upon hanging up the phone, "I am definitely not going into psychiatry."

Ob/Gyn was also quick to join the growing list of eliminated specialties. Again, the free clinic at Baptist Hospital, although a great learning opportunity for all kinds of obstetric and gynecologic problems, was not the nice-little-happy-expectant-parent kind of setting. The clinic was a hive for sexually transmitted diseases and full of women who did not indulge themselves in much personal hygiene. If they were pregnant, they were often unhappy about or even unaware of their prenatal condition.

Mark had actually been taught how to perform a pelvic exam during his first emergency room rotation prior to his brief break from school, and learned what the "chandelier sign" was on his first exam. The resident had explained that if a woman has gonorrhea, when you touch her cervix with a cotton swab, as one would do when performing a Pap smear, she will yell and reach for the chandelier, because her cervix is so tender. Mark's first patient followed the script exactly, as did many of his later patients in the Ob/Gyn clinic.

Neurology had been the first specialty to spark any sustained interest, due in some part, to the fact that this was the first rotation where the young student felt that he was respected and appreciated by the rest of the house staff as well as the attendings. The intern taught him how to do a lumbar puncture (LP)—or spinal tap, as it's commonly called—and permitted Mark to do as many LPs as were presented over the next several weeks. As a result, by the time he began his internal medicine rotation in January, he was experienced and good at the procedure and became sought after to perform LPs by interns and residents who either had "tough sticks" or didn't especially like doing them.

Anatomically, thinner people are easier to "stick" because the outline of the lumbar spine is easier to see and feel. Placement of the needle to obtain spinal fluid has to be precise in order to collect the specimen. Mark described to me an incident during that first medicine rotation when the resident called on him to do an LP on a gentleman who was a particularly difficult "stick" due to the fact that he weighed about three hundred pounds. The young student amazed the medical spectators by guiding a three-inch needle toward an imperceptible lumbar space and successfully collecting the clear fluid specimen. Unfortunately, when it was analyzed in the lab, the fluid turned out to be urine.

Internal medicine, being adult general medicine, encompassed a great deal and covered a wide range of illnesses within a multitude of different specialties, such as diabetes, hypertension, gastro-intestinal problems, heart problems, infectious diseases, and so on. The students had to begin to learn when it was appropriate to diagnose and treat problems and when to consult a subspecialist. The interns and the residents were further honing those same skills. It was generally felt that in order to be a good internist, an internal medicine student needed to learn as much as possible about all of the medical problems encountered regardless of the separate subspecialties they might represent.

The third-year students were assigned wards and a specific number of patients to follow on that ward. Once the intern had interviewed the patient and obtained his/her own history and physical, the student independently did the same thing. The intern's findings became the official history and physical that went into the chart. The student's write-up was turned in to the resident and graded or critiqued. The other job of the student was to track down all the lab results in the early morning and get them back to the chart before hospital rounds were made, also in the early morning. Nothing was computerized at that time, but Alexander Graham Bell's invention and athletic running shoes got great workouts.

Rounds were often made with the whole entourage from students through interns, residents, and attending physicians, walking from room to room. The group, in varying lengths of white coats, students in short ones, residents and attendings in long ones, would stop outside each door to discuss various things before entering the room and chatting with the patient. Discussions inside the patient room as well as outside the room ranged from updating the attending with new information about the patient's condition, to "pimping" sessions, whereby one of the higher members in the chain of command would ask a lower member a question like, "Why does such and such an illness produce a certain symptom?" Since the student was always on the lowest rung of the ladder, there was any number of questions that could come his or her way from any member of the group. Students were often tasked with looking up something in the medical library and giving a five-minute report the next morning to the group.

Often, the group would break in the mornings around eight or nine for coffee in the cafeteria. Mark was one of the rare medical students who never learned to drink coffee. He always felt that the wonderful aroma of coffee belied its bitter taste, and he also thought the time it took to consume a hot drink was a supreme waste of time, since he had so much to do. If rounds were not completed before the break, he had to persevere and pass the time with his own preferred beverage. But the fact of the matter was that a cold can of Pepsi could be found in any number of vending machines scattered throughout the hospital, taking mere seconds to obtain as well as consume on the run, resulting in a much more practical means of imbibing caffeine and sugar by the sleep deprived.

In addition to their clinical duties, third-year students were also expected to research a particular illness and present it at a medicine meeting in front of the entire hospital medical staff. Due to these types of continued academic pursuits, the students were not expected to follow every patient on the ward. Those responsibilities fell to the interns and residents.

Lupus was the topic of Mark's research. After the presentation of his research to the medicine meeting, he was honored with one question.

> *The chairman of the department, asked me, "If Lupus is a systemic illness, why does the butterfly rash, so characteristic of Lupus, appear on the face as opposed to some other portion of the body?" I did not know the answer to that question, but I thought for a few seconds and answered confidently that I thought it must be due to the fact that since the blood vessels in the cheeks were so close to the surface, the effects of Lupus were more readily seen there. The chairman nodded briefly and said, "Good answer." I still don't know if he liked the actual answer or if he just liked the confident manner in which I took my stand.*

Mark's yellow copy of his internal medicine rotation student evaluation form signed by that same chairman of the department has check marks straight down all twelve categories of performance in the "Acceptable" block. The comments are "Inquisitive, dependable performance. Excellent paper on Lupus." His rotation ended without fanfare on March 13, 1976.

During the next two months, he did one more brief stint in psychiatry and Ob/Gyn, as the plans for our upcoming June wedding intensified. It was during this time period that we renewed our discussions of what kind of doctor he should become. He wondered if "it was written in the stars" that he should become a cancer doctor. Oncology had become a true subspecialty since the early days of his own illness. To become an oncologist, one had to complete a three-year internal medicine residency, pass the board, and complete a two to four-year fellowship, depending on whether or not one wanted to also be trained in the subspecialty of hematology. Although he had not rotated through oncology yet, he had already been able to observe that the hours were long, and call was busy and unpredictable. Also, oncology and dealing with death were inextricably linked.

The urgency of the looming decision would become greater over the summer as the upcoming fall approached, bringing with it internship and residency interviews for the fourth-year students. Some time would be allotted for students to briefly leave their duties at the hospital to travel to other teaching hospitals to assess and be assessed by residency programs anywhere in the country. The relatively brief introductions to the various specialties to which they had been exposed would have to suffice as the basis for their decisions.

In addition to oncology, dermatology, and pathology remained possibilities. Unlike oncology, both dermatology and pathology seemed to have professional as well as personal lifestyle advantages. Their lack of emergencies meant that the "on-call" hours outside of the office as well as hours spent in the office seeing patients were much more controllable, resulting in a more predictable schedule. As far as the "writing in the stars" went, both specialties did deal with cancer in some way. His own primary cancer had begun as dermatologic in nature, and pathology was almost always the definitive answer in diagnosing cancer in all its various forms and stages.

By the time my hometown newspaper had published our wedding announcement article—which ended by stating, "The groom, a fourth-year medical student, plans to do a residency in dermatology"—the groom had already changed his mind. While in New Jersey, just prior to the wedding, we had taken the opportunity to visit various dermatology programs in the surrounding vicinity, such as Monmouth, New Jersey; Brooklyn, New York; and Hershey, Pennsylvania. The multitude of rashes and other skin disorders unrelated to cancer did not fulfill Mark's still-evolving medical practice needs.

The one constant that we could depend upon during this phase of trial and error was our plan to be together forever, and we wanted all aspects of our wedding to be reflective of who we really were, and who we intended to be. That desire made the first song we would dance to as a married couple extremely important to us, and it was a given that it would have to be a Beatles song. Because of Mark's crazy schedule, it was my duty to research the lyrics and present the possibilities as to which Beatles song would become "our" song. Together we would achieve consensus.

Although the Beatles' repertoire offered several wonderful possibilities, John Lennon's words from "In My Life" were selected as the most appropriate, because Mark and I felt that we were soul mates whose differences complemented each other. One of our differences had to do with the way we viewed the passage of time. The past was very special and important to him, and he held his memories close to the front of his mind so that time would not erode them. I relished the present and was more than content to let time work its magic on the past. On June 5, 1976, we bravely stepped into the future together.

After a three-day honeymoon in Wildwood, New Jersey, we returned to Winston-Salem to face the last year of medical school. The fourth-year student rotations were set up as electives so the future doctors could both continue to experience different specialties and concentrate in areas of their own choosing. Late summer provided exposure to pathology and a superior mentor. Dr. Robert Prichard proved to be both a "regular guy" and a gifted pathologist who was devoted to both his specialty and to WFU basketball. Mark had pointed him out to me many times at the basketball games. He was easily spotted since he sat right behind the Deacs' bench.

In addition to being well respected, Dr. Prichard was a "Joe" of a guy, with a great personality. He and his specialty gained Mark's admiration, especially in the area of cancer. As a pathologist, Dr. Prichard made the call. He was the guy who decided whether a biopsy specimen was a basal cell or a malignant melanoma, a primary liver tumor or a liver metastasis from a primary colon cancer. Specific treatments depended on his decisions. Perhaps here was the medical specialty for Mark.

Focusing his intentions on pathology, Mark scheduled interviews at various institutions seeking the requisite four-year residency program. The night of the United States presidential election in November of 1976 found us in a room at the Pine Barn Inn in Danville, Pennsylvania, in preparation for an interview with the pathology department at Geisinger Medical Center the following morning. We had arrived around nine, been granted a late bite to eat at the inn, and decided to check on the election results before retiring. I remember falling asleep around midnight having seen on TV that Gerald Ford had been elected. By the time we awoke the next morning, however, Jimmy Carter was our new president.

That wasn't the only surprise. Having arrived in the very small town of Danville well after dark, we had no idea of the topography of the area or the proximity and size of the medical center. As we stepped outside into the clear autumn morning, we were struck by the breathtakingly beautiful scenery in the mountains of Pennsylvania. The quaint little Pine Barn Inn sat up high and looked down over the mountains where the trees were dressed in spectacular fall finery and contrasted with the clear vivid blue of the sky. As we turned around and glanced upward, we were astounded to see a rounded structure looking very much like a gigantic pale-colored stone spaceship carved into the side of the mountain directly behind and above the inn within walking distance; Geisinger Medical Center sat totally out of sync with the rest of the landscape as well as the size of the town. It was clear that the medical center was the single largest employer in the town as well as the surrounding area, and that all the businesses in town on the single main street relied on it for their customer base.

As a tertiary care center, people from all over Pennsylvania as well as people from the surrounding states were referred to Geisinger. It had an excellent reputation as a teaching hospital in several different medical specialties, among them pathology. After his interview, Mark was reasonably confident that he was a good candidate for the program, and he returned to Bowman Gray having made his decision. He would apply for residency in pathology, and Geisinger was his first choice.

Residencies and internships were applied for through a program known as the match program. All the medical schools and all the teaching hospitals in the country participated in the match. The process consisted of each one of the fourth-year student candidates filling out a match form on which he or she listed, in order of priority, the residency programs he or she desired. The teaching hospitals also filled out a form on which they listed the individual candidates they desired in order of priority. The forms were turned in on a given day in November. A central agency matched everybody up according to the priority lists from both parties, student to program, program to student.

When all the data was compiled and analyzed, the final results were tabulated and made known in March. This meant that students did not know where they would be located for residency, and programs did not know whom they would get until March.

The whole process was shrouded in secrecy, although rumors of verbal commitments for some lucky students traversed the grapevine. All the medical students and all the programs in the entire country found out the same day at the same time. Match day was huge, and as the prior months crept toward the day of reckoning in March, stress levels were high, and location woes were main topics of conversation.

Mark spent the months preceding match day rotating through oncology. It was during this time period that he was able to work with his old doctor, Dr. Spurr. The hours were long, the clinics busy, the patients sick, the memories of his own chemotherapy nauseating. But there was a spirit of camaraderie among the nurses and the staff of students, residents, fellows, and attending physicians. The cancer team was strong.

From an academic standpoint, he witnessed the clinical research in the form of trials with various combinations of chemotherapeutic drug regimens that was ongoing. The hope that abounded came not from the research itself, but from the patients and the team, the hands-on, handholding, compassionate, worthy team of cancer caregivers. By the time match day rolled around, and he found out that he had matched with his first choice, he was beginning to question his decision to become a pathologist.

Over the next few weeks Mark elected to do one final rotation in clinical oncology, and on Monday, May 16, 1977, medical school was over. He graduated on the Wake Forest University lawn, the Quad in front of Wait Chapel, the recipient of his MD and the C. B. Deane Memorial Award, which was given to a student for outstanding achievement in oncology.

He was four years out from chemotherapy, he was a nine-year cancer survivor, and he was finally a doctor.

Mark and I at our rehearsal dinner with
his parents, Jeanne and Charlie. 1976

Our wedding day, June 5, 1976.

Mark and I at his med school graduation on the
Wake Forest University Quad. 1977

CHAPTER 12

GEISINGER

As we loaded up the U-Haul truck with the aid of our close friends, Dick, Mary, Fred, and his wife Gail, there were sad good-byes, a few tears, several hugs, and quite a bit of grumbling about my piano. We were feeling somewhat envious of their situation, and as we packed and lugged and lifted, we all discussed our plight. Fred, a year ahead of Mark, had elected and matched to stay in Winston-Salem at Bowman Gray for his surgery residency, a five-year program. The remorse Mark and I had about leaving such a nice town, our Wake Forest sports, and the friends we had come to know so well, was further complicated by an increasingly obvious fact. Bubbling near the surface of realization in Mark's head was the knowledge that he was not really meant to be a pathologist. All of us felt it, but the match program was a signed contract, and Mark had an obligation to fill the slot at Geisinger that awaited him. It was with brave smiles, some resolve, and a looming question that we drove away from the condo in Winston-Salem towards Danville, PA with all of our belongings in the U-Haul and the TR-6 in tow.

It was late June, and the pathology residency, like all other residencies, was scheduled to begin on July 1. The one thing we were eagerly looking forward to was income. The house staff position at Geisinger would be Mark's first paying job as a physician. The air force was happy to defer Mark for his civilian residency, meaning he would serve his four years of committed active duty after his residency, but they discontinued the four-hundred-dollar monthly stipend they had paid during medical school in accordance with the original scholarship agreement.

I was also between jobs due to our move. Unable to secure a teaching position as an English teacher in or around Winston-Salem,

I had taken a job at JC Penney just after my graduation in '75. The company had offered me a promotion opportunity one year later, but the location was in Durham, ninety miles away. I found the driving distance unacceptable, and knowing we had only one year left in medical school and not knowing where we would be located through the match program, I took the liberty of quitting and accepted a job as a waitress at a steak and ale place called Le Chateau, not too far from the hospital. I donned the flowered, scoop-necked, short-skirted uniform with its attached little vest that laced up the front just under the bust line along with the bright orange stretch panties that were worn under the skirt to complete the ensemble. To my surprise, I found myself working with two other WFU graduates who were married to medical students awaiting location information and at the mercy of the match program.

We made much more money than any first or second-year teacher, by golly. But then, schools didn't force their teachers to wear uniforms that automatically entered them into the legs contests held in the bar. It wasn't really the actual job that I hated; it was more the entitlement to which much of the general public felt they had to be rude to the wait staff. There were the touchy-feelie butt pinchers, the leering jack-asses who would smirk, "How married are you?" as well as the self-appointed kings who would loudly proclaim, "Get me this or get me that, and I want it yesterday." Then, there were those who demanded special one-of-a-kind treatment: "I don't want a whole spoonful of that stuff; I want two blueberries on my cheese cake, exactly two, not three, not one"—this asinine demand was to blueberry glaze served table side.

And I have always loved being told what to do by my so-called superiors. On one such night, having finished closing out the early section, a designation given to the more isolated room off to one side of the main dining room, I was literally walking out the door when the manager grabbed my arm and told me there was a situation, and I was going to have to stay. "Ah, pray tell."

"There is a large group here," he hissed, "about eighteen."

"So what," I hissed back. "There's plenty of room in the main dining room."

"No. You have to take this group in the side room."

"Why me? The side room's clean. It's my night to leave early."

"No, you don't understand. They're too grungy to be in the main dining room."

"They're too what?"

"They're in tee shirts and grungy jeans. Some of 'em got long hair."

"Guys have been wearing their hair long since the Beatles got here."

"No, these guys look pretty rough, but they say they can pay their bill. Come on, help me out. I think they could cause some real trouble"

"Oh boy, my favorite."

The "grungy" group of ruffians, unrecognized until I showed up to take their drink order, turned out to be none other than Billy Joel and his band. They had played at Wake Forest that night, and he and his band were hungry and had been directed to the "best restaurant in Winston-Salem." And I had them all to myself in the side dining room. Even the chef stopped griping about having to cook that many dinners so late at night, after I told him for whom he broiled. It did my heart good to see my judgmental manager roll up his sleeves and run about the kitchen; he didn't dare step foot into the dining room either, after he had been such a horse's ass to them at the front door.

The conversation in that side dining room is a good memory also, because Billy Joel was not quite as well known then as he is now. *Piano Man* had been out for two or three years, and was still his best known song, at least in my circles. The radio stations I listened to played it more than any of his newer songs, and I had already identified it as my theme song for my year of waitressing.

The band was anxious to know how popular they were down South, our way. They wanted to know if I could name any other songs of theirs other than *Piano Man*. *The Stranger* had not yet been released, but they did have another whole album out. And they asked the question that all bands who played at Wake Forest asked.

"Why do they hold their concerts in a church? That was weird, man."

Wait Chapel was the largest gathering area at Wake, and the inside of the chapel could be very believably converted into a concert hall with the front becoming a large stage. The students were used to it, and the WFU community saw a lot of good bands there over the years. But the organ's huge majestic pipes were difficult to hide, and there was no mistaking the outside with its tall, beautiful steeple. It was probably weirder for Iron Butterfly, when they played there back in 1970. That performance, unfortunately, predated me, but that's where Mark saw them. Imagine "In-A-Gadda-Da-Vida" blaring right out of Wait Chapel!

Le Chateau was a nice restaurant with good food. In fact, before I worked there, it had been Mark's and my favorite, and on the rare occasions that we splurged and went out to dinner, that is where we dined.

I am proud to say that I am a wait-staff survivor. After several years, I was able once again to go out to dinner and enjoy myself. But there are scars; I have to tip at least thirty percent, more if I have lingering conversation after dinner preventing table-turnover, and more if the server fosters a relaxing dining experience. And sometimes, I feel the need to sneak an extra tip to the server if I am not the one picking up the tab because I have no way of knowing what was deemed a suitable tip.

Waitress days behind me, I was hoping that the job market for teachers was better in Pennsylvania than it was in North Carolina, and knowing that PA had reciprocity with NC for the type of teaching certificate my Wake Forest education had earned me, I had already made application with the state for my PA certificate. I would soon find out that there was a so-called teacher glut in Pennsylvania in 1977 as well. In fact, one needed a PA teaching certificate just to substitute teach, and substitute teachers could only sub within their certified specialty. And the state had a six-month backlog. As it turned out, there were no jobs to be had in or around Danville for me, except one night-shift file clerk position at the hospital, to which Mark said, "no" on my behalf.

It was a good thing we had opted for the Geisinger housing that had been offered to us. The medical center owned about eight houses that were on its "campus." The best thing was that they were within walking distance of the hospital—actually within the shadow of the hospital, with a sidewalk that was a few hundred yards long and lead right up to the very door of the center. Interns who had elected to do specialties that required them to spend their call-nights overnight in the hospital had preferred status as far as acquiring one of the little houses. One of the nice things about the pathology residency, including its first year, was that there were no overnight call-nights required to be spent in the hospital, meaning call was allowed to be taken from home. Only seven of the little rental houses had been spoken for by the interns who had first dibs, leaving one for us.

The worst thing about the little "tin" houses was the brown institutional tile with which they were all floored. Also, they were without washers, dryers and air conditioning. But the price was right. In fact, Geisinger deducted the rent right out of the paycheck, and you couldn't beat the location. We set about brightening the place up with some purchased rug remnants and my homemade curtains, and our little three-bedroom, one-bath bungalow became home.

Best foot forward, Mark started work as scheduled, and I joined the house staff wives' club. The pathology internship was set up as two six-month rotations: surgical pathology, which involved working in the lab with surgical specimens, and autopsy. Mark and the other first-year pathology resident flipped a coin to see who would work in which area first, and Mark won autopsy. There were never any emergencies in autopsy, so Mark got to walk home for lunch every day at noon, and walk home for dinner every night at six. After two weeks of examining stomach contents in dead people, he eliminated from his menu soups, stews, and anything that was all mixed up together before it was eaten.

Jobless and bored, I found the house staff wives' club to be a welcome diversion. They were warm and friendly and engaged in reprinting a second edition of their cookbook, *Pleasing Prescriptions*, the proceeds of which would go to a worthy community project. My favorite recipes for banana bread and pumpkin muffins are still found in this book. Despite my sojourn into charitable work, I was still bored, and our little neighborhood, except for the bachelor surgery resident, close as it was, was mainly focused on getting pregnant.

Mark and I opted for a six-week old puppy, and so began a love affair with a black and silver German Shepherd we named Augie, so Mark could be "Doggie Daddy" like the old *Augie Doggie and Doggie Daddy*[*] cartoon. An impersonated Jimmy Durante was the original cartoon voice of Doggie Daddy, and in his legendary gravelly voice, he used to talk about Augie, his cartoon son. Our Augie was a daughter, and she lit up our lives. She learned the daily routine very quickly, and when it was time for Mark to come home for lunch or dinner, she would patiently wait on the sidewalk in front of our house to catch sight of him. Just as he set foot onto the walk, she would bolt and run as hard as she could to meet him. No finer greeting could there be.

In the field behind Geisinger, Mark taught her to catch frisbees like a champion and tennis balls that he would throw straight up so high that I could barely see them. The eagle-eyed dog, totally focused on her task, never lost sight of the ball and would jump up to meet and catch it in her teeth every time. She was a superb athlete and would run as fast as she could before leaping and cavorting in the air to catch a frisbee.

I taught her to read. No kidding. Mark had seen a demonstration of German Shepherds who could supposedly read a couple of years earlier back in Winston-Salem one day at the mall when he was waiting for me to get off of work. He had been so intrigued that he had bought the manual entitled *Stop! Sit! And Think* from

---

[*] Augie Doggie and Doggie Daddy animated cartoon produced by Hanna Barbera. Doggie Daddy's voice was done by Doug Young. Augie Doggie's voice was done by Doug Butler.

the owner/author Charles P. Eisenmann. From the time Augie was a puppy, we had always talked to her in full sentences like she was another person, and she always acted like she understood everything we said. She loved to help. She did everything from helping me carry in groceries from the car, to helping me put laundry away. I knew we had an extraordinary dog and decided to give reading a whirl, unbeknownst to him.

He was surprised and probably briefly worried about my sanity one night, when I got out Augie's flash cards, and she proceeded to sit at attention and then perform the commands thereon. He thought at first that she must be reading my body language or that I had a secret hand signal. Then, he decided that she must be recognizing something about the general outline of the letters on each flash card, but not really reading. When I was able to take an ordinary sheet of paper and write down simple commands such as "sit" "shake hands" or "lie down" in various sizes of print, and she performed, he was finally convinced. The scientific community can be a tough sell.

Despite the reading dog and the offers to go flying with the bachelor, wild-man, pilot-turned-doctor, surgery resident, future astronaut, who lived behind us, autopsies were not living patients. Mark hated to fly, and he really missed living, breathing patients. I was bored at home, and he was bored at work. Towards the end of the unusually hot summer, we made a startling discovery. I was pregnant. That wasn't supposed to be possible post-chemotherapy. Perhaps there was something in the water in Danville, or perhaps just the water in our little neighborhood. Out of seven couples, there were four pregnancies in addition to mine. I became the only one to miscarry later that fall. So the chemotherapy questions remained after all.

It was near the end of September when Mark wrote to the chairman of the internal medicine department back at Bowman Gray to inform him of his desire to seek a residency in internal medicine when his year of obligation to the pathology residency had been fulfilled, and to ask for his advice. After many discussions, we both realized that pathology was just not going to work for him. He had finally determined what he loved best about being a doctor—the relationship with his patients. I had finally determined that the need for that particular doctor-patient relationship was an integral part of who he was. Our very orderly and predictable days were numbered; so were the autopsies.

The first snowfall began very quietly on the evening of October 16 and deposited six inches on the ground. It then snowed at least a little everyday and continued to add to the initial amount until it was piled up to our roof. The walkway was kept clear by the grounds staff at the medical center so that there was a clear narrow path to the hospital, but one could not see over the steep white wall of snow on either side of the path. The TR-6 just stayed buried under the snow parked on the little street that ran behind the neighborhood. It was not really a car designed for use in the snow anyway.

We actually never saw the ground again in Danville; Mark got a call at the end of January from the medicine residency director at Baptist Hospital, who said an open slot in the internal medicine residency had just been created because an intern had had to take a sudden, extended, medical leave of absence. He wasn't sure that Mark could get out of his contract at Geisinger, but the need was great at Baptist Hospital, and he thought he could transfer six months of credit towards Mark's medicine residency from his pathology residency and offer him a full three-year internal medicine program. He would still have to do a full year of a rotating internship, but six out of his seven months of pathology could be substituted for six months of electives in the latter part of the internal medicine residency. The result would be that he would finish up one month later than normal in August of 1980 rather than in July.

Mark was sure that the air force would allow him to change specialties and locations, which they eventually did rather easily. He was equally sure that he was going to get out of his contract at Geisinger one way or another, but he was dreading his discussion with the chairman of the pathology department, because he had been a nice guy and ran a top-notch program. As Mark had guessed, his boss at Geisinger was not happy about his resident's desire to leave the program or with the contact from Baptist Hospital. "I don't *have* to let you out of your contract, you know." But he did let him go. Having to deal with a disgruntled first-year resident would do neither his program nor the young doctor any good.

The elation at the other end of the phone, when Mark placed the call to let the residency program know that he was able to accept the open position at Bowman Gray, went a long way towards helping Mark to ease the memory of having disappointed the people at Geisinger. We quickly dug out the TR-6, loaded up a Ryder truck, and put Danville, PA, in our rear-view mirror. Of course, what Mark mostly saw in his rear view mirror was me driving his TR-6 laden with several house plants and one German Shepherd who was much too large for the little two-seater car. It was fourteen degrees and snowing as we wound our way south through the mountains, so he probably saw a little fishtailing also. I know I saw some ahead of me.

As we neared our turn onto Route 81 leaving Sunbury, the snow, which had become ice, suddenly exploded into millions of dazzling diamonds as the sun issued us a sudden and unexpected welcome. At the same exact second, the car radio played "Here Comes the Sun." I could tell that up ahead Mark was having the same Beatles experience in the truck, and I knew that we were both thinking, "It's a sign." A sign that we had made the right decision? A sign that we were going to survive the trip? Perhaps any or all of the above, but whatever the omen represented, we knew it was a good one.

Twelve hours later, we found ourselves back at the Stone Bridge condo in Winston-Salem with the same crew of friends who had helped us move out. Somehow, the furniture and boxes seemed lighter this time, although the piano sustained about as much grumbling as before.

CHAPTER 13

INTERNSHIP

The internal medicine internship at Bowman Gray was set up as a straight medicine internship, meaning the first-year resident (intern) rotated through twelve required specialties in adult medicine a month at a time. The house staff was broken down into teams per inpatient ward within a particular medicine subspecialty, each team usually consisting of one or two interns, one or two second-year residents, and, hopefully, a couple of medical students. The third-year residents were involved with patient care only as consultants.

The intern usually saw the patient first, did the physical examination, took the history, and did the write up for the patient's chart. It was reviewed by the second-year resident, and diagnostic tests were discussed and subsequently ordered by the intern. Depending on the patient's condition and preliminary tests, the need to consult other specialists often arose. In such cases, the intern requested the consult from the appropriate service, and the actual consultation was done by the third-year resident who was assigned to that specialty. Occasionally, the patient might need to be transferred to another service, such as surgery. But as long as the patient remained an internal medicine patient, it was the intern's job to be that patient's primary doctor for the length of the hospital stay or the end of the rotation, whichever happened first.

An intern's morning began by six o'clock with the hunting and gathering of test results, which was referred to by the house staff as "scut" work. Scut work involved the actual tracking down of labs, scans, and other diagnostic tests that had been ordered the previous day, which in the pre-computer days of the late seventies, meant visiting various parts of the hospital to physically obtain a piece of paper or film. Consequently, as much scut work as possible was assigned by the interns to the medical students on the team, in the interest of having an up-to-date patient profile in the patient's chart by the time morning rounds began with the rest of the team around eight or nine.

Continuing medical decisions and appropriate questions and team discussions were dependent on timely, accurate reports to assess the status of their patients. Everything needed to be well underway by the time afternoon rounds were made with not only the team of interns, residents, and students, but also the attendings and/or fellows.

The second-year resident's primary job was to serve as a back-up resource for the intern with most, if not all, of the hands-on medicine done by the intern. Hopefully, the intern would have learned how to perform most of the diagnostic procedures required within the realm of internal medicine as a student. But there were bound to be missing pieces of the puzzle, depending on everything from the types of patients to the types of interns and residents one had been exposed to as a student. Interns were expected to learn any unfamiliar or unpracticed procedures from another intern or resident, and then to teach them to another intern or student. Everybody tried to help everybody else gain as much practical experience as possible, and due to the overwhelming work load, a "see one, do one, teach one" philosophy prevailed. For example, if the intern was rotating through the oncology service and had never done a bone marrow biopsy and aspiration before, another intern or second-year resident would show him or her how to perform the procedure by doing it while instructing and narrating the sequence of steps involved. The next time a bone marrow came up, the intern who had watched just one would, under supervision of either another intern or resident, attempt the bone marrow procedure and, hopefully for all concerned, succeed. It then became his or her duty to teach the procedure by example to someone else who had not yet done one and then supervise someone else's first attempt.

The interns and second-year residents were also required to be on call for admissions to the hospital every third night, and call had to be taken within the hospital. Day one and day two would begin at six in the morning and end anywhere from six to ten or eleven at night, depending on the subspecialty and particular patient load. Day three as the on call day would start at the same time, but from five in the evening until six the next morning, the additional responsibility of taking all the new internal medicine admissions to the hospital was assumed. At 6 a.m. after a night on-call, day one began the cycle all over again, meaning that the interns and residents who had been on call the previous night would remain in the hospital to work the entire day before going home. It was very common, especially for the interns, to have been up all night. Due to sleep deprivation, it was a challenge just to look and function like real people all day. By the time they were driving home in the evening, they had often been up for thirty-two to thirty-six hours. The house staff looked after each other and tried to shoo anyone who had been on call the previous night out the door at a reasonable hour, around 5 or 6 p.m., by picking up any unfinished work the tired docs might still have to do.

Beds were provided in call rooms that slept four and contained a house phone. Pagers or beepers, as they were commonly called, were required to be on at all times. Four doctors multiplied by four beepers multiplied by four individuals talking on the house phone to answer the beeper calls left few uninterrupted minutes of sleep during the night. Second-year residents had their sleep interrupted according to the experience level of the intern under them. Consequently, nobody got very much sleep in July when medical students became interns, and interns became second-year residents.

Mark had to hit the ground running in February of 1978 and slip into the slot vacated by the intern who had left the program. Whereas the other interns had already had seven months of experience on the wards and were essentially winding down their first year, his first year was just getting started. Once again, he found himself on the low rung of the pecking order, and this time, he was seven months lower than the other interns. He was very aware of the possibility that the second-year residents who had just started getting a little more sleep, albeit in the hospital, might not be looking forward to playing back-up for the brand new intern taking call.

Everybody, including Mark, would hope that he had learned most medicine diagnostic procedures when he was a student and remembered them. Autopsies had afforded no bone marrow biopsies, no lumbar punctures, no central lines, no plural effusion taps, and no procedures of any kind performed on living patients.

I could not have been assigned to a better second-year resident. Realizing my position as a late starter, he took me under his wing and agreed to get me up and running as soon as possible by filling in any gaps and making sure I knew how to do all of the procedures required of a doctor taking care of internal medicine patients, as quickly as possible. Any time there was a procedure to be done that he wasn't sure if I knew how to do, he would call me to check and see if I wanted to come and do it. He taught me all kinds of tricks of the trade to doing expert procedures, meaning getting good quality results with as little discomfort to the patients as possible. I in turn passed on my newly acquired expertise to a student or another intern in need.

One night during my first month on call, one of the other interns in the room got a page from one of the floors. He turned to me and said that we had a guy who needed to have a central line (central venous catheter that is inserted into the jugular vein for the purpose of delivering certain types of medications and measuring central venous pressure) *put in, and he wanted to know if I had ever done one before, and did I want to do this one? I told him I had seen some done before as a student, but I had never done one myself. He said, "Well this one will be a good one for you to learn on because this guy is comatose."*

They let me do the whole thing while talking me through it. Everything went perfectly from start to finish. Even though the guy was comatose, we numbed him up, just in case, and proceeded to put the line in place. Just as we were sewing the line in place at the very end of the procedure, the resident walked in. He said, "How are you guys doing? Do you need anything?" We said, "No, everything went fine. We're just finishing up." He said, "Well, you know the patient is not breathing?" We said, "What?" He said, "The guy is not breathing." We checked, and sure enough the patient was dead. He was a DNR (do not resuscitate), but we did not want to be the cause of his death. We reviewed our entire procedure, but nobody could determine why he had died— whether it was the result of a complication from the proce- dure, or whether he would have died anyway. All we knew was that he had been alive at the beginning of the procedure and was dead at the end of it.

I went back to my call room to go back to bed that night and rehearsed the entire scenario in my head over again. "Okay, I put the introducer in and pulled out the guide wire. I put my finger over the opening so that no air could get into the line. Did I not have my finger all the way over the opening? I know that I did. Then I inserted the catheter, pulled out the introducer, kept my finger on the opening and hooked it up. I must not have had my finger over the opening all the way. What other complication would have caused his death if it wasn't air in the line? I know I had the line blocked off. But what if I didn't? Did I kill this guy?"

That was a long and sleepless night for Mark, but he was in the thick of the jungle of internship, and once daybreak rolled around, there was only time to think of the pressing need of each minute, and as the clock ticked, experience grew.

Sleep deprivation was a huge problem. Since the call rooms were really communication hubs with two sets of bunk beds, the young doctors learned to sneak into unoccupied patient rooms to grab any real sleep. They kept their beepers on, and there was a phone in the room to use when they got a page, but with only one doctor's beeper going off, there was a much better chance of catching a few more winks. This practice was, of course, against hospital rules because the patient rooms were already made up for patients who might get admitted. The nurses got angry when they found a sleeping resident in one of the empty rooms because they had to remake the bed and change out anything else that had been used before allowing occupancy by a patient. Still, an empty room was an empty room, and the house staff camped out as often as possible.

On the home front, the best chance interns had of seeing their spouses at any predictable time was on the day after call. However, due to the lack of sleep, one could not plan on very much coherent conversation before eating a meal and falling into bed. A good night's sleep was always had that night, and then day two began. Day two had no guaranteed ending, but being able to sleep at home was still the reward at the end of it. Then it was day three again, call day.

Foreseeing days of fragmented conversations, unrequited nights, lonely dinner candles burned to nubs, and more contact with my husband's dirty laundry than with him, I decided, very early into this new schedule, to busy myself with a career change that would begin with the two-year MBA program at Wake Forest. The graduation date would coincide with the end of his residency and seemed a perfect fit. Even though I had just barely dipped my toe into the business world with my year at JC Penney, I discovered that I really enjoyed the competitive atmosphere, and I saw all kinds of opportunities for creative thinking. Hopefully, my creative thinking in the future would pay for my incurred debt now. Having survived on the shoestring budget of a first-year resident at Geisinger, we knew that we could manage my proposed student status if we were willing to secure a loan large enough to totally pay for my graduate school. That decision made, I immediately began a job search to fill the six months or so before school was scheduled to begin.

That's how and when I met Dr. Spurr, Mark's old cancer doctor. All the cancer doctors at Bowman Gray knew that Mark had come back to join the internal medicine program as an intern, and they were very excited that their walking miracle had returned, still cancer-free nearly five years out from chemotherapy. What's more, he was now on the "right" road. They considered him too much of a people person to be closed away in a pathology lab. It was during a "welcome back" conversation between Mark and Dr. Spurr that my job status was addressed, and it just so happened that the oncology staff had two attendings/associate professors who needed a secretary. Dr. Spurr asked to meet me, and I paid him a visit in his office shortly thereafter.

Dr. Charles Spurr was the Chairman of the Oncology Department with a long history of cancer research behind him. According to Mark, he had even been involved with what were possibly some of the earliest chemotherapy trials in the United States, experimenting with injections of nitrogen-mustard into a Hodgkin's Disease patient, prior to coming to Bowman Gray.

Despite my excitement at meeting Mark's former cancer doctor, I entered the office with some trepidation, somewhat daunted by the prospect of working for this man. What I found was a tall, kindly, grandfather-like gentleman dressed in a long white coat, with silvery-white hair swirled around a generous amount of bare scalp. His handshake was warm, and he seemed genuinely enthused to meet "Mark's wife." He walked me around the department, introducing me to the other oncologists as well as the two secretaries, who occupied desks in the central common area of the office suite.

Both secretaries appeared friendly, extraordinarily busy, and extremely competent. They also seemed to be in control of the offices and kept their respective doctors "straight." I could tell by the interaction between colleagues and staff that all of the oncologists were greatly admired and respected. I also detected a very dry wit in Dr. Spurr that caused his eyes to sparkle in his own amusement.

Dr. Spurr already knew I had a degree in English, and after asking me how fast I could type, he hired me on the spot, bypassing the human resources department, evidently much to their chagrin. Three weeks into my job, my presence was demanded in the temporary trailer, which housed human resources outside the hospital, where I was rudely subjected to a typing test and the "normal and customary interviews that should have taken place" previous to my employment. Well, Dr. Spurr was Dr. Spurr. Just for the record, I did pass the typing test.

After a few orientation weeks of working in Dr. Spurr's office with his secretary in preparation for working for the two doctors whom I had yet to meet, a strange malady began to afflict me. I awoke one morning to find that I was a bit under the weather, with vomiting, headache, and fatigue. Assuming I had the flu, I took a couple of days off, but when the symptoms refused to abate, and having had no fever, I went back to work hoping to hide my discomfort while visiting the ladies' room every hour of the mornings. My intern husband and I got to see each other every day since we both worked at the hospital, and our meetings occurred in the cafeteria for lunch whenever he could take a break. By lunchtime, I was usually able to eat without nausea and keep the food down, but by early evening, the nausea would return and prevent me from eating dinner. Finally, with noticeable weight loss on my little frame, and fearing some terminal illness, I allowed Mark to order some blood work to be done at the hospital lab.

Somehow that little miracle that wasn't supposed to be able to happen, that had happened once before at Geisinger as "perhaps a fluke," had happened again. Chemo or no chemo, I was pregnant again, and I was so much sicker than the first time, that I rather suspected that this pregnancy just might be viable. But we really didn't know, and due to Mark's medical history and my former miscarriage, and the fact that I had just started this new job, we decided not to tell anybody, except the person I dreaded telling the most, Dr. Spurr. Dr. Spurr had predicted that I would enjoy my job so much that I would never actually start the MBA program, and he had professed no fear at all upon hiring me that I might actually leave in six or seven months as planned.

I confessed my condition to him the next morning, somewhat tearfully (I must have been hormonal). To my surprise he was genuinely congratulatory and happy to know that I was not ill, as I had not been quite so clever as I thought to hide my growing symptoms. I told him I had not so much as suspected my pregnancy when I was hired, and I asked him his opinion of the role Mark's chemotherapy might play in this scenario. For instance, what if I did not miscarry this time? What kinds of birth defects might his former chemotherapy cause in our baby? His answer was, of course, that nobody knew. No one with Mark's history had survived long enough to find out. But since sperm are manufactured continuously rather than being present from birth, as eggs are in females, the sperm were *probably* healthy. He concurred with the previous opinion given me at Geisinger that I *probably* would not have gotten pregnant at all if there was anything wrong with the sperm. He was very optimistic and tried to reassure me, but probability was one thing; a baby was another. I still had one more burning question that I kept to myself, and later pondered with my husband: Was it fair to our future baby to risk that kind of unknown?

Although Dr. Spurr had vowed to keep our secret, and I believe he did, there are no secrets in the hospital. News, especially news of a secretive nature, spreads more rapidly than any other kind of noteworthy event. It wasn't long before everybody knew, and since interns spent so little time with their wives, jokes abounded. Everybody teased Mark, "Who'd you get to do it for you?" And everybody teased me, "When did y'all have time for that little trick? Must've happened here at the hospital somewhere??!" (Not.)

Most people didn't know how close to home some of their comments were to Mark because they didn't know his medical history. He was no longer on chemo when he entered med school, so only a select few of his classmates became privy to his background. Most of the residents were from all over the country and could not have known. All of the students were new. There were many new doctors on staff from all over the world. So most of the people in the know were his former doctors, a few friends who had stayed at Bowman Gray for residency, and the select few who were told. Much had changed since his brain tumor operation in 1968. Dr. David Kelly who had performed the operation was now the chairman of the neurosurgery department, and Dr. Richard Janeway, who had been Mark's neurologist, was now the dean of the medical school.

I don't really know if Dr. Spurr or any of the other doctors in the know worried during the next seven months; if they did, they never let on. The atmosphere was one of celebration and expectation, as well as nausea and vomiting for six hours every morning. Everybody said that would pass. Such was life when I finally met and went to work for Drs. Hy Muss and Doug White. They had both served in the army during the later years of Vietnam as doctors and returned to the United States to do their hematology/oncology fellowships on the GI Bill. Fresh from fellowship they had come on staff as attendings/associate professors at Bowman Gray a few years earlier, and I became their secretary.

They were both great guys and compassionate and knowledgeable docs. Other than that similarity, they were night and day. Dr. Douglas White was tall and thin with dark hair and as laid back and quiet as they come, although it was not difficult to uncover his sense of humor or solicit a smile. Dr. Hyman Muss was shorter with auburn hair and as energetic and springy as a Jack Russell Terrier. His sense of humor was vibrant and almost never concealed. He was hardly ever stationary, but he would unfailingly call his wife every day after lunch and in loud rapid succession blow about ten to fifteen kisses to her through the phone, before rushing out of the office to round with the residents or meet with the fellows or see patients. Sometime after 4 p.m., he would reappear in his office and dutifully return all phone calls of the day. Dr. White, who had the dubious honor of having an office through which the chimney to the hospital crematorium ran, would methodically go about his business and then quietly slip away late in the afternoon to pursue his hobby at home of disassembling and restoring antique cars.

Both doctors were involved in a great deal of clinical research developing and initiating chemotherapy drug trials, and it became a large part of my job to prepare the manuscripts that documented their research, first for peer review, and then for publication. The suite of three small offices where we worked was on a different floor than the other oncology suite that housed Dr. Spurr. We were on the fourth floor just down the hall from the anatomy lab where the blended smells of formaldehyde and brewing coffee at seven in the morning promoted and prolonged my morning sickness. The ladies' room was half the length of the hall and around the corner from the office, and I learned to time my nausea-based dashes to that ladies' room just right. I am proud to say that I made it in time every time.

One thing, among many, that Dr. Spurr was right about was that I did really enjoy my job. The additional thought of trundling into class in August, nearly eight months pregnant and having a baby halfway through the first semester, convinced me to put the MBA program on the back burner. When grant season hit Bowman Gray, I was called upon to leave my fourth floor duties to someone else and go back to work for Dr. Spurr in the new oncology research center, which had recently been set up in some newly vacated temporary space located in the basement of the hospital. The research center housed Director Dr. Spurr, who had moved his office from upstairs, his secretary, a tumor registrar, and various people who helped collect and collate research data. There was a brand-new data processing machine that people were learning how to operate, and the promise of a data/word processor which none of us had ever seen. In 1978, desktop computers had not yet been implemented, and all "word processing" was done on electric typewriters.

"Grant season" referred to the last couple of months prior to the October 1 deadline for federal grant applications to be filed with the National Cancer Institute. Without grant money to fund it, cancer research could not continue. My new job was to work on the team to put the applications together and get them submitted on time. There were only a few electric typewriters banging away, updating curriculum vitae of people involved, editing and retyping submitted manuscripts of ongoing and proposed research programs, and filling in application blanks with required information. Some of the applications were over five hundred pages long, and I was informed that there was always a scurry and flurry at the end of September, no matter what. True to their prediction, on the day the applications were due in DC, I found myself driving two copies of our application to the little airport in Winston-Salem, where I hand delivered them to the courier and watched them get loaded into the plane. I then returned to my office and waited to receive confirmation that they had indeed been received at their destination on time.

During all the hubbub of federal grant season, and the customary workload of internship, a very special anniversary had come for Mark. On September twentieth at lunch, he said, "Follow me." He led me upstairs through the neurosurgery department in search of Dr. David Kelly. Not finding him in his office, Mark picked up a piece of blank paper from his desk and wrote him a note:

9/20/78
Dr. Kelly,
Do you remember where you were and what you were doing 10 years ago today?

Mark Ellis

Later that day he received a page from Dr. Kelly. He said, "I know exactly where I was and what I was doing. I'll never forget. I can't believe it's been ten years since your operation." Mark said, "I just wanted to thank you, again."

By mid-October, we received notification that Bowman Gray's application had been approved, and on the sixteenth of October, ten days before my baby was due, Dr. Spurr took the grant team to lunch to celebrate. That night a very tired intern appeared at our house, having had no sleep the night before in the hospital and having worked an unusually long day after. At 11 p.m., he fell into bed and saw his baby album that I had been looking at earlier. He glanced up at me and said, "Please don't let it be tonight. I've been up for thirty-six hours straight." Fifteen minutes later, my water broke.

While the overly tired prospective father slept, Augie and I paced the hallway and the new nursery, brother Steve's former room which I had transformed from gold walls with black trim to yellow walls with white trim and homemade nursery rhyme drapes. Finally, around 6 a.m., with the contractions closer together and more intense, I awakened Mark and told him it was time. He wanted to know if I was sure. Silly question. A few hours later, a perfect baby daughter answered our prayers. Although his beeper went off several times during the labor and delivery, and the necessary phone calls were made, my intern husband was present at her birth, and when she looked up at him and curled her tiny perfect fingers around his pinky, he was enraptured and captured for life.

In addition to Mark and the obstetrician and the obstetric nurses, there had also been a couple of student nurses, two medical students, a resident, two paramedics, and a taxi driver present. And they had all stood around at the foot of the table on which I was trapped in labor, staring up at the part of my body where all the action was from the depths of their vantage point. One of the medical students suddenly remembered that he had forgotten a portion of his initial examination, and thinking it would be a good idea to examine the pupils of my eyes while I was bearing down and pushing, exchanged his position at the foot of the table for the head, placing his face and a scope directly in front of my eye. What he heard through my clenched teeth when I could speak is not fit to print, but it involved the placement of his lighted instrument rigorously within his own body.

As a result of my performance to such a large audience, I decided that I had fulfilled my teaching responsibility during labor and delivery. For the rest of my hospital confinement, I made sure that any medical students, nursing students, residents, or any other superfluous beings who thought they needed to see my episiotomy changed their minds. My body was open for inspection on a "need to know" basis only.

Four weeks after Lisa was born, I gave notice to the oncology research center that I would not be returning. I elected to become a full-time mother, not knowing how well my brief foray into the administrative world of cancer care would serve me in the future, and being unsure of this moonlighting thing that Mark had planned to begin as soon as he became a second-year resident in February in order to supplement his income and replace my paycheck.

Life had changed, yet internship continued. We could not see each other every day, since I no longer worked at the hospital. The quick lunches we had been able to grab together, even on call days, were impossible now. Fortunately, we had become a two-car family about ten days before Lisa was born, which meant that I had more independence and could function around the baby's schedule instead of his. Better still was the fact that Fred, still a surgery resident, and Gail had become new parents to a baby daughter just twelve weeks ahead of us, and Gail had also elected to become a full-time mother and had given up her teaching job.

Fred and Gail lived within walking distance to the hospital because surgery residents were allowed to take call from home and were not required to spend every third night in the hospital. That is not to say that their sleep didn't get interrupted, or that Fred was not up all night working on one or more cases in the operating room many nights. In fact, I have it on good authority that "Red Fred" became "Code Red Fred" during his surgery residency because he could always be counted on to dive into the middle of a trauma mess and do what needed to be done, and he loved doing so.

We lived about fifteen minutes apart, and Gail, Jenny, Lisa, and I learned how to become mothers and daughters together. We also learned how to adapt ourselves from our "working girl" roles to our domestic positions as doctors' wives, which meant we would have to make "executive decisions" about the running of the household, parental matters, car repairs, and social engagements—everything from the most important to the most mundane. Our husbands' presence, unless we were on out-of-town vacations, would never be able to be depended upon, and we would be responsible for teaching ourselves and our children how to function independently, be adaptable, and think empathetically about the doctor/husband/father we would always share with others. Indeed, internship and residency was every bit as much a dress rehearsal for spouses and children as it was for the young doctors.

Conversely, the doctors would have to learn how to miss all the aspects of home life they would like to be a part of as well as how to shoulder the guilt of missing things they thought should fall to their responsibility rather than to that of their spouses. They would have to learn to trust that the decisions made in their absences would be the same decisions that would have been made had they been able to take part in the decision process, or they would have to learn how to accept the judgment of their life partners. Although they would be regally treated to favorite meals, romantic gestures, and the best of the baby playtime when they were home, in reality, the docs in training wore no crowns either at work or at home.

CHAPTER 14

Residency

Whereas the jump from medical student to intern had been a giant leap, fraught with both the anxiety and the hope of rising to the level of expectation, the transition from intern to second-year resident was a stride marked with confidence. Mark was no longer a doctor merely on sheepskin. He was also a doctor by experience, and what's more, he knew he was competent. He characterizes the year of internship as comparable to the formative years of a child between the ages of one and five.

Even though I hailed the end of his year of internship as a benchmark of what he would never again have to endure, having seen the sleep deprivation and the frustration with the lack of any real time outside the hospital, those thoughts would not be foremost in his mind. What would stand out in his mind, then and now, was the supercharged feeling of acquiring practical medical knowledge at rapid-fire pace, in an atmosphere of necessary efficiency and camaraderie. In fact, he remembers internship as one of the best years of his life.

February of 1979 marked the beginning of his second year of residency, once again, seven months behind the other second-year residents, or five months ahead of the other interns, depending on the point of view. He had worked with both groups as an intern, and he would again work with both groups as a second-year resident. For the next five months, the residents who were used to him being an intern would have to recognize his newly acquired duties, and the interns who were used to him being one of them would have to recognize him as their boss and mentor.

One of the uniquely good things about assuming the duties of a second-year resident in the middle of the year was that the interns Mark had to supervise were already very experienced. Their chart work, their decision making, and their expertise at procedures was much more advanced than it had been in July when they first made the leap from student to doctor. This meant that, among other advantages, he would have less interrupted sleep during call nights than he was used to having. . .at least for the next five months until July rolled around again and ushered in an entirely new group of interns.

The schedule of call nights for second-year residents was a little different than it was for interns. It was every third night during the week Monday through Friday and every other weekend. The second-year residents separated the weekend schedule from the weekday schedule, and since there were usually two second-year residents sharing a given service, there were two working weekends and two off-weekends per month. This meant that during weekends at the hospital, the second-year resident was supervising someone else's interns in addition to his or her own. This "taking of the reins" for another doctor's patients and interns allowed for scrutiny of one another's supervisory skills as well as medical decision making skills and was good training for future life as a physician. Most physicians would always share call with another physician, meaning they would have to be able to surrender their patients for a temporary period of time, such as a weekend or a night, in order to have any off-time. In order to do so, one had to develop a level of trust for the other physician's medical decisions and manner of dealing with patients, not so easy in later life as it was now, when the feeling of being in control or "at the helm" was new.

With the newly found freedom of two weekends per month out of the hospital, Mark decided to follow the lead of other residents who were moonlighting to supplement their incomes. There were several residents who, like him, were young married parents who had lost the second incomes from their spouses and welcomed the opportunity to make some "real" money. And there was no quicker way to make the extra cash.

Moonlighting was a very specific term that only applied to one type of work, being the in-house, on-call, emergency room doctor at one of several outlying hospitals for one or more nights on a weekend. It was forbidden by the residency program, discouraged by most attending physicians, hated by spouses, and indulged in by residents who were hungry for income. Spoken of usually in code by the residents, the network of young doctors all knew who among them spent their free time moonlighting. In fact, several residents staffed the same emergency rooms and rotated shifts around their primary schedules at Baptist.

The shifts at the various hospitals, some of which were two hours away, were twenty-five hours each beginning Saturday morning and ending Sunday morning, and then beginning Sunday morning and ending Monday morning. Once in awhile a half-shift could be picked up on Friday night. Sometimes two shifts were worked together for a total of fifty hours in one weekend. The going rate was twenty-five dollars per hour. Working just two shifts netted more money than working the entire month at a resident's salary.

The major problem for the residency program as well as for the eager young doctor was a true lack of sleep. Although an on-call room with a shower was provided for the doctor, there was very little sleep. Patients came into the ER at all hours of the day and night with any number of complaints and situations requiring the attention of a physician. The schedule was especially difficult if the moonlighting weekend occurred just after or just prior to a regular call night at Baptist.

If the resident had been on call at Baptist Friday night and was scheduled to work the Saturday ER shift at another hospital, he or she would have to drive directly to the other hospital upon being released from duty and begin the twenty-five hour shift there. If little sleep was had Friday night, there was sure to be less during the next twenty-five hours. This made for a very tired resident who returned home on Sunday morning to fall into bed, get up in the early afternoon, spend about eight waking hours at home, return to bed and go back to work on Monday morning.

Although the schedule was grueling enough in that scenario, it really only affected the resident's home life and the outlying ER. When a Sunday shift was worked, the residency program was directly affected due to a very tired second-year resident beginning work at Baptist on Monday morning. It was worse if the resident was on call Monday night because he would have to work through Tuesday before going home, meaning that by Tuesday at 6 p.m., he could have been awake for fifty-eight hours, all the while being responsible for his interns and their patients. Attempts were always made to avoid back-to-back call nights, but there was really no way to totally avoid these situations. Once the resident was plugged into the ER schedule, the hospitals, which were small, understaffed community hospitals, became dependent upon the young doctors, all of whom had the same scheduling issues.

Moonlighting was always a bad idea to me. We very strongly disagreed about the topic. I thought it was bad for the program because of the fact that medical decisions were being made by people who were overly tired. I thought the sleep deprivation imposed by the program itself was fundamentally wrong, and moonlighting only compounded the problem. Mark argued that he would get more sleep as a second-year resident, especially in the middle of the year, than he had as an intern, and could always stop moonlighting if things did not go well. "Everybody else is doing it, even Fred, and besides, maybe we can even save some money." It was very difficult to make ends meet on the meager salary of a resident, and most months they didn't exactly meet. I didn't enjoy using Visa to pay off Mastercard and Mastercard to pay off Visa, but we both considered our financial situation temporary, and I would rather have had less money and more of his presence at home.

Mark had developed a very strong, very stubborn desire to be a good provider for his family since becoming a father—not exactly a character flaw—and as he pointed out to me, there was no way that I could make six hundred twenty-five dollars in one twenty-five hour span of time. Although he was speaking from a practical standpoint, his statement angered and hurt me and made me feel rather helpless, perhaps a character flaw in me. Nevertheless, it was true. The one point we agreed upon, without question, was that the best job for me was to be a full-time mother, at home with our baby. I wanted to be a poorer one, financially speaking, considering the short period of time our daughter would be a baby; he wanted me to be a richer one, considering the short period of time that he would "need" to moonlight.

In the end, he decided to moonlight two shifts per month, giving us an extra twelve hundred fifty dollars per month or fifteen thousand per year. Lisa, Augie, and I would see less of him for the next two years than we had during internship. I made the decision to throw myself into my "job" and be the best parent I could be. I became determined to never allow Lisa to be adversely affected by his absence or my reaction to it. Gail and I had many discussions about the absent doctor syndrome while our daughters played together, she believing that "it would always be like this, so we needed to get used to it," and me hoping that it would not, and looking forward to the end of residency.

It was the best of times and the worst of times, I suppose. I reveled in motherhood. I loved watching Lisa discover life. She was so delighted in her daily discoveries. There was something new and beautiful without fail in every single day, and Lisa and Augie became the best of friends. We were a very happy trio, but I do admit to some loneliness, and I regretted that Mark could not share all the baby's "firsts" and little daily happenings that made life so worthwhile to me.

I have to admit that there were some good things that grew out of the moonlighting experience other than the extra money. I became more independent and developed the fortitude and confidence as a parent to handle any situation that might arise. I realized once again that if my destiny in this life was truly to be a partner with a man who felt his destiny was along this particular path, then the last thing he needed at home was a whiny, dependent wife. What he would need at home was strength, organization, nurturing, and love. And I dedicated myself to creating that atmosphere.

When Mark was home, he played ball and frisbee with the dog, who was tireless in his presence. We had some semblance of family dinners, choosing foods that could be cooked ahead of time and warmed up on short notice in pre-microwave age in which we lived. We took walks to the park where he pushed Lisa in the swing and played with her in the sandbox, much of the time while throwing the ball for Augie. Sometimes he and I would try to play tennis. We would enclose everybody within the fenced tennis courts, seat Lisa in her stroller with a toy to play tug-of-war or hide-and-seek with Augie, and commence a game. The dog was great for retrieving stray balls, but sooner or later, she insisted on playing net for either him or me, and she was just too good at it. Lisa was not happy being constrained in an audience seat for very long anyway, so tennis was a short game, but we always enjoyed our time together.

Fortunately for Mark, not so for me, Lisa was a "night owl." No matter what time he got home, they could count on each other for some quality time together. When he was home, I often woke up to find them sitting on the couch watching late night TV and sharing forbidden chocolate ice cream, and I often went to sleep hearing the clicking sounds of the baby swing keeping rhythm for Mark's acoustic guitar while he sang "Rocky Raccoon" to his baby daughter.

The good thing about moonlighting for Mark, other than the sense that he was being a good provider, was that he was the boss in the ER, and as such, was depended upon and appropriately respected by the staff. He gained invaluable experience in making practical medical decisions, expediting care, and handling expected as well as unexpected situations without the kind of backup support from a hierarchy that existed only in a teaching hospital.

Typically in the community hospital, the resident from Baptist who was working the ER shift was the only doctor present in the hospital on the weekend nights. Backup support existed in the form of private practice community physicians who covered for one another by taking call from home. The emergency room doctor was expected to assess patients and to do as much as possible for them according to his or her level of expertise and training. Much of an ER shift was spent performing real hands-on medicine and treating and releasing patients, or treating them to a point and admitting them to the hospital. Their care would then be transferred to the appropriate community physicians later that day or the next morning depending on the time of day they presented in the emergency room.

Patients who required more urgent care from a community doctor resulted in a phone call from the emergency room to the doctor on call. The ER doctor would explain the situation to the on-call physician and either receive instructions over the phone as to what to do, or request the presence of the on-call doctor, depending on the situation. For example, a questionable appendix would result in a call to the surgeon. Heart attacks resulted in a call to the cardiologist, if there was one. Sometimes communities had few, if any, specialists and had to rely on general practitioners for everything. Some doctors had nobody with whom to share call and were just on call every night.

There was reluctance on the part of the ER doctor to "bother" the on-call doctor, especially at night, knowing firsthand what it was like to be sleep deprived, and some doctors were reluctant to come back to the hospital or didn't appreciate having their sleep disturbed. Their vulnerability was often determined by the type of resident manning the emergency room. Whereas a surgery resident would be able to handle certain types of injuries better than a medicine resident, a medicine resident would be able to handle certain types of illnesses better than a surgery resident. When Mark worked the ER shifts, most of the outside physician contact he had was with surgeons.

Eden, North Carolina, is a small town located about an hour and a half northwest of Winston-Salem and was home to one of the community hospitals in which several of the residents from Baptist Hospital moonlighted, including Mark. One night while he was on duty there, a young man came into the emergency room with a broken ankle. After assessing the situation and determining that a surgeon was needed, Mark made the necessary call. A short time later, a middle-aged guy in well-worn jeans and mud-caked boots showed up and introduced himself as the surgeon. Looking more like a rancher who had spent a long day with his herd, he rolled up his sleeves as he clomped across the floor and went in to see the patient. As he prepared to set the bone, he called Mark into the room. He said, "See this? You know what kind of fracture this is? It's a trimalleolar fracture. You know who else had one of these? John Wilkes Boothe. It's the same kind of fracture he got when he jumped onto the stage after shooting President Lincoln."

Amazing what you learn in the middle of the night from a crusty dude wearing cowboy boots. And he could not have picked a better guy to be teaching about John Wilkes Boothe's broken ankle. It just so happened that this here resident working in the ER had paved Bean Town Road right in front of the historic home of Dr. Samuel Mudd, the famous physician who had set that trimalleaolar fracture in the ankle of John Wilkes Boothe.

Yes indeedy, Mark had had a summer job after graduating from high school working on a road crew. "The best thing about that job was that when we ran out of asphalt, we would have to wait for another truck, and while we waited, somebody would go get some crabs, and after we ate, we would stretch out on the side of the road under a tree and take a nap." The schedule played well into the hands of a young, almost-college lad who enjoyed drinking beer and chasing girls with his best buddy Robert until three in the morning. He had to get up at six. Of course, after he mistakenly threw a shovel full of hot asphalt onto one of the other guys, he won the job of flagman. (I really think he should leave that part out when he talks about it, but he never does.)

He probably told the surgeon the whole story; he has told it multiple times to his family. If one takes the back way, route

301 from Virginia up to DC, Bean Town Road is not too far off the beaten path in Maryland. His paving masterpiece has been proudly displayed to the captive audience trapped in the car on several occasions. . .the same audience time after time.

As impressive as that story undoubtedly was to the surgeon he had called in, Mark, years later, learned a little tidbit about that surgeon, who had not looked the part, but had expertly fixed the patient's ankle. He had not only graduated from Wake Forest, but he had also played football there and had been good enough to be drafted in the NFL. He had opted to go to medical school instead and had become an orthopedic surgeon and chosen to live in and serve the community in little 'ol Eden, North Carolina.

Events and situations in the small-town emergency rooms were not all as informative or friendly as that particular one was. Some of his most memorable emergency room nights involved a drunken young man who had just about been scalped by a cue stick in a billiard room brawl, a cockroach stuck in someone's ear canal, and a motorcycle gang leader's girlfriend who had a sliced cheek needing stitches. The latter would not be nearly as memorable if the burly, leather-garbed, gang leader had not threatened Mark, "If you leave a scar on my girlfriend's face, I'll find your wife and leave a scar on hers." One of the saddest nights involved a shooting victim who turned out to be a tech who worked at the ER and who arrived DOA.

The variety of patients and the potential problems were infinite. Usually, however, he was getting coughed on by crying kids or patching up drunks who had been fighting, as he plodded from one curtained cubicle to another to answer the needs of the steady stream of humanity that trickled in through the revolving emergency room doors.

When his twenty-five hour shift was done in the mornings, he would interrupt his drive home to stop at a gas station and grab a soda to keep himself awake on the road. He would also call me from the pay phone (pre-cell phone days) to tell me he was leaving and to give me his ETA. I always worried about him going to sleep while he was driving, but he always arrived safely home, gave the dog, the baby, and the wife a kiss and stumbled up the two flights of stairs where he fell into bed.

Somehow, someway, despite the crazy schedule, before the end of his second year of residency, I was pregnant again. By the time he crossed over into his third year in February 1980, we were expecting four life-changing events to take place in the upcoming summer: a new baby, the end of residency, a move to somewhere as yet unknown and the beginning of active duty in the air force. Timing is everything, so says the great council of They.

The third year of residency was when the six months of Mark's prior pathology credit kicked in, meaning that although Mark had come onto the consult service enjoyed by the rest of the third-year residents midyear, he was instantly elevated to their status. They would all finish in the summertime, them in July, and him in August.

The consult service was a welcome reprieve from the demands of primary responsibility to patients. The third-year residents still had to continue with their outpatient clinics two or three times a week as they had done throughout their residency, but they had no patients of their own in the hospital to follow. The third-year residents rotated through various services for which they did the internal medicine consults. For example, if there was a general surgery patient who appeared to have a related or non-related medical condition, an internal medicine consult was sought by the surgical resident. The medicine resident would see the patient, work him or her up for the problem, make a diagnosis, and recommend appropriate treatment. The patient would continue to be followed on the surgery service by the surgery resident, with backup from the medicine residents on a PRN (as needed) basis. Sometimes, the problem would require transfer of the patient to a medicine service, but once the initial work-up and recommendation was made, the patient belonged to whatever second-year medicine resident and intern were rotating through that particular medicine specialty.

The third-year residents also spent less overnight call in the hospital. . .which meant they could moonlight more often, which meant more money.

One of the reasons that having some money to save was so important to Mark as a provider, was that he had no life insurance. Here he was, a father and sole provider for a very young and expanding family, and he had no financial protection to offer them if something happened to him. Due to his medical history, no company would insure him. We had been through the process for four years with several companies, including those who offered guarantee-issue life insurance policies; what a laugh. Part of the process was the "in your own home physical" in which a doctor comes to your home, does a brief physical, takes a urine sample, a blood sample, and a history, which in Mark's case was long and complex. The doctors who heard the story were incredulous to be sure, but they also recognized the huge importance of the passage of time.

Five years without a recurrence was pretty standard for defining the term "cure." In 1980, it had been twelve years since Mark's brain tumor, and he had had no recurrences. He had brain scans, lung scans, and supporting letters from his former oncologists to document his perfect health, but to no avail.

The process always began and ended the same way. Once the examining doctor was over the initial shock that he had survived this horrendous illness, the doubt would set in. "You couldn't really have had a brain tumor that was malignant melanoma. You may have had a malignant mole and a brain tumor, but the tumor could not have been melanoma. You would be dead now." They would recover themselves and generally go to bat for him, but the underwriters would take up the song, "You couldn't have had malignant melanoma. . ."

Mark finally "stole" his own medical records from the hospital. In those days, medical records were so confidential that the patient couldn't even have access to them, (unless, of course, one was in the military, where the patient was entirely responsible for them and carried the originals from one military location to the next). At any rate, being a doctor at Baptist Hospital, Mark had access, and he took them for safekeeping and for copying, to prove his case to the insurance companies.

Although the records served as documenting evidence for the length of time he had been disease free, they also served as documenting evidence that he truly had had a malignant melanoma brain tumor with additional metastases. The underwriters changed their tune to, "You have a very poor prognosis. We cannot offer you life insurance at this time."

Even with all the documentation, all the recommendations, the passage of time, the perfect health, and the fact that he was considered a good enough health risk for the United States Air Force, the insurance companies were unyielding. We must have been very optimistic people, because we continued our lives as though we expected them to continue. Mark trotted along his medical career path as sole provider of our family, and I marched along my path to the expiration of my teaching certificate and the hibernation of my future earning potential. What if the insurance companies were right? What if his cancer came back?

I only remember one time when Mark showed any emotion other than that of eternal optimism about his prognosis. Way back when he was in medical school and I was in college, we had been studying up in his room at the condo. I was reading, seated on his bed propped up with a couple of pillows, and he was seated at this huge desk he had gotten from some surplus store, with his back to me. He suddenly picked up the three-inch thick book he was reading and threw it across the room and then stomped out. It was pretty early in our relationship; I think we were already engaged, but I wasn't sure what had just happened. I ventured over to pick up the book, a seventh edition of *Harrison's Principals of Internal*

*Medicine** and found the area he had been highlighting. It was a small section, only two pages on malignant melanoma, which basically stated that he wasn't really alive and had no hope of being so:

> *Cutaneous Malignant Melanoma, however, is virtually untreatable by chemotherapy or x-ray, and, so far, hope for survival has been based on surgical excision during the very early primary stages before deep invasion occurs.*

At that time, Mark was nine years beyond his primary melanoma, seven years beyond his brain tumor, two years beyond his five years of chemotherapy treatment, and thankfully, very much alive. When he walked back into the room a few minutes later, he started and finished a brief conversation with me:

> *"That really pisses me off. Did you read that?"*
> "Yes."
> *"Well, don't worry about it. It's obviously bullshit."*

He wasn't worried. He was just mad. . .at the textbook.

Medical or health insurance had not been a problem for him or for us, although it had been a bit of a problem for his father. Back in the sixties and seventies, health insurance existed only as major medical, which covered hospitalizations and emergency room expenses. There were no plans for preventive medicine or coverage of doctor visits or prescription coverage. Those were cash transactions payable at time of service or billed monthly on payment plans.

Since Mark was a dependent when he first got sick, and since his dad had good health insurance through the United States Department of Defense, the health insurance company could not drop him, even when he came of age to transfer to his own policy, due to the fact that he was still on chemotherapy. So he had stayed on his father's policy until he was off treatment and until his father

---

* *Harrison's Principles of Internal Medicine*, "Malignant Melanoma," Thomas B. Fitzpatrick. Published by McGraw Hill, Inc. 1974. Quoted with permission.

successfully found a policy to which Mark could transfer that would not deny him benefits for a pre-existing condition if he ever had a recurrence. When we got married, I was added to his policy, which included maternity benefits, and off we went. Of course, since he never had a recurrence, the policy was never put to the test.

Life insurance was a pickle, and Mark just kept at it, until one day just before we went on active duty, he was finally offered a rated policy. A rated policy meant that there was an additional fee attached to the premium due to an identified health risk. There were several levels of ratings—the higher the health risk, the higher the rating, and the higher the premium. With his level of identified risk being the absolute highest, the policy was nearly unaffordable on our income, but if we took the policy, paid the exorbitant premiums on time, and stayed healthy, the policy would be reviewed in a few years, and the rating gradually reduced as time went on.

It wasn't for that much life insurance either, only about $25,000, but it would "bury him" and provide a small nest egg. More importantly, it was kind of like establishing credit. Once he got his foot in the door, other companies would be more likely to follow suit and eventually offer him better policies, increasing the total amount of life insurance.

That seemed like a racket to me, but at the same time, I wasn't earning any money, nor was I protecting my own earning potential. I was just being a young mommy and a homemaker. Mark was determined to eventually amass enough life insurance to take care of his family in such a way as to provide his children with a mother who would have the ability to continue to be a homemaker if and when his fatal cancer ever came back. So he continued to moonlight, and we began to pay the exorbitant premiums.

It was around this time that Mark was offered a hematology/oncology fellowship opportunity at Bowman Gray about which we were very excited. It meant that he would defer the four-year air force commitment yet again for three years, the length of the program, and he would serve all of his active duty years as a hematologist/oncologist at one of the major military tertiary care centers, probably in the United States.

We had already been discussing air force locations, and initially we were excited about an opportunity to serve outside the continental United States, like Hawaii or England or Germany. But when we found out about the quarantine restrictions necessary to take Augie with us, it became very important to us to stay stateside. The quarantine period for her varied depending on location, from three months to six months, but we would have been unwilling to kennel her for any longer than two weeks. She was, after all, our first-born.

The United States Air Force saw things a bit differently. They informed us that their need for internists was greater than their need for oncologists, and that we would definitely be coming on board as soon as Mark's residency was finished. If we wanted anything to say about our location, we had better fill out our top three choices on their official form rather quickly.

Mark was disappointed because he knew that the oncology program at Bowman Gray was excellent, and having been in Winston-Salem for so many years, we were both very comfortable there. When Bowman Gray said that he would be welcomed back for the fellowship after his four-year commitment to the air force had been fulfilled, he was somewhat assuaged, and we adjusted our plans to begin to try to get excited about where we might wind up living for the next four years. We filled out the "top three form":

1. Myrtle Beach AFB, Myrtle Beach, South Carolina
2. Tyndall AFB, Panama City, Florida
3. McDill AFB, St. Petersburg, Florida

There were, of course, no guarantees; this was the military. We settled in to wait.

In the meantime, Mark was assigned to Hickory, North Carolina to fulfill his four-week outreach program requirement by Bowman

Gray. It was June, and I was hugely pregnant, expecting our baby in mid-July. The good news was that family living quarters were provided at an apartment complex close to the small community hospital, and even Augie could go with us. The bad news was that they were roach infested with old dirty long shag carpeting and no place to run the energy off of a young German Shepherd. With a fair-skinned active toddler, even the over-crowded pool did not offer enough entertainment.

After one week, I took Lisa, Augie, and my rapidly enlarging midsection to Myrtle Beach to stay with Mark's parents. Augie had long ago adopted Pop Pop as her favorite relative and fortunately won his heart, and Lisa, who called herself Sassy, (for reasons that became evident later in her life) was their only grandchild. We were graciously received in the little town house at Possum Trot to which Mammaw and Pop Pop had recently retired and were treated like we were on vacation.

Mark's parents were avid golfers, and Lisa was an avid golf cart rider. Before or after golf, we ran the dog at the beach. She loved the surf and would bound in through the waves to retrieve a frisbee or a tennis ball, swimming back with strong strokes and demanding that we challenge her to further distances out into the ocean. I was able to take an afternoon nap, which Sassy had given up when she was nine months old and which in my condition was almost mandatory, and Mammaw and I played scrabble and cards during quiet times. Poor Mark slugged it out in Hickory.

During one of Mark's off weekends, he visited us at the beach, and we went out to an air show at the air force base where we were hoping to be stationed. The hospital was small, and internal medicine was the highest level of specialty there, which meant the internists practiced a little of everything, or as much of anything that they could handle. Perhaps it was not the ideal hospital situation for an aspiring oncologist, but the location was great. . .the beach, mild weather, and a set of grandparents.

About a week after our return to Winston-Salem to finish the last two months of residency, the fourth of July rolled around, and my fifteen year-old sister joined us to await the arrival of the baby and to be the on-call babysitter while I was in the hospital. The holiday weekend wasn't nearly as celebrated in Winston-Salem as it was in our hometown of Roebling, New Jersey, so Amy and I decided to have our own little party and watch the fireworks on TV.

Mark was moonlighting for the entire weekend, and we were by ourselves. Strawberry daiquiris seemed like a good idea; a couple of blueberries garnishing the top of the frozen red concoction made it a very suitable tribute to Independence Day. We had so much fun that night, catching up on all of my sister's teenage dramas, and latest bands, and talking about the new "disco fever" clothes and whether or not I'd ever be able to get back into my Gloria Vanderbilt designer jeans, that we continued the celebration the following two nights.

It was some sort of justice, I suppose, that I had to list my last meal as a strawberry daiquiri when I checked into the hospital in labor around five in the morning on July 7. There was no time for an epidural, and the alcohol had long since been metabolized. Mark almost missed the delivery, but he managed to appear minutes before the baby that would share his name was born.

Six weeks later, residency was over, and the condo at Stonebridge was empty, our furniture having been picked up and trucked to a storage facility in Panama City, Florida, courtesy of the United States Air Force. Mark, having had a pre-active duty physical—which, for him, included more testing than the average bear, with a brain scan and a lung scan—drove to Sheppard Air Force Base in Texas to complete a four-week officer training program with yet another clean bill of health. On the way, he stopped off for two days in Dallas and took the internal medicine boards. I, with my two babies and no home, decided to split time between New Jersey with Grandma and Pap Pap and Myrtle Beach with Mammaw and Pop Pop.

I kenneled Augie and flew to New Jersey and reunited with the dog and Mark's parents two weeks later in Winston-Salem, where we picked up my car and drove to Myrtle Beach. After our stay at Myrtle Beach, Mammaw, the dog, the babies, and I drove to Panama City. Armed with milk-laden breasts, toddler snacks, diapers, Dr. Seuss books, crayons, and a tennis ball stiff with old dog slobber, I sat between the two baby seats in the back of my burnt-orange Cutlass station wagon with Sassy, Mark Jr., and Augie. Some of the baby paraphernalia was in the way back with the dog, and some of it was in the front seat on the passenger side of the car. Part of the baby swing hung over the back of the back seat on one side, and part of the dog hung over the back of the back seat on the other side. We drove straight through, about twelve hours. My mother in law insisted on doing all the driving.

One of Mark's favorite sayings is, "Mama Ellis didn't raise no dummy." That's because Mama Ellis ain't no dummy.

CHAPTER 15

TYNDALL

We couldn't wait to see Mark, and I guess he couldn't wait to see us either, because when he drove up to our motel, he was still dressed in his newly acquired air force uniform. Lisa had been anxiously watching out the window with Augie by her side. As soon as he rumbled into the parking lot in his TR-6, she yelled, "Daddy!" and before he had stepped out of the car, the dog burst out of the ensuing bottleneck at the motel door first. Navigating Augie's great wagging tale, and shouting, "You're home!" Sassy, yellow curls bobbing, ran straight into her father's arms where she was whisked high above the gleefully yipping German Shepherd. She then giggled, "Daddy, you have no hair!"

That was the first time any of us, excepting his mother, had ever seen Mark with short hair. It was really short too. It was buzzed. One of the first things that had been required of the new officers at Sheppard Air Force Base, probably reminiscent of freshman football days to Mark, was to achieve that military cut. But, hair or no hair, I always was a sucker for a man in uniform. We made him put on his hat and show us his salute.

Baby Mark had been asleep just inside the motel room, which had a door that opened out into the parking lot. By the time we went inside, Lisa was wearing the hat and chattering like a magpie, and baby Mark was awake. When his father leaned over the bed and gently said, "Hi, Markie," the baby stared intently at him with his dark brown eyes wide open and didn't make a sound or move a muscle. He had been six weeks old when his father had left to report for officer training in Texas, and four weeks later, he had no idea who this stranger was. I felt bad for Mark, who had driven all night so he could reunite with his family as quickly as possible.

Our first order of business was to move into more suitable quarters and put Mammaw on a plane heading back to Myrtle Beach. Since we had no house prospects yet, we booked ourselves into an extended stay motel with a kitchenette and a playground for both the dog and the toddler. We could have stayed at the visiting officers' quarters (VOQ) at Tyndall, but the base was located on its own little island and was the furthest point from anything. So we decided that we would stay at a more central location from which we could make shorter, more toddler/dog friendly scouting missions to peruse neighborhoods and houses for rent. We intended to buy our first house as soon as we could, but we needed immediate housing and did not want to live at the motel a day longer than necessary. Our real estate agent thought that a rental would be able to be located and processed much faster than a sale. Of course, we were looking for a rental that would allow two babies and a large dog, something we feared might be extremely difficult.

In the civilian world from whence we came, we probably would have met with difficulty in our attempts, but the military world was different. As we soon discovered, the air force community extended far beyond the base. Our agent took us out to view neighborhoods. Let me rephrase that: Our agent drove her car, and we followed in the station wagon with the babies and the dog. We didn't normally take the dog everywhere we went, but we didn't want to leave her in the motel room and chance an unsuspecting motel staff member wandering into our room to find a one-hundred-twenty-pound German Shepherd protecting our stuff, and we thought that we might have to prove how well-behaved Augie was to a rental owner. We knew that if one could look beyond the size and breed of the dog, that she was personable enough to win anybody's heart. We were young.

We found a new neighborhood, most of which was still being built, called Grimes Estates. Our agent had billed it as a military neighborhood. I didn't really know how a community that was located twenty minutes off base could possibly be a military neighborhood, but we were new to all this air force stuff.

The new homes were mostly brick ranchers with three or four bedrooms built in about five or six different models with adjustable floor plans and customized features. One three-bedroom home with a two-car garage and a fenced-in backyard had just been vacated by a family who had been stationed at Tyndall and was for rent. The house was perfect for us. The most outstanding thing about the house was the color scheme on the inside. The carpet was brick red and actually matched the color of the bricks outside. The kitchen vinyl was a Spanish mosaic pattern with the same brick red to match the carpet as well as the colors amber and black. The kitchen appliances I had never seen before; nor have I since. They were vermilion. . .the stove, the refrigerator, and even the dishwasher. I thought they were beautiful. So did Mark.

The best thing about the house was that the owner was willing to give us a six-month lease with an option to renew if needed. We would have bought it on the spot if it had been for sale and we had had enough money for a down payment. . . which it wasn't and we didn't. But what a find! And no problems with the dog or the little ones. That was our first lesson concerning military families. Military families were good to each other.

What a great neighborhood. There were kids and dogs and cats and stay-at-home moms. Most of the husbands were air force and worked at the base. The neighborhood was friendly and easygoing. Nobody had any pretense. The pilots were wild men, but that was accepted, expected, and enjoyed. We immediately decided to build our own house there, and we found easy financing through the federal credit union, with a VA loan, again a military plus.

We had a steady paycheck on which we could make ends meet with NO MOONLIGHTING! Mark was a captain with a captain's salary plus an additional medical corps bonus. We eagerly signed a contract to build a house with the same floor plan that we were renting. The foundation already poured, the house was projected to be done in six months. Perfect. The VA loan meant that we had to put very little money down, and the captain's salary meant that we could easily afford the monthly payments at eight percent.

That was in September of 1980. By October the interest rates had climbed to ten percent, and rates were so unstable that the credit union would not allow us to lock in the rate until thirty days before the closing date. But things were still okay. We could still swing the payments, and everything else was working out well. Lisa turned two on the seventeenth of October, and even though we had been in town for less than three weeks, the neighbors helped scare up a birthday party for her in our new backyard with more than enough little kids and presents.

Mark's job was going well. He and his partner Steve, who was also new to Tyndall, were the only two internists at the hospital, which meant that, like the hospital we had seen at Myrtle Beach Air Force Base, they were the highest level of specialists stationed there. They were both fresh from their residencies, confident in their medical skills, and inexperienced in daily medical practice administrative issues outside of a training program. They had a lot to do and more cardiac cases than they cared for, but Steve was a great guy—laid back, smart, and fun. His wife, Robin, was tall and pretty and another Beatles fanatic on the same level of fanaticism as Mark. We got along famously, and their son, David, who was about three years older than Lisa, tolerated her well and was an expert on *Star Wars*. He had a model of the Millennium Falcon that he knew inside and out and could rattle off almost as much trivia about *Star Wars* as Robin and Mark could banter back and forth about the Beatles.

Life was good. I learned how to shop at the commissary. . .never on the day after payday, which was once a month. The military ID check line to get into the commissary was incredible on that day as well as the check-out lines, and the aisles were packed with shoppers—not a good day to take babies to get groceries. But the prices couldn't be beaten, and there was no sales tax, although you were expected to tip the baggers a percentage of the total bill. Somewhat problematic was the LARGE size of everything. From laundry detergent to dry goods, things came in big sacks and boxes. Storage at home was both an art and a science.

I learned how to shop from the more veteran air force wives, once every two weeks, sometimes once a month. I tried to learn how to freeze milk and bread, but I didn't have enough room in the freezer. In order to fit everything in the cart, the military wives had the system. Plastic-entwined six-packs, which were how all the soda and beer was packaged within each case, were removed from the case a six-pack at a time and hung over the top sides of the cart by splitting the six cans long ways so that three cans hung on each side. There was virtually no other product that could ride like that; therefore, if you tried to put cases of drinks inside or under your cart, you were wasting space. The sides of the carts, or "buggies" as they are called in the south, could hold two whole cases worth of six-packs if you dangled them in that manner, saving the bottom of your cart for other bulk necessities, like a hundred rolls of toilet paper or a case of dog food. In reality, the commissary was similar to what Sam's Club is like nowadays, although I don't believe bulk shopping was available to everyday civilians during the early 1980s.

There were rumored to be alligators in the bayou behind our house and stories of the beasts getting into garages and hiding under cars, but I never saw any. The chain link fence around the back yard would have protected the dog anyway, and the toddlers were never outside by themselves, fence or none. Augie even took a mad dash into the bayou one day during a walk when we had let her off her leash to play ball and stick. Like she had done in the ocean so many times, she plunged into the water to chase down a stick that had gone awry. Although we worried and desperately tried to change the dog's mind before she got too far out into the water, she managed to come out in one piece, stick in mouth. I am sure that alligators did live back there. Panama City, Florida, had all manner of bothersome critters, like the "no-seeums," little unseen flying insects that were small enough to fit through window screens and bit like hell. I learned quickly that they staged their attacks late in the day, so four in the afternoon was the daily end of outdoor fun for the kids.

Steve and Robin had even had a scorpion come up out of the drain in their bathtub during the night, and Steve nearly stepped on it at 6 a.m. when he sleepily stepped into the tub to turn on the shower. Fortunately, he spotted the critter out of the corner of his eye just before his bare foot landed on top of it, and disaster was averted. He trapped the thing in a jar, and he and David preserved it in alcohol. They also had a snake that managed to get into their heating ducts somehow in the garage, and it crawled all through the system, terrifying Robin by poking out its head from ceiling registers in various rooms, before a game warden finally caught it.

Florida was an adventure, and despite the creepy-crawlers, we had fun exploring and adapting to the area as well as to our new military life. I surprised myself by liking the air force. Having grown up when I did and come of age with all the hippies and flower children, I wasn't sure I was going to have much appreciation for the regimentation of the military. But I did. I rapidly got used to the lack of hair on men's heads, and I began to like the clean-cut appearance even out of uniform. It certainly answered Mark's old curly hair problem for him. No frizz, no muss, no fuss.

I also found appreciation for the mutual respect, the open acknowledgement of a superior by the salute. The rank was there for all to see, and it told a fair amount about a person: length of time in the service, pay grade, education. There were additional pins and insignia to indicate medical corps, legal corps, pilot, flight surgeon. As a result, everybody knew how much money everybody else made. Instead of feeling exposed, I felt very comfortable, even though there were the inside jokes and jabs at the doctors for not "really" being military people like the rest of the crowd, since they had risen up through the ranks largely by mail, along the extensive education path they had taken to become doctors.

Mark liked the same aspects of the military that I did, and he liked seeing the patients. He was less enamored with the way the hospital ran. He and Steve were both frustrated with the "red tape" that they had to go through to get certain supplies or to make any changes in the way their clinics were run. He also did not like the fact that his staff—i.e., nurses, lab techs, receptionists, etc.—were not really under him. All the nurses in the entire hospital as well as in all the clinics, for instance, answered to one nursing supervisor who was a colonel and made all staffing decisions. The doctors had no say in whether or not a nurse got pulled for a different hospital duty on any given day.

Mark was always butting his head against the wall, so to speak, trying to improve the system. Steve would always tell him, "That's just the way they do things. Just don't let it get to you. You're not going to be a lifer in the air force anyway." Despite the fact that Mark had an oncology fellowship opportunity four or so years into the future, he persisted in taking that old medical school approach he had adopted in which he would try on his present job like he planned to do it forever. For him, being a lifer in the United States Air Force was a legitimate possibility. . . if a few things changed. What's more, because he was new to active duty, he really didn't know if the problems he encountered were specific to Tyndall or whether they were standard air force problems or military problems in general.

In early November, a great thing happened for Mark. He still had his TR-6, and he enjoyed his twenty-minute commute to and from work because it was his down time, and he loved driving his sports car and listening to good music. He came in one evening from work, made his greetings, extended both hands straight up into the air raising his face to the ceiling and said, "There's finally real music on the radio again!" Having never fully recovered from the break-up of the Beatles, and having no real appreciation for the disco music of the late seventies, he felt that the music scene had been relatively stagnant and disappointing. However, he found a beacon of hope on the way home from the base that night when he heard Bruce Springsteen's new song, "Hungry Heart." Music was still a very important part of Mark's daily inspiration, and the Boss had answered a long-awaited need.

Since things were about to get a little rocky, some good old rock 'n roll was going to be very useful. The first bump in the road occurred when the interest rates shot up uncontrollably. When they hit fourteen percent, we no longer had a valid contract, because we could no longer afford the monthly payments for the house we were building. Since the contract was contingent on obtaining financing, as most real estate contracts are, we and the builder were out of luck. We were really disappointed and unsure what we would do about housing, because we really had our hearts set on the house, and more importantly, we loved the neighborhood.

I discovered that I hated socialized medicine, which was really what military health care was, in my opinion. Mark Jr. was prone to ear infections, and the waiting room in the pediatric clinic was always jammed with runny-nosed, coughing children. Since the wait to see the pediatrician was never less than three hours, probably due to lack of adequate staffing as well as lack of adequate space, the baby with the painful ears cried while the toddler who was forced to accompany us acquired germs for all manner of illnesses. The prescribed antibiotic was always the same, ampicillin, in reconstitutable pink powder form in a semitransparent plastic bottle. Prior to mixing with water, the antibiotic powder had a very long shelf life, and I would always complain to Mark, "Can't you just bring some home to have on hand?" I knew when my kids had ear infections; after being up all night with a wailing baby, I didn't need to wait three more excruciating hours or make my baby wait three more excruciating hours to have a doctor or physician assistant look into his ears and tell me he had an infection. Dah! I argued that membership had its privileges, but to no avail. He insisted on playing by the rules, the first rule being that he was not our family's doctor.

The next bad turn of events was more than a bump in the road. On December 8, during the Monday night football game, Mark was standing in the kitchen watching the game on TV in the attached family room as he put the shine on the red-orange stove after doing the dinner dishes. Despite his busy job, after a round of "hop on pop," he was very helpful in the evenings when he was home and often preferred kitchen cleanup duty to bathing the kids. I think he found the instant gratification of putting the spit-shine on the kitchen while he watched or listened to a television program therapeutic.

I had just finished reading to the kids and putting them to bed and walked into the family room to sit down to watch the game. Before I got to the couch and before Mark could put down his dishtowel, Howard Cosell announced that John Lennon had been shot outside his home at the Dakota in New York City. We both stood there as if struck by lightning, motionless and disbe-lieving. My mind was reeling; "Maybe he's not dead, maybe he's not dead, maybe he's not dead," but Cosell's next announcement confirmed the worst. John was dead on arrival at a hospital in New York City.

That moment is frozen in time for both of us, a niche on both of our time lines, the injustice of his violent death and the pass-ing of a musical genius washing over us and combining to form the dark realization that the world would never be the same. The impact was overwhelming even before we realized that the Beatles would truly never play together again. Mark's usual optimism towards life became somewhat clouded that night. The Beatles, all of them, had meant a great deal to him and had been a huge influence in his life.

Swirling through the fog were the other bumps which had sud-denly been reduced from disappointments to inconveniences. Even the "dagger in the heart" notification that Mark had flunked the internal medicine boards he had taken in Dallas on the way to officer training school paled in the light of John's passing. He recalled the "kiss of death" conversation he had had on the eleva-tor with the chairman of internal medicine, back at Bowman Gray just before he had finished residency, in which he had shared his insecurity due to his lack of time to prepare for the upcoming boards. The good doctor had assured him, "Don't worry, nobody from Bowman Gray has ever flunked the internal medicine boards. You'll do fine." Jinx.

After realizing the dubious honor he now held, he had shoved the notification into a drawer in his nightstand and onto a shelf in the back of his mind and continued working. He would deal with what to do about that later. When he found out that his partner had also not passed the boards, he was surprised, but neither doctor was in any mood to make any immediate decisions concerning what that meant or what they would do about it.

The sun did come out again. Another military family up the street got orders to report to a new base, and decided to sell their house. The housing market was still very slow due to the prevailing high interest rates, but because their VA loan had been taken out a couple of years earlier when rates had been at seven percent, they had a hot commodity. VA loans were assumable without having to qualify through the regular process, and because we were eligible for a VA loan ourselves, we could assume theirs and give them our eligibility so that in the future they could again obtain a VA loan. We had to give them their asking price, of course, meaning we had to come up with some equity, but fortunately, they were asking a fair price for their house, and they didn't have that much equity in it. And I think Mark's dad lent him a little cash.

We became the proud owners of our first house. It wasn't like the one we had rented and hoped to build, but we decided we liked it even better. A contemporary California "A-frame" redwood house, it was the only custom specimen in the neighborhood, and it was flooded with light through all the glass in the big "A" portion of the frame that was the front wall of our living room. It had two twin decks off the back of the house, one from the kitchen and one from the master bed room, and a backyard that was twice the size of the rental backyard; it extended even closer to the bayou. We fenced it.

The real bright spot was when the family that was building across the street from us moved in. We became instant best friends, all of us: kids, moms, and dads. They even learned to like Augie. The Goyden family was a family of four just like us except their oldest child who was Lisa's age was a boy, Chris, and their youngest was a girl, Jenny, a few months younger than Mark Jr. Mike was also a captain in the air force who had graduated from the Air Force Academy and worked in the building at Tyndall that had no windows. We never knew exactly what he did because his stuff was classified. We knew that his job was with computers, and we knew it had to do with air defense.

Jan was a stay-at-home mom like me, and we did everything together, from kids and commissary, to kids and picnics, preschool, and playtime. Jan and I were even addicted to the same soap, *All My Children*, and while the kids were napping, or having quiet time in their rooms, we would call each other to discuss the latest soap developments and try to predict the future scenarios for the various characters. We enjoyed a rather high rate of accuracy, too, with our predictions.

One thing that the neighborhood did not have was a park for the kids, so Mike and Mark went out and bought swing sets for the backyards. They helped each other plant those poles into the ground in such a way that they were guaranteed to be safe for the kids. Between the amount of cement and the cross board configuration they came up with for anchoring the swing sets, it's probably safe to say that the underground portions of those sets are probably exactly where they were placed twenty-five-plus years ago, and they are never coming out.

Video tape players were becoming the hot new thing then, and Mike and Mark each got one and began to tape everything. *Annie, Wizard of Oz, Star Wars,* and *Mickey & the Beanstalk* played at our house all the time. Our kids have no idea of the impact of the invention, but we could not believe that we no longer had to wait for reruns or risk not seeing a particular show by not being home in time to see it when it aired. All you had to do was set the timer, and voila. What's more, you could control what your kids watched on TV and when they watched it and use it to your best advantage. Of course, the ability to see a movie or a show over and over again to the point of memorization would probably have some effect, but it didn't necessarily follow that the effect would be deleterious. It might even prove beneficial.

Once, every other month, we would combine funds and get a babysitter for all four kids and have a grown-up double date night out. We usually went out for dinner to a restaurant we could not afford and ate and drank and laughed and paid by credit card. (Cash went to the sitter.) Neither Mike nor Mark had to talk "shop," since neither of them was in the same field of work, which was a welcome relief to both of them as well as us wives. There were never any career politics of any kind involved. It was a wonderful time, when friends were friends, for real.

Mark and Steve's main job at the hospital was to take care of everybody who got admitted to the internal medicine ward or who walked into their offices, which were located right at the hospital. They also did consults for the family practice physicians. Most of the patients were retired military or dependents of active duty military personnel. They read EKGs, ran and interpreted treadmill tests on cardiac patients, took care of GI bleeds, and performed the wide scope of duties that good internists could possibly handle. Anything that really could not be handled at the base hospital got "Champused out" to the community hospital or to a civilian subspecialist, Champus being the military health insurance that covered a dependent or an active duty person who needed care from a civilian facility. They tried never to have to Champus people outside the system because it cost the military (federal government) additional money.

The cost of all medical care including Champus was entirely borne by the military. Military personnel, both active duty and retired, as well as their dependent families paid zero for their health care, including prescriptions and medical supplies. That was the up side. The down side was that a patient had to be patient. There was a finite supply of doctors and an infinite number of patients. The patients could not go outside the system to expedite their care unless they were Champused out or were willing to pay the entire cost. They could not choose what specialty center they might be sent to within the military system, and if they were Champused to a civilian center, the center had to accept Champus as an insurance, or the patient would have to bear the entire expense. Not all civilian facilities accepted Champus because the reimbursement for services was a set fee, usually below what the facility charged, and the patient could not be charged for expenses that Champus would not pay. Again, this was essentially socialized medicine, to my mind, and it had advantages and disadvantages. To me, the military served as an accurate illustration of what large-scale socialized medicine was in some parts of the world and what it would be in the United States, if ever instituted for the population at large.

All doctors had to take emergency room call, MOD (medical officer of the day), no matter what their specialty. This meant that pediatricians had to handle heart attacks, and internists had to handle little kids. Bad medicine. Uncomfortable medicine. The hospital was a forty-bed facility with no obstetric or gynecologic capability. That was a good thing for the doctors who staffed the hospital, since none were Ob/Gyns, and later, a good thing for me.

As the top specialists at Tyndall Hospital, the internists, either Mark or Steve, had to be on call at all times. They divided their call duties by each taking a week at a time. Usually, call meant phone consultation advice rather than actually having to get called into the hospital after hours, but there were always a few sleepless nights per month due to having to get up and go in the middle of the night, as well as several other less-than-restful nights just from the sheer number of calls or the serious nature of a particular patient's problem. I remember one Christmas Eve when Santa's bag for Lisa was full of dolly furniture and such that needed to be assembled, since the elf in charge of assembly had been too busy to even start the task before nightfall of the twenty-fourth. As Santa was on call and got called to the hospital around 9 p.m. and the elf was nowhere to be found, Mrs. Santa had to stay up all night by herself and figure out how to screw which bolt in figure A into which slot in figure B with which tool. She had no use for the little metal washers left lying around and threw them out; they looked like choking hazards to her.

Keeping such a schedule did not afford any real study time for the two internists who had not quite made it by the boards on that first go-round even if they had wanted to study. Steve had originally proclaimed that he was not going to take the boards again. At that time, the specialty boards were not much more than a status symbol and not required by anybody except academic institutions who wanted an elite staff of physicians with credentials that leant a high degree of legitimacy to their publications. Or if an internist wanted to subspecialize (to become an oncologist, for example) the fellowship program required a passing grade on the internal medicine boards.

Passing the boards was determined by a bell curve, meaning there was no predetermined percentage of correct answers that represented a pass. The top thirty percent of the scores were high passes, the middle thirty percent were passes, and the bottom forty percent were failures. You were measured only against the other people taking the test at that time, and it was given once per year. When your scores came back to you, a series of asterisks showed into what percentile your score fell. Steve had only missed passing by a partial asterisk. Mark had missed by two and one half asterisks.

Mark, who still wanted to be eligible for an oncology fellowship, knew he would have to take the boards again, and he thought Steve would appreciate the status of being a board certified internist in the private practice he planned to have when he finished his air force commitment. He basically talked Steve into taking them again. They decided that they would not take them until their third year at Tyndall and planned to spend their second year studying. To keep each other honest, they planned to meet at alternate houses on one night each week to "pimp" each other to make sure that they had retained the reading assignments they had assigned to each other the week before and to give each other confidence that the necessary ground had been covered.

Actually, the plan was more concrete than a weekly assignment. They had decided that they were going to reread *Harrison's Principals of Internal Medicine* in total in preparation for the upcoming test.

Having a year in which to prepare themselves, they mathematically divided up the pages and came up with their schedule. If life was busy before their academic pursuits, those twelve months were jam packed, and nothing was permitted as an interruption to the schedule. It was carved in stone.

What a time to get pregnant! And what a time to get a pair of phlebitic legs to go with the pregnancy. At six weeks, I had phlebitis (inflammation of the veins) in one calf; at three months, both of my legs looked like spoiled hamburger meat from my butt to my ankles, the whole way down the backs of both legs. Not only was the condition incredibly painful, but it was also potentially life threatening, since the chronic venous inflammation made suitable conditions for a DVT (deep venous thrombosis or blood clot) to develop and possibly travel to my lung or heart. I was commanded to stay off my feet by my obstetrician, and since I was not to sit with my legs down, I was not supposed to drive. Now, that just wasn't possible with two babies and a husband who had the kind of responsibilities and schedule that Mark had.

My doctor was in private practice and was very familiar with the air force and the way Champus worked, since he took care of all the Ob/Gyn needs for Tyndall. His orders to me were to be up for no more than two hours scattered throughout one twenty-four hour period and to immediately be fitted for a pair of compression panty hose to be worn at all times except for nighttime sleeping. The prescription didn't sound too complicated, and he explained that I would be measured at Tyndall medical supply and fitted with custom compression hose.

The fitting session went very smoothly, but the order had to be filled somewhere else and shipped back to Tyndall. The waiting period was four to six weeks, during which time Mark added the bimonthly shopping at the commissary to his other duties and tackled the dinner dishes every night that he was home. I used my two hours per day of stand-up time to prepare meals and get as much housekeeping done as I could, but I could not stand for more than a few minutes before my legs filled up, turned purple and became intensely painful. I spent most of my time scooting around the house on my behind or doing a crab walk so that I could keep up with the kids and get from one room to another.

When six weeks had passed and my compression hose were still not in, medical supply at Tyndall traced my order and found that it had been lost. In fact, I had to begin the process all over again and get re-fitted and once again wait the requisite time period to fill the order. I was seven months pregnant when I finally received my hose, and what a world of difference they made. I was once again able to be on my feet and active without the phlebitic pain. The hose were very tight as well as hot since it was summertime, but our lives got back to normal, and they saved me from further inflammation.

During the months of confinement, I worked on a piece of crewel artwork for Mark's office that was a well-known Norman Rockwell magazine cover depicting a doctor examining a little girl's doll, and while I stitched, I remember listening to Mark and Steve cross examine each other as they continued their review for the upcoming internal medicine boards. It was the summer of 1982, and they were scheduled to take the test in the fall. Sometimes when they were done studying for the night, they would discuss future plans. Neither of them wanted to stay in the air force as internists by that time. Steve wanted to go out into private practice as an internist, and he really wanted Mark to join him. Mark, once again, was willing to "try on" that possibility because he really liked Steve both as a doctor and as a friend. He was somebody Mark felt he could work with very easily for his entire career as a doctor.

It was the internal medicine specialty itself that presented some issues which caused Mark to question whether or not he would really be happy spending his physician career as an internist. Primary care of adults was vitally important, but it did present the opportunity for what Mark considered abuse of the doctor by patients who were not really sick—hypochondriacs, or in more typical physician lingo, "crocks." If there was anything Mark couldn't stand, it was a crock. And he had some world-class doozies at Tyndall.

They drove him bonkers. The other kind of patient he did not enjoy was the patient whose illness he considered self-inflicted, such as drug addiction. He did not feel that he had the required patience or compassion to deal with those types of patients long term.

There was also a logistical problem. Steve and Robin really wanted to stay in Florida, even Panama City, but Florida's summers were too hot and muggy and buggy for me, and I really missed the four distinct seasons found a little further up north. Mark was not sold on Florida either, although it had some pull for him because his brother lived in St. Petersburg. We both loved the bright colors of autumn, which were nowhere to be found in Florida, and football season didn't feel like football season to Mark without the crisp cool weather of the fall he was used to having. Steve and Mark did, however, agree to begin investigating opportunities for a future practice together.

Our third baby was due in mid-July, but on the 29th of June, my doctor told me the baby would be born within twenty-four hours. There was a mad scramble up in New Jersey, since my mother had agreed to come down as soon as the baby was born, as she had done with the first two. She was able to get an earlier flight than previously planned and bravely appeared at our house ready to take on the task of helping with the newborn as well as with her other two grandchildren.

Four weeks later, on July 26, I packed my bags, marched/wad-dled into my doctor's office, and told him that if he didn't rupture my membranes, I was going to do it myself. One hour later, in the comfort of Gulf Coast Community Hospital, our perfect red-haired baby boy was born. There were no nursing students, medical students, taxi drivers, or extraneous personnel. Everybody knew what he or she was doing, and everybody was comforting and compassionate. I didn't feel like a science experiment. I didn't feel like just one cow amidst the cattle. I felt like people wanted to do a good job and make things so pleasant for me that I might consider coming back. Two days later, with a teeny, tiny tee shirt that said, "I got my start at Gulf Coast Community Hospital," Robert Christopher Ellis and I went home.

We were welcomed by our brand new video camera that we had splurged on in honor of Robbie's future birth, because we didn't want to miss out on the opportunity of having family movies with audio, now that the new technology was readily available. Consequently, not only were we able to capture the new baby's homecoming, we were able to capture Mark Jr's first word ever and preserve it. As I came through the door, baby Robbie in my arms, to the great barked greeting of Augie, and to Sassy's "Mommy, you're home!" and to Grandma's quiet relief, two-year-old Mark pointed to Robbie and yelled, "Baby!"

Five weeks later, Mark and Steve went to Tallahassee to take the internal medicine boards, knowing they would have to wait until November to hear the results. They were confident that they were much more prepared this time, and I was certain that they would both pass with flying colors. Soon after they were notified of their passing scores, Mark and I had a discussion one night after we had gone to bed and turned the lights out. Lying there in the darkness, listening to him wonder once again, like he had done so many years earlier, if there was some cosmic reason why he should become an oncologist, I knew that he was not destined for private practice as an internist.

He was conflicted about what to tell Steve, because as their third year in the air force progressed, Steve had begun to get excited about setting up their own practice in about a year and a half. He said he had tested the political air around Panama City and found it to be receptive to two new internists. In the meantime, Mark had talked to Bowman Gray to make sure there would still be a slot open in their oncology fellowship program. Although he was assured that there would be a spot for him, he realized that the salary would be far from adequate now that we had three children and were used to living on a captain's salary, and he was no longer willing to moonlight.

He once again thought about private practice as an internist, but added to his list of possibilities a fellowship within the air force, which would mean he would not have to take a cut in pay. On the contrary, the longer he stayed in the air force, the higher in rank he would rise, and the higher his corresponding salary would be. He would also incur an additional active-duty commitment once the fellowship was done, but if the training was good, the disadvantage of deferring civilian life was well worth the financial advantage of staying in the military longer than originally planned.

He began to look into air force fellowships to get his name out there early and was surprised to get a call from Walter Reed Army Hospital in Washington, DC, saying that they had an open fellowship slot, not in '84 when his commitment to Tyndall was done, but in '83, in six months. Walter Reed's fellowship was a three-year program that combined both hematology and oncology, preparing the fellow to sit for both subspecialty boards. Mark really liked the idea of having both certifications, and the reputation of Walter Reed's program was outstanding. But what to do about his air force commitment to Tyndall?

In some instances the different military branches are very connected and work very well together. This was one instance. There were very few large teaching medical centers in the entire military, and they shared each other's doctors depending on the need. When the army hospital commander (a general) at Walter Reed, the most renowned military medical center in the world, asked the air force hospital commander (a colonel) at Tyndall, a small base hospital, to release Mark a year early to serve as a fellow at Walter Reed, he was released. The agreement between the two branches of service was that the army would train him for three years and return him to the air force to fulfill the rest of his active duty time.

The beauty of the deal was that all the branches of the military looked on a fellowship as a necessary service to their medical centers as well as a training program for the individual. For this reason, the remaining one year of active duty that Mark owed the air force for medical school, which he would have been serving at Tyndall, could run concurrently with his first year of fellowship training at the army hospital. In return for his next two years of fellowship training at Walter Reed, he would owe two years of active duty somewhere in the air force at one of their tertiary care medical centers as a hematologist/oncologist when he finished the program.

Essentially, that meant that Mark was really only being charged one extra year of active duty for three extra years of training. It was an offer he couldn't refuse, and it meant we were leaving Panama City a year earlier than expected.

This was bad news for Steve and bad news for our good friends the Goydens. Military people understand when you move around from place to place; it comes with the territory. But in this instance, nobody, least of all Mark and I, had expected it. We all kind of got the news at the same time, and there was really no other decision to be made. It was a great opportunity, and we had to move on. Cosmic plans are like that.

In January, the Redskins won the Super Bowl against the Miami Dolphins. Although we had been invited across the street to the Goydens for a super bowl party, we had to decline, due to the fact that it was the Redskins in the super bowl. That would be one of those rules governing Mark's fanaticism that I should have known, but I confess that I was every bit as surprised as our friends were. After all, nobody was going to be rooting for Miami.

It had already been an odd football year anyway due to the strike and the scrubs playing. However, Mark did prove his decision to be the correct choice. If we had gone to the Goydens for the Super Bowl, he never could have spent the entire game on his hands and knees two feet in front of the TV set praying to the television gods, face buried in the carpet, like he did in his own home. On the other hand, in that position he could have missed John Riggins' game-turning, unbelievable run when the diesel broke the tackle by Miami's number twenty-eight and ran for a touchdown. (I'm not really good enough to remember the number of the Miami player; the moment is immortalized in a picture on the wall in Mark's study.) As it turned out, he did not miss it when it happened, and I'm sure the party across the street heard him shouting, "Holy shit! Go! Go! Run!"

In February, we took some leave time to house hunt in the DC area and drove up to Myrtle Beach for a brief stopover visit with Mammaw and Pop Pop. We then drove all the way to New Jersey, where we abused Grandma and Pap Pap by dropping all three kids off for a few days while we braved the two feet of snow in the DC area to locate a worthy future home. We were hoping for a door-to-door move this time. We found a nice new neighborhood in the middle stages of being constructed in Derwood, Maryland. After selecting a family-oriented cul-de-sac location, we chose an available four-bedroom floor plan, wrote the required small deposit check, and drove home, comfortable in the knowledge that our new home would be ready in late June in preparation for Mark's fellowship program, which began on July 1. I wonder how long people get to legitimately blame their decisions on youth.

Later that spring, I remarked to my husband that the strawberries that I had struggled to plant way back in a garden area closest to the bayou, but inside the fence, didn't seem to be coming up. These strawberries were special strawberries. One day when I had been expecting Robbie, who was now nine months old, I had been resting with my bum legs up while Markie napped and Lisa had quiet time in her room. The doorbell sounded, and after I had hushed Augie and limped quickly to the door, I was confronted by a lady I did not know with a large box of strawberry plants in her arms. She said that God had told her to give them to me. I said, "Who are you?" She said it didn't matter who she was and that she was new to the area. She just stood there looking at me, offering no other information. When I finally asked her if she was sure they were for me, she said, "I prayed about it, and God said they were for you." I said, "God must be mistaken, because I'm six months pregnant, and my legs are not in any shape to do anything, let alone plant strawberries." She said, nevertheless, she had no choice but to leave them with me. "God never makes mistakes." With that, she set them down on the porch, turned around and walked away.

I still had no idea who she was, and I never saw her again. But I couldn't just let the plants die, and Jan didn't want them, especially after she heard how they came to me. Mark said, "Forget about them; they're just plants." But I couldn't forget, and one aspect of the several weird things from which to choose concerning her visit was that strawberry ice cream had been my one and only craving the entire time I was expecting Robbie. Well, to Mark's consternation, while he was at work, I struggled to plant those plants despite my legs, and they grew and bore fruit that summer.

But where were they this year when I was strong and healthy again, my last year to enjoy my two little strawberry fields? Mark looked a little sheepish when he admitted that he had forgotten about them and run over them with the lawn mower a few weeks earlier, which meant he had also forgotten them and continued to run over them each successive week. I don't know what that means in the overall scheme of things, but I know that out of all the nebulous cosmic vibes, one undeniable fact emerges: If you continuously mow over young vegetable or fruit plants with a lawn mower, they won't grow.

We cried when we left Panama City. It was the summer of 1983. Lisa was four and a half, Mark was ready to turn three, and Robbie was eleven months old. Robbie didn't cry. His best friends were there in the car with him. The doc didn't cry. He was a man about it, and it was time to move on. For Lisa, Mark Jr., and me, it was just too tough leaving Jan and Chris and Jenny standing on the sidewalk in front of their house, crying and waving.

The Goydens may have had an additional reason to cry because they were the ones left behind to explain why our house was now purple. We had painted it to put it on the market after taking a sample of the existing wood color to the paint store to have it matched. The man at the store said the match for it was called garnet and mixed up the number of custom gallons we would need. We should have known that with a name like "garnet" we weren't going to get "redwood," but we assumed that the paint store guy knew more than we knew about paint.

Mark painted the house himself. When the first side didn't look right, we decided that it was merely the contrast between the old paint and the new paint. He painted a second side. It still didn't seem right, and the brown roof began to look orange against the garnet. He decided that painting the third side would really prove whether it was going to work or not. The roof was definitely orange now, in terrible contrast to the rather purple sides, but there was only one more side to go. The paint went on with Mark lying in precarious positions on the roof to brush the uppermost wooden peaks, and I was determined to prevent his having to be up there again. From the ground, I told him it was looking better and better. We both knew it was a lie. The day we left Panama City the house was freshly painted and hideous, but somebody bought it anyway.

The Goydens called us after it sold and told us that the first thing that the new people did after they moved in was to repaint the house a redwood color. The second thing they did was to cut down the magnolia tree I had planted in the front yard.

**Mark with Lisa, Mark Jr., Robbie (the baby),
and Augie during "pop" time. 1982**

Tyndall days. Mark (again in Redskin jersey) and
I with kids out for a neighborhood stroll. 1983

"I MORPHED BACK INTO A SPONGE TO SOAK UP EVERYTHING THEY HAD TO OFFER."

CHAPTER 16

FELLOWSHIP

Military moves were interesting. Everything was paid for by the military up to a certain pound limit set according to rank. Packers were always included in the move, and they were extremely efficient. You did not need to have anything ready except what you planned to take in the car with you. On the appointed day, they came armed with packing paper and boxes and began unloading cabinets, closets, garages, everything. They were not allowed to take spices or alcohol, but they would pack everything else, including trash, that was still in your trashcans.

As we were still aiming for a door-to-door move, we had followed behind the movers, cleaning each room as it became empty, and pretty much backed out the front door, cleaning the foyer floor last as the truck was preparing to leave. Except for the rocking chair on top of the car, we bore a strong resemblance to the Beverly Hillbillies when we pulled up to Mark's parents' townhouse at Possum Trot in Myrtle Beach, where we had decided to spend a few days to visit and break up the trip to our new destination. The sight of my burnt sienna station wagon with the U-haul storage box strapped on top and the TR-6 attached by a tow bar, with two kids in car seats and one in a booster seat, plus a large shedding dog and two weary adults, should have been enough to strike fear into a sane person's heart. I strongly doubt that Mammaw and Pop Pop's friends felt very much envy as they watched us trying to park and then witnessed our troop emerge from the car.

As usual, however, Mammaw and Pop Pop seemed undaunted and welcomed us into their two-bedroom town home. We treated the break as a vacation and sent Lisa and Mark Jr. off to play golf with their grandparents a few times, which to them meant pretend-driving the golf carts and looking for alligators in the water hazards. The dog gave her expert swimming and frisbee catching exhibitions at the beach, and we fulfilled our promise to the two older kids to take them to see *The Empire Strikes Back*, which was being rerun in Myrtle Beach.

Little Mark and Lisa had *Star Wars* already memorized and could not wait to see the sequel. When Darth Vader's larger than life, total screen encompassing image suddenly appeared breathing in that ominous style for which he is famous, Little Mark levitated out of his own seat and into his father's lap, burying his face into Mark's chest. Lisa hid her face in my sleeve, and all of our popcorn spilled onto the floor. By the time we left the movie theater, Little Mark had a new hero, Lando Calrissian (Wando Calwisian in three-year-old speak) and all of us thought we might die waiting to see the just released *Return of the Jedi* to free us from the dark note on which the second movie in the promised trilogy ended.

During all the summer fun, we had a great deal of trouble making contact with our realtor, from whom we had received monthly updates on the progress of our house during the past five months. We were growing concerned because our last update had placed the house about two weeks behind schedule, which placed our new "end of June" closing date dangerously close to Mark's July 1 start date at Walter Reed. Our furniture was somewhere en route; we didn't really know where, because the movers always combined pick-ups with other moving families and took a circuitous route to the new location.

Just before we departed Myrtle Beach for another brief vacation stay in New Jersey with my parents, our realtor called to say that she had been in contact with the contractor, who said that the house would not be ready until mid July. This was bad news indeed. We humbly asked my parents if we might extend our vacation stay to three or four weeks, to which they graciously, if not happily, agreed, in case the estimate was true. If it was, we would also have to figure out how Mark was going to start work on the first.

On the way to New Jersey via Maryland, we decided to stop in Derwood to see our new house and show it to the kids for whom we had tried to build excitement at the prospect of a new neighborhood, new room, new friends, and such. We drove to the cul-de-sac location that we both remembered, but could not find the house. The last time we had seen the neighborhood, it had been buried under two feet of snow, so we thought that perhaps we didn't recognize it. According to the new street sign, we were on the right street, but there was definitely no house. Finding an attractive, perky young woman manning the construction office, we asked for directions to the address of our new home and described where we had been, and she assured us that we had been in the right place after all. We knew that this could not be the case, so we asked her to come with us to show her where we had been, and when we arrived at the cul-de-sac location, she pointed to the hole in the ground that held a freshly poured foundation and cheerily said, "That's it!"

We may have been fools more than once, but even we could tell that the house was not going to be ready in three weeks. . .six months, maybe. Evidently, the builder had "forgotten" to build our house, and the realtor had never eyeballed it the entire construction period and relied on updates from the lying contractor via telephone. So much for a door-to-door move; we would deal with the contractor later. Our immediate problem was to face the fact that we were homeless. We did not look forward to imparting such news to my parents, and the kids remained unimpressed.

Later, the contractor didn't bat an eye when he told us that he wasn't *that* far behind. He could have the house done by November, and he had no intention of giving us our deposit back. We found that date to be unacceptable and hired a lawyer to change his mind. In the end, he was forced to refund our deposit and pay our legal expenses, but that money would stay tied up for several months and not be available for our present housing struggles.

During the last week in June, while I stayed in New Jersey with the kids, Mark went to DC to house hunt with a new realtor. Prospects were exceedingly dim. The cost of housing in the DC area was very high, as were the mortgage interest rates, and even with the additional military housing allowance allotted to a captain for being transferred to a high-cost living area, the question we kept getting from the realtor was, "Do you want an eat-in kitchen or a garage?"

July 1 came and Mark started his fellowship at Walter Reed, first by commuting from New Jersey to Washington, DC, daily. That plan quickly changed after two days of commuting three hours each way, to staying at the visiting officers' quarters at Andrews Air Force Base and traveling to New Jersey on the weekends. The Fourth of July found him in DC, house hunting with yet another realtor who was more optimistic about our pursuits. She had contacts in the mortgage business who were very familiar with creative financing, which was becoming increasingly popular, and she had located a special house, in a new neighborhood called North Farm in Rockville, Maryland.

The houses in North Farm were way beyond our budget, but there was one brand-new, completely finished house that was a "failed sale" on which she thought the contractor would give us a good deal. Mark really liked the house and the location and worked with the realtor's financial contacts to come up with some truly creative financing, all the while acclimating to his first week of his brand new fellowship at Walter Reed.

July 7 was Little Mark's third birthday, and Daddy who had been gone for a week was excitedly expected back for the poolside celebration. My dad had taken the trouble to build an inner fence in the backyard to block direct access to the in-ground swimming pool from the house, in preparation for his three non-swimmer young grandchildren's extended visit. In Mark's absence we had set up common sense rules concerning the pool: Gate is never left unlocked, kids never allowed in pool area without an adult, etc., with the fail safe rule being that no bathing suits were allowed on the kids until the inflated arm bands we called "water wings" were on their arms first.

Besides me, there were four adults who regularly used the pool and from whom the kids sought permission for various activities: both of my parents, my sister Amy, who was now eighteen, and one of her girl friends, Julie. My parents also owned a large German Shepherd named Jessie, who happened to be Augie's littermate. Both dogs always acted like they knew each other and played and romped and got along beautifully, but with the addition of our three children all under the age of five plus Augie and me, mayhem was likely to break out at any minute of any day.

I obsessively checked the gate to the pool area every night before I went to bed out of fear that the kids would awaken early without my knowledge and decide to have an adventure in the pool. I never slept soundly, and I was always the first one up. On Little Mark's birthday, however, conditions were confusing enough— with the party being set up in the pool area and everybody coming and going back and forth, and the kids highly charged with excitement—that extra caution was necessary.

In the midst of all the preparation, Daddy arrived home from DC for the celebration and went upstairs to change, not knowing the failsafe rule about the water wings. Little Mark went up to join him, and knowing that he was safely in a room with his father, I went into the kitchen to join my mother, Robbie, and Lisa. A few minutes later, I went upstairs to brief Mark about the failsafe rule I had designed because I knew that Little Mark had a new bathing suit that he was dying to put on, and he knew he was not allowed to change into it until it was time to swim. When I opened the door to the bedroom, I noticed that my little boy was not in the bedroom.

"Where's Mark?"
"He went downstairs to find you."
"When?"
"A minute ago."

Noticing our son's clothes in a small heap on the floor, and spotting his water wings on the bed, I said, "You didn't let him put on his bathing suit, did you?"

I was running as fast as I could go before I heard the answer, down the steps through the family room, out the door, and through the garage, preparing to fling myself into the pool to save my child. I arrived poolside just in time to see Julie, Amy's friend, holding little Mark's hand, as she walked the dripping three year-old along the edge of the pool away from the ladder. His hair was soaked, his eyelashes were dripping, and his big brown eyes were round as saucers. I was close to fainting. He was smiling. Julie was gently chastising him, "You know you are not supposed to get into the pool without your water wings, Markie."

There were no steps into the pool. The only entrance was the ladder at the deep end unless you jumped from the shallow end, which was three feet deep, or from the diving board. I knew that one of those three things had happened, but I didn't know which one. I also knew that Julie had been sunbathing on a raft in the pool during the party set-up, and thank God for her tan. She explained that she had thought she heard something and opened her eyes in time to see Little Mark descending into the pool on the ladder. She said, "Markie, aren't you supposed to have your water wings on?" The child had said nothing, made no sound at all as he let go of the ladder and silently sunk. Julie immediately jumped off of her raft and pulled him up, actually so fast that the child wasn't traumatized at all. He didn't cry. He wasn't scared. Indeed, he was smiling. He had no clue that Julie had just saved his life.

After that experience, I was willing to take any house anywhere as long as it did not have a pool, and I agreed to the three mortgages Mark had worked out with three different institutions to purchase the house I had yet to see. The first mortgage was a negative amortization mortgage; the second, a smaller mortgage that was a second lien; and the third, a five-year balloon secured by yet a third lien on the house. It was 1983, and creative financing was the name of the game.

On July 15, we left New Jersey, headed to our new house at North Farm in Rockville, knowing that we were stretched beyond what we could reasonably afford and knowing also that at the end of Mark's fellowship in three years, we would owe the bank more rather than less on the house. Our closing date was not until September 1, but the builder allowed us to rent it from him until we closed, using the rent as our down payment. We were excited, despite the financial constraints under which we would be living, and Mark kept telling me that the neighborhood was worth it, that he was sure it was the right thing to do. Housing prices were going up, not down, and the realtor, who seemed highly knowledgeable, had convinced him that the neighborhood would be a good value because the houses would appreciate at a more rapid rate than our negative amortization loan could add to our owed principal. Mark boasted to the kids and me that he had noticed lots of kids and happy families going about the business of living, and he felt like it was the next best thing to our former neighborhood in Panama City. That last boast piqued everybody's curiosity and gave us hope.

The house was beautiful. All the houses in the neighborhood were beautiful. The outside of it was a pale orange brick with harvest gold wood accents and olive green shutters. The front door entrance was off of a long covered front porch and opened into a foyer from which you could see the step-down living room straight ahead and the two half-sets of stairs to the left that led up to the three bedrooms and study, or down to the family room which opened into the backyard. To the right of the foyer was the entrance into the kitchen, which did have a small eat-in area and an entrance into a formal dining room. The living room had a huge stone fireplace that ascended all the way to the cathedral ceiling, with two sliding doors on either side that would eventually lead to a deck. There was also a two-car garage and a full basement.

As nice as our new home on 32 Hollyberry Court was, it was the environment that made our financial restraints worthwhile. The people of the neighborhood were a friendly young group of family-oriented professionals with dogs and cats and kids and busy lives. There was a wide cultural diversity of doctors, lawyers, businessmen, nurses, and teachers, as well as one of the Redskins' football players. A middle linebacker lived a few doors from us in the only other house like ours on the street. That fact made me suspiciously wonder if Mark had somehow been informed of this juicy little tidbit in advance, and it had influenced his decision to take on our three mortgages.

The very best thing about the neighborhood was 33 Hollyberry Court, the house right next door, because it was the home of our future best friends. The couple who looked to be about our age had a little girl, Jenny, who was Mark's age (about to turn three in August), and they had a German Shepherd a little smaller than Augie named Sissy, who was also friendly and adept at ball and stick. Jerry was a financial consultant who had gone to Maryland and graduated in '75, and Carol, his wife, was a math guru who worked for a satellite communications firm and had gone to Wake Forest. As soon as we saw each other, we recognized that we had seen each other somewhere before, and when we realized we had the Wake thing in common, we knew where. As she stood there in her short hair and pregnant condition, and I stood there in my short hair, my life's work of producing progeny done, we reminisced. "Didn't you used to have long blonde hair?" "Didn't you used to have real long dark hair, like down to your waist?" She had lived one floor below me in the same dorm for two years and graduated in '76, one year after me. It was one of those "small world" moments and the beginning of a long and fulfilling friendship for us all.

The kids' first meeting of the neighborhood kids also had its own memorable beginning. On the first night in our new house, the doorbell rang just after dinnertime, and upon opening the door, I was faced with four little smiling girls' faces, with one of them anxiously asking me if there were any kids who moved in today at our house. I said, "Yes there are!" and called out loudly, "There are some kids at the door." Lisa and Robbie quickly appeared at the door and began a round of introductions. Little Mark was up the half flight of steps in the hall bathroom taking a bath. But on hearing the kids and being so ready to make new friends, he sprang up out of the tub, his slippery naked body eluding his father's grasp, dashed down the six steps, and ran up to the wide-open front door dripping wet and exclaiming, "Hi! I'm Wuke Skywalker!" The little girls were all between the ages of three and six, and none of them had brothers.

The girls, of course, were surprised by the sight of the little naked boy standing unabashedly at the door talking to them, and they giggled and pointed at his maleness, and I felt so heartbroken for him in all of his innocence and hopefulness of finding friends. I was surprised at his new name. I don't know when he decided to take on the name of Wuke Skywalker, but from that day forward until he turned four, he refused to tell anybody his real name. He did shortly meet and become good friends with some little boys from the neighborhood and rapidly forgot about the first impression he had made. But I'm not so sure that those little girls forgot it.

Mark was one of the few military people in North Farm and stood out in his air force blues against the civilian crowd who survived the DC rush hour everyday to return to the neighborhood around 6 p.m. or so. One of the joys of his fellowship was that there was no real night or weekend call. He had so many levels of house staff under him that when he did get called, the caller was usually a second or third-year internal medicine resident who could handle most situations with some additional advice given over the phone. Having to jump into the car and head back to the hospital was not the norm. He also had no rounding responsibilities on the weekends even when he was on call. Since the calls were not frequent, uninterrupted sleep was standard except for the usual middle of the night disruptions that occur when one has three young children and a dog: Somebody has a bad dream; somebody wets the bed; somebody throws up; the dog hears something and loudly defends the household. . . .This three-year stint would be the first time since medical school that Mark had enjoyed regular predictable hours.

The daily schedule of a fellow in the combined hematology/ oncology program at Walter Reed largely took place between the hours of eight in the morning to five in the evening, Monday through Friday. He had daily half-day clinic hours for seeing outpatients, as well as scheduled rounding time on inpatients with residents and attending physicians. A fellow was also expected to attend a number of conferences and tumor boards of various kinds that occurred once per week. In fact, there were so many different kinds of conferences and tumor boards, that there were few days when there wasn't some required presence in a meeting of some sort. (A tumor board is a meeting of a group of doctors and certain support staff who represent various specialties that might all have been involved with a cancer patient, such as the pathologist, surgeon, radiation therapist, tumor registrar, etc. They take turns presenting certain interesting cases and hashing out the various approaches to treatment for the patient. Tumor boards are required by any hospital that has a cancer program, although academic institutions have a much larger array of kinds of tumor boards.) At Walter Reed there were breast tumor boards, lung tumor boards, colon, ovarian, prostate etc. In addition to the oncology solid tumor boards, there were hematology-oncology conferences on leukemias and lymphomas. There were pure hematology conferences on anemias and a seemingly endless number of weird blood disorders totally unrelated to cancer. Fellows were also expected to be presenters and not just listeners during these conferences.

During certain months, fellows had research opportunities at Walter Reed Army Institute of Research referred to as WRAIR. During research months, fellows did not see patients. Instead, they assisted in some type of hematological research and spent the time studying hematology. Hematology was more academically oriented due to the humongous amount of minutia that had to be learned, and due to the fact that many of the disorders a hematologist needed to know were rare enough that they might never be seen in a real patient during fellowship. Oncology was much more hands-on, and although there was a great deal to read and study in oncology, and although there are several very rare cancers, much of what one could read about would also be occurring in one of the patients who would be seen during the three-year program.

The main duty of a fellow was to learn all that he or she could during the fellowship. A great deal of knowledge needed to be packed into three years and filed away in the brain, and the fellow's schedule was designed to afford him as much opportunity as possible to learn the material and study for the upcoming subspecialty boards.

Hematology and oncology were separate subspecialties, each with its own subspecialty national board given in November of alternate years. Each board required the fellow to have had at least two years of fellowship before sitting for the board. The quickest way to complete the process was to take one board while still in fellowship and the next board one year later, a few months after the fellowship had already ended. In the combined hematology/oncology program, the fellow usually took whichever board was being offered at the time he or she first became eligible. A passing score was required to be able to sit for the other subspecialty board. For Mark, oncology would be his first board in November of 1985. If he did not pass it the first time around, he could not take the hematology board the following November, and since each board was only given in alternate years, a failure would require waiting two years to retake it. So failure was not an option, and he set up his home study schedule to supplement his study schedule at work from that standpoint.

At work, Mark saw cancer patients in the mornings and read as much as he could about their cancers in his textbooks and journals in the afternoons. He was also assigned to a mentor-attending physician.

> *Fellowship was another great learning time for me. Because military personnel were sent to Walter Reed from all over the world, we saw everything. We had the opportunity to see more of the weird coagulation disorders, anemias, and rare cancers than most fellowship programs afforded, and I considered myself very lucky to be there. Of course, I was the only doctor in a blue uniform in oncology, and I had traded my large office on the Gulf of Mexico and the status*

of being one of the only two specialists at Tyndall, for a small desk in a closet and being the new kid on the block again at Walter Reed. But it was worth it, and I morphed back into a sponge to soak up everything they had to offer.

I had a great schedule. I saw consults in the hospital and then picked up those particular patients to follow in my outpatient clinics. I worked out during my lunch hour by swimming; Walter Reed had a beautiful Olympic-sized pool. I studied, read journals, prepared talks, and went to lectures the rest of the time. One of the good things about being an air force guy at an army facility was that when the army docs had to dress in fatigues and go out and march in the parking lot, I wasn't required to participate. And I didn't.

I do remember that there was pressure to publish like there is at any academic medical center. As fellows, we wrote up cases and collaborated with attendings on research papers that were published in various oncology journals and presented at national meetings. I was impressed with the amount of publishing that some of the attending doctors produced, but I wasn't that interested in publishing myself. I did enough to accomplish being the first author on enough papers to be a productive fellow in the program, but I was more interested in the "meat and potatoes" of practicing oncology, and I knew that I wanted to go into private practice as opposed to joining the staff of an academic institution.

At home, we had a defined schedule. Daddy would get home around six and we would all have dinner together at six-fifteen. After dinner, Mark cleaned up the dinner dishes while I bathed the kids. As soon as all three kids were bathed and clad in their pajamas, they would meet Daddy in the kitchen for the nightly cookie party. Mark, the kids, and the dog would all sit on the kitchen floor and have cookies for dessert and talk and laugh and have a great time. After the cookie party, he went upstairs to his study, which connected to the master bedroom as a sitting room but had double doors to close it off from the bedroom. He spent a few hours reading, outlining, and catching up on whatever study he had not completed during the day at work.

He always tried to take Friday nights off, and on many Friday nights, either we all would go next door to the Graves, or they would all come to our house, where all the kids would play in one room, hopefully settle down on the floor with pillows and blankets at some point, and watch TV before falling asleep. Carol, Jerry, Mark, and I would play Trivial Pursuit, pop popcorn, and drink beer, which always made the trivia game much more fun and our discussions very lively. We expounded upon our amazing and some not-so amazing feats in high school and college, and told coming-of-age stories, which might have been painful at the time they had actually taken place, but were hilarious now, from our side of experience. At the end of the night, the parents who were visiting carried their sleeping children back across the yard to tuck them into their own beds. It was a wonderful time in our lives, and we are all still great friends. We have the type of friendship that no amount of time or distance changes. Whenever we see each other, we pick up where we left off and keep on going.

Life was very busy and active and fun. The kids had tons of activities in Rockville and participated with other kids in the neighborhood in everything from tumbling classes at MarvaTots to the diving team at the neighborhood pool. Lisa started kindergarten, Little Mark started preschool, and Robbie went to "mother's morning out." Since the Montgomery County schools and the preschools were so good, we were very happy with the educational start of our children. We also now held the two very coveted Ellis Family Redskins tickets, since we lived so close to DC, and on Sundays during football season, Mark and I went to all the home games. I think that is when I really made the conversion from the Eagles to the Redskins. I found it impossible to live in that town and not catch the Redskin fever. As the kids got older, they all got to go to one game per season with Daddy.

In January of 1985, Mark's home study program got cranked up a notch since the oncology board was scheduled for the upcoming November. He wrote down his study plan on two index cards and taped them to the back of his Devita textbook, which had nineteen hundred pages in it. The first thing on the first card is the date, of course, Jan. 1985. Immediately under the date is written the title of the card, because all index cards need titles. "Oncology Boards Study Plan: RELAX!" (Which I just find hysterically funny now. I wish I had known that then. I didn't even know about the cards bearing the schedule until I started writing this chapter. We will have a good laugh over that one of these nights.) The remainder of this card says:

Devita-Read and outline with cards Jan-Aug,
Charts, tables, chapters.
Use Haskills as supplement during the year.
Journals: Review articles (Seminars, Cancer,
Annuals, NEJM, JCO, etc.)
(Files and library rounds once per week)
Continue conferences (Lymphoma Board,
H/O management)
New Fellows lectures
Concentrate on and document weak areas.
Sept/Oct: Review cards, charts, tables
(Devita)
Re-evaluate study plan
Review articles (files) (over)
(Sept-Oct cont.) Review notes from
Fellow's lectures etc.
Board Review course.
Concentrate on weak areas & Board
favorites:
    Epidemiology
    Chemo Pharm & Toxicity
    Staging - get flash cards

Know all chemotherapeutic drugs – <u>COLD</u>!

The second index card is a breakdown by month of the specific pages and topics to be covered:

Month *Pages* *Topic(s)*
  Jan 1331-1582 *Lymphomas/Leukemias*
-Metabolic Ca
  Feb   1582-1822 *Onc Emergencies*
Radiation Sensitizers
  March   1822-1886 *Radiation Sensitizers*
  0-198   Chemotherapy
  April   198-475 *Clinical Trials*
ENT Ca, Lung Ca
  May   475-731 *Mediastinal Tumors*
GI Malignancy
  June   732-971 *GYN, Breast Ca*
  July   971-1254 *Endo Ca, Skin Ca*
  Aug   1254-1331 *Childhood Ca*
  Sept   Chapters of other chemo books
  Oct   Hit weak areas etc. Re-eval study
plan.
Read M-Tue-W-Th 15 pages per night
Catch up on weekends.
Areas to concentrate on: Staging
Epidemiology
Chemotherapeutic agents (Pharm)
Kinetics

The study plan became the priority. He used every free moment to study. The kids and I understood that there were never to be any interruptions, and there were not. Mark and I declined social engagements, friends' invitations, and anything socially that required both of us. Financially speaking, that was a good thing, because our adjustable mortgage rate was ever climbing, and the paycheck was not. Even some Redskins game tickets went to friends. The kids didn't really understand why they could not interrupt, and friends didn't really understand why the schedule for an upcoming test that was still many months away had no flexibility in it. But, I knew exactly why. That first internal medicine board haunted him, and he was determined that he would not repeat that unfortunate mishap on the oncology board. The months crawled on towards the date of the board, November 19, 1985.

Mark always had a certain way that he studied, which was quite the opposite of mine. He studied until a day or two before a big test, and then took the preceding day and night completely off and did something to purposely relax him. Sometimes he would go to a movie. I, on the other hand, studied right up until test time, hoping to memorize one last fact. On the night before the oncology board in 1985, the Redskins were playing the Giants at home. Since it was a night game, Mark did not want to go due to the hour he would get home on a night when he needed to be well rested. So he suggested to me that I take Carol to the game, and we excitedly made plans to ride the subway to the stadium and have a girls' night out. On the day of the game, he began to worry that I would not be able to come into the house in the wee hours of the morning without waking him or making the dog bark and such. So I gave the tickets to Carol and Jerry so that they could both go and resolved to watch the game on TV that night at home with Mark.

However, since Redskins games were never relaxing to him, and since his mood for the entire week was determined by the outcome of Redskins games, he decided not to watch it. Unfortunately, he didn't stick with that decision. He couldn't stand it. He rationalized that he was more uptight knowing that it was on and he wasn't watching than he would be if he just watched, and he had nothing else to do to pass the time to make sure he was tired enough to sleep to get his rest for the big day tomorrow. He planned to only watch the first half and then go to bed, to not chance having to deal with a negative outcome of the game, which would be a bad omen for his test the next day.

The Redskins had a great team that year, and with Joe Theismann at the helm, they were bound to win; this is the fact that I pointed out to him. Of course, later that night we watched in horror and disbelief as Theismann had his leg horribly broken during a sack. The replays in real time and in slow motion were graphically clear. I think I have heard Joe Theismann say in interviews since then that he was not in any actual pain right after it happened, but anybody, Redskin fan or not, who saw that leg snap right in the middle of his shin and bend so unnaturally grabbed their own shins that night and felt actual pain. Mark was horrified. He was crestfallen for the Redskins and for Joe, whose career was immediately ended with the injury. He was sure it was an omen about the next day's oncology board.

Board day came and went, but the oncology board results would not be known for four months, and since he couldn't really get psyched for studying for the heme board scheduled for November of 1986 until he knew the result of the onc board he had just taken, Mark relaxed and decided to get the most out of the last few months of his fellowship, and our talks about where we would spend the last two years in the air force began. The Gramm-Rudman-Hollings Act had passed Congress, and it had huge ramifications to the military. The act was aimed at balancing the federal budget and reducing the existing deficit to zero by 1991, and federal spending was slashed. Part of the reduction in spending was a limit placed on all branches of the military regarding relocation of military personnel. Instead of moving troops around the country every two years, as was the norm for many military families, tours of duty would now be for a minimum of four years, saving millions of dollars spent by the military in relocation. So we ushered in the New Year celebrating the assumption that we would be stationed at Walter Reed for the last two years of our air force commitment. That was great news to all of us. By now, Lisa was in second grade, and Little Mark was in kindergarten in one of the best school systems in the country. We loved our friends and DC and hoped to stay in Rockville permanently.

Things in our perfect little world got a little rocky in Rockville starting on Jan 28, when everybody in the country, including most schools were grouped around television sets to watch the Challenger Space Shuttle take off. Our second grader was no exception, and she had already determined that she would be an astronaut when she grew up. She was so excited about the woman teacher, Christa McAuliffe, who was to be the first person in the Teacher In Space Project to go into space. She was devastated and shocked along with everybody else when we all witnessed the horrific explosion of the shuttle seventy or so seconds into the flight. It dampened everybody's spirits. The world just seemed to be on tilt.

Sometime in February, we began to hear rumblings that we might not be able to stay at Walter Reed regardless of Gramm-Rudman. There was need for an oncologist at Travis Air Force Base in California, and it appeared that Mark would be that oncologist. As exciting as California would have been to us before the kids were in school, it was not in the least exciting now. None of the kids wanted to leave their friends in Rockville. The final verdict was not in yet, but Walter Reed was not a sure thing anymore.

In March, we got some great news. Mark had not only passed the oncology boards, he had blown the doors off of them. He had scored in the ninety-ninth percentile. He was on cloud nine. Location woes went out the door. He could rationalize just about any move knowing that the location would be temporary. The air force would not have him for any longer than two years. After that, we would be free to go into a private practice in civilian life wherever we wanted. And he had the most important board under his belt; he didn't really need the heme board certification in order to practice oncology. So if he didn't feel ready for the heme board when it rolled around, he didn't really have to take it.

In April and May, our location destination changed almost daily from Walter Reed to Travis, from Travis to Walter Reed. The story that we got was that a general in the air force demanded that Mark be "returned" to the air force, and he expected him to be ready to go to work at David Grant Medical Center on Travis AFB in California. This demand was despite the pleas from Mark's commander at Walter Reed, and despite the allegation that the commander had involved the top general in the army.

To assuage ourselves while we were facing our impending destiny, we determined that we would at least come back to the DC area even if we had to relocate to California now. We tried to work out our finances so that we could just rent out our house for two years and then come back to it. Back to the home that held so many memories, the gardens that I landscaped from the tiniest baby plants which I faithfully nursed into recognizable small shrubs, the house that I had slowly decorated a few wall paper rolls at a time, carefully choosing them, saving the money for them, hanging them a couple of sheets per night after the kids went to bed while Mark studied. Back to the house that had the best playroom in the world, which was the full basement that I had sealed myself with crayon green sealer paint on the floor, and white sealant on the cinder block walls that housed Barbie's dream house and He-Man figures, Transformers, and Star Wars stuff, the playroom where the kids could ride their big wheels, and toddler buses and trikes on rainy days. The playroom that bore the seal of approval from the Ellis kids who had dipped their hands in primary colors of paint and stamped them on the walls as "wallpaper" all around the playroom during the two weeks when they all had been quarantined with chicken pox at the same time. Back to the house so perfectly situated next door to 33 Hollyberry Court.

But. . there was no way to be able to charge enough rent to cover the ever-escalating cost of our three mortgages. Finally, near the end of May, fearing that we could wait no longer to put our house on the market if we had to make a move, and sadly knowing that we had no choice but to get out from under the horrible mortgages if we did, we made the decision to list it. We listed it high, according to the realtor. Better to start high, she said.

We had bought the house in 1983 for $145,000 with the afore-described mortgages. Due to the negative amortization mortgage, we now owed $149,000. We listed it for $235,000 one sunny, fateful Saturday late in May.

An hour later, it was sold, full price.

Twenty-three years later at Jenny Graves' wedding, we met the folks who bought our house. They still lived there. I told them that the shrubs planted on the side of the house closest to 33 Hollyberry Court, which the Graves had already told me had flourished and were about six feet tall, had been about three or four inches tall when I first planted them, and that I had driven Jerry nuts with the sprinkler in the predawn hours sounding its chc-chc-chc-chc-chc under his bedroom window. Mark, chuckling, asked them how long it took them to paint over the kids' stamped hands on the wall in the playroom. They said, "They're still there. We just had our kids add their own handprints to the wall."

We also thanked them for saving our friends' lives. One night, years after we had moved away, there was a thunderstorm early in the evening. When the Graves all went to bed on the second floor hours later, they did not know that there had been a light-ning strike to their attic during the storm, and they did not realize that a small fire smoldered, ever growing above their heads. At 2 a.m., their neighbor in our former house was up ironing a shirt in preparation for a business trip the next day. The master bedroom in which he was ironing had a sliding glass door that led to a future balcony, which faced the house behind them, and there were no windows on the Graves' side in that room at all. When he looked up from his ironing, he noticed a fire blazing in what appeared to be the house behind him. He rushed over to the sliding door, and realized that the house behind him was not on fire at all; its windows were reflecting the huge fire that was blazing through the roof of the house next door to him, the Graves'. When he was unable to awaken the Graves by phone, he rushed over to the house and began beating frantically on the front door and ringing the doorbell. The commotion roused the German Shepherd who immediately began barking, which in turn roused the Graves. There was no smoke in their bedroom yet, and the smoke alarms remained silent. The neighbors' wife was still trying to reach them by phone, and I don't know who told them that their house was on fire first, but I know that they raced into all three kids' rooms grabbing up their sleeping children, and everyone including the dog made it safely outside of the house a few mere seconds before the ceiling above the crib in the baby's room collapsed and set the rest of the house on fire.

If we had still lived there, chances are that none of the Ellises would have been up at 2 a.m. to notice the fire. Blessings come in many forms. Sometimes we just don't recognize them at the time. And, maybe, some things are written in the stars.

Mark and Lisa in Mark's legendary red '73 TR-6. 1980

CHAPTER 17

CALIFORNIA

Once again, we found ourselves backing out of a driveway waving to friends we were leaving behind, as we began the first leg of our trip to our new destination. As had become customary with our moves, our immediate destination was to my parents' home for a brief stay. The trip from Rockville, Maryland, to Roebling, New Jersey, was only three hours long, almost not enough time for the tears to dry. I don't know how long the boys cried because we were split along gender lines in our two cars. Lisa, Augie, and I were in my old burnt orange station wagon, and we cried all the way to Baltimore and then made a pact with each other that we would stop crying by the time we emerged from the Baltimore Tunnel on I-95. It was a beautiful sunny day in June, not conducive to crying at all, and I am sure we could have kept it up longer if the weather had been more reflective of our moods.

Mark had an additional reason to be sad. He had finally made the decision to sell his beloved TR6. It had been driven so much since he bought it in 1974, twelve years earlier, that it had finally gotten to the point where it needed to be owned by somebody who loved to tinker with cars. Although he had always planned to develop working on the TR6 as a hobby, he had never found the time to devote to it. Carol's brother and brother-in-law loved to work on cars and had always admired the little red sports car that was no longer manufactured. They were only too happy to take it off of his hands for $500. (About five years later, Mark's car appeared on the cover of a car magazine, which they proudly sent to us. There it was in all of its gleaming glory, fully restored, worthy of its classic status.)

Lisa had spent a great deal of special time with Daddy in that car. One of our favorite pictures of her is a picture from when she is about eighteen months old dressed in her bathing suit, over-sized sunglasses, and floppy sun hat sitting up proudly in the car seat anchored into the passenger side of the TR6, top down. She has a look on her face like she owns the world. Losing that car was a blow to her also, and she said that when she grew up, she was going to buy it back. She had just finished second grade.

As we continued on our short jaunt to Roebling, I began to talk to Lisa about her upcoming trip with her father. The station wagon we were riding in was to become my sister's car when we left New Jersey for California, leaving us with only one car, a white Honda Accord, which we needed to get across the country. Since the car was a five-passenger car, and the one-hundred-fifteen-pound German Shepherd was our sixth passenger, Mark had decided that he and Lisa would take the great cross-country journey of a lifetime by themselves with only Augie as the passenger in the backseat. The boys and I would remain at Grandma's and Pap Pap's for the week of the journey, and then fly out to California to join them. (Little Mark, now almost six, had learned how to swim in Rockville, thank God, but Robbie, not quite four, had not. Needless to say, I didn't like the plan.)

Our reunion with my parents was typical, with the two German Shepherd sisters romping and the grandparents happily exhausting themselves in the enthusiasm of the grandchildren. Cherry picking season was in full swing, and the kids all helped to harvest the sour cherries, or "chah -llies" as Robbie called them, from the two Montmorency and North Star trees that grew in the yard. Cherry season meant that the best "chahllie" pie in the entire world would be rolling off of Grandma's rolling pin and baking in the oven in no time. The rest of the revered sour cherries would be pitted, bagged, and frozen, destined for future pies the rest of the year. How my parents managed to yield from a mere two dwarf trees the number of cherries which could fill twenty deep dish pies year after year, I will never know and will always be frustrated trying to duplicate.

My dad could exact more produce from a third of an acre corner lot in the middle of town than anybody I have ever known.

His strategic placement of fruit trees and vegetables at various places around the yard allowed the plants to be both ornamental and highly productive. Pole-limas wound their way up string that was attached to contraptions that only my father could invent, around the perimeter of the chain-link pool fence. Tomatoes and peppers grew in between rose bushes wherever there was room. Yellow squash and zucchini grew inside the pool area along with my mother's two beloved cherry trees, and pear, apple, peach and fig trees grew in whatever area offered the right conditions, the fig trees having also been requested by my mother. The figs never seemed to realize that they were being asked to grow in a climate with rather cold winters, and they flourished just like all the rest of the fruit trees and wound up in my mother's favorite Christmas cookies each year. Summer produce, such as the best corn in the world, that was not grown at home was grown in the country not more than ten minutes away, and all worthy produce from home or country farm was canned or frozen at peak season for use the rest of the year amidst lip smacking discussion by the family labor force regarding just how good that summer succotash or cherry pie or pear sauce was going to taste at Thanksgiving and Christmas. There was no time to harbor any gloom about a move in such homey warmth and activity.

Having traced the cross-country route on a map and determined the approximate overnight stopping points, the day for the great father-daughter-dog sojourn arrived, and the trio set out, father and daughter waving, seated in the front seats, and dog eagerly seated upright in the backseat. I was pretty nervous about this whole thing; Mark said, "No sweat." The deal was that the trio would call in every night to let us know where they were and how they were doing.

The first night was spent somewhere in Ohio, where Mark reported that they were staying at a Holiday Inn. No, he had not mentioned to them that they were traveling with a dog; nobody asked. Yes, Lisa was doing fine; she was a great traveling companion. "Here, Lisa. Talk to Mommy." Lisa reported that Daddy had let her order a grown-up dinner, a prime rib which had taken up the entire plate, and she had eaten the whole thing all by herself. What I thought was, "Why do you want to teach a seven year-old child to eat an expensive sixteen-ounce piece of meat? Is this father-daughter bonding?" What I said was, "Oh, that's nice. Please put Daddy back on the phone."

The duration of the trip was to be five days. The second day went well also, with both dog and child doing well. The third night they had a little problem. Having gotten caught trying to sneak the dog into the motel, they had to alter their plan and find another place to stay. Unable to endure any more time in the car, and being in some little town in the midwest, they were forced to stay at a very small motel that didn't care about the dog at all. It was one of those little truck stop motels where you could drive right up to your door. Being extremely hungry having passed the usual dinner hour searching for a place to stay, Mark unlocked the door and ushered the dog inside the room along with her water bowl and a tasty dish of dry Purina dog chow, deciding to satisfy the human urgent need of eating a meal before unloading the bags from the car.

The surrounding area turned out to be devoid of eating establishments, and after searching for an hour or so, the weary pair bought some junk food to see them through the night. Upon their return to the motel, when he unlocked and opened the door, instead of the usual greeting from the large black and silver German Shepherd, they were met with a swarm of buzzing flies. The dog was nowhere to be seen. Mark immediately propped the door open to let as many of the nasty masses of airborne insects out as possible, placing the uneaten dog food outside on the sidewalk, and called out to Augie. No response. "Daddy, this is gross. Where's Augie? I have to go to the potty." Worrying about the missing dog, a zillion things going through his mind, wondering what he would find in the bathroom, he guided Lisa through the flies, swatting as he went with a magazine. The toilet and the sink actually seemed to be reasonably clean, but when he pulled back the shower curtain for inspection, he jumped back in complete surprise. The entire length of the bathtub was taken up by a very large silent dog who appeared to be cowering, head down, ears folded. The giant guard dog was terrified of the buzzing flies. She was shaking head to toe and refused to come out of the tub. In addition to the flies, she was terrified of her "papa" slapping the magazine around everywhere to get rid of them, having been trained as a puppy with a rolled-up newspaper that we used to swat against our legs to make a frightful sound when she was out of order.

Fortunately, I didn't know any of this. All I heard that night was a rather vanilla report that father, daughter, and dog were enjoying a snack in front of the TV in their room and were looking forward to crossing the great Rockies the next day. It wasn't a very nice motel, but it would suffice.

In a town that had no place to get dinner, it naturally follows that it had no place for breakfast either. So, armed once again with junk food, father, daughter, and dog began their trek into the Rocky Mountains. They stopped along the way at a gas station that was manned by an old crusty cowboy complete with dirty dungarees, large scuffed boots with real spurs, and a sweat-stained wide-brimmed cowboy hat. His leathery face deeply grooved by years of sun, wind, and dirt, he was the scariest sight Lisa had ever seen, and when they approached the counter to pay for the peanut butter crackers and Pringles, he looked right at the little girl, narrowed his eyes, and drawled, "That'll be one thousand, two hunnert, and seventy dollars." She was too terrified to speak or to even look away and just stood frozen in place for what must have seemed like an eternity to her. Then the cowboy laughed, revealing tobacco-stained teeth, and said, "I'm just joshin' ya, little lady."

The crackers weren't very fresh, and the Pringles were downright stale, but the Pepsi was good. They hit the top of their first mountain and were about halfway down in their decent before Lisa vomited. What's a guy going to do driving a Honda Accord down a narrow road with no real shoulder while his little girl is throwing up Pringles and the dog is stretched out, the front of her great hulking body hanging over the front seat, and dutifully cleaning up Lisa's face and upper body with her tongue?

The call I got that night was a little different from the other calls:

"I need some mommy advice."
"Okaaay."
"Lisa says her tummy hurts."
"Well, where does it hurt?"
"I can't tell."
"What does she say?"
"Everywhere. I'm really worried about her, and I don't know what to do."
"Let me talk to her."
"Mommy?"
"Hi, honey. Daddy says you have a tummy ache."
"Uh-huh."
"Do you feel like you might throw up?"
"Not anymore. It just hurts now."
"You already threw up?"
"Yeah, in the car."
"When?"
"In the afternoon."
"What did you have for lunch?"
"Pringles."
"What did you have for breakfast?"
"Pringles."
"Honey, put daddy back on the phone, okay?"

That's when the whole story came out as easily as pulling teeth, rewinding of course, from the up-chucked Pringles in the mountains all the way back through the fly-infested motel, with a generous helping of, "Well, that's because. . ." sprinkled in between the segments of the story in response to my questions, "Well why didn't you. . .?"

The good news was that they were still on schedule and would descend into California the following day if Lisa wasn't having an appendectomy somewhere in Nevada. The appendectomy fear was only from her father. Doctor Mom was completely comfortable with her own diagnosis and had prescribed some Pepto Bismol that she had packed, to be followed up in the morning with saltines for breakfast and a suitable nutritious lunch no matter where they had to drive to get it.

Back at Grandma's house, the excitement was building for the boys, who were looking forward to their own great adventure on an airplane. We had been hoping yet again for a door-to-door move, but our furniture was stalled somewhere in Texas and would not be showing up to California for another week or two, which meant we would be temporarily moving into the VOQ (Visiting Officer's Quarters) on Travis AFB. We had already bought a house in California in what was reputed to be the best public school district in the county, shortly after we had sold our house in North Farm, during a whirlwind three-day trip to Fairfield, California, where Travis was located.

Those three days had served as our introduction to the realtor, to the neighborhoods surrounding Travis, to David Grant Medical Center on the base, and to some of the other doctors at the medical center. It had been a great trip, one of the very few we had taken without the kids, and we had not only chosen a house, but we had also met the other oncologists. What a great group of people. They were young and fun and smart, and it was clearly evident that they were all good friends as well as good doctors—compassionate, well trained, and down to earth.

Several of the medical center doctors and their spouses had taken us out to dinner to their favorite sushi bar. Neither Mark nor I had ever eaten sushi and were hoping that there was something edible on the menu. The first edible that we came across was in the form of adult beverages, which everybody had in quantities sufficient to loosen inhibitions. Peer pressure got the best of Mark, and he decided to try whatever community sushi platters the others ordered as they passed them around. One of the other wives named Kelly and I moved to our own table and ordered chicken teriyaki.

Kelly was an easy-going, pretty, blue-eyed blond, from West Virginia who had gone to college at Marshall University in

Huntington. She had actually been in school there when the college suffered the terrible tragedy of losing the football team in a plane crash, which I could tell had carved a niche on her timeline. We had a lot in common; she had a flair for art projects, was a former schoolteacher, and had a daughter just the right baby-sitting age for the Ellis kids. Kelly was easy to talk to, and I knew that I liked her right away, and that she would become a good friend.

As we talked and laughed and got to know each other, the raucous medical table across the room began to yell out for more and more daring sushi items. One of them began to yell out to the waiter, "We want suckers! Bring us stuff with suckers on it!" I could not believe Mark was eating barely dead oceanic creatures, and as I sat there knowing that there was not enough alcohol in the world to induce me to kiss a mouth that had eaten raw fish and squid and octopus, into the restaurant rushed our realtor, Pat. Upon spotting me, she breathlessly asked, "Where's Mark?"

"He's among the drunk doctors over there eating octopus and doing shots. Why? What's wrong?

"There are competing contracts for your house! If you want it, you need to sign this counter-offer from the owner right now! The first one back to the listing agent gets the house!"

Holy Cow. It's eight o'clock in the evening; nobody is sober except the realtor who has somehow tracked us down, still pre-cell phone days, and we are going to sign a contract to buy a house. That's exactly what we did. We signed it amidst jovial drunken shouts from the medical crew, "Don't worry, Mark, you're signing it under duress! You got a good attorney? Ha ha ha ha ha! Good luck, buddy!" Pat was the first one back to the listing agent.

It was after that crazy visit to California, just a couple of weeks before we had to leave Rockville, that we had begun to realize that our dreaded move could prove to be yet another golden opportunity that had the potential to be as wonderful as we would allow it to be. And that thought was what we held fast to as our little family reunited and moved into the VOQ on Travis.

If you ask any of the kids what they remember about the VOQ at Travis, they all say the same thing, "*Jaws!*" The VOQ was a throwback to the early fifties in décor, not superbly maintained, dark as well as dingy, and the dusty floor-to-ceiling drapes were torn and ugly. But the suite had one out of two TVs that worked, and *Jaws* was just coming on when we switched on the working set. Having given up swimming in the ocean after I saw the movie back in the mid-seventies, I didn't think it was a great idea for the kids to see it, but I was overruled by Daddy and the gang of kids who were jumping on the bed and siding with him. So we popped some popcorn and settled down to watch the movie all together. I think the kids understood my point of view by the end of the movie. Little Mark wondered if sharks ever got into swimming pools. Robbie wondered if there was any possible way a giant shark could get into the VOQ. I went to bed laughing as I heard Mark in the next room explaining how distant we were from the ocean and trying to convince the kids to not all sleep in the same bed and to turn out the lights.

In about a week, our furniture showed up, and we were able to move into our house, which had four bedrooms this time instead of three, meaning that we could split the boys if they did not want to share a room. But they loved their bunk beds and chose to stay together, giving us the opportunity to have a real guest room. Everybody liked the house and excitedly opened boxes and reunited with toys and stuffed animals that had been packed up for four weeks. I was excited about the majestic English walnut tree, which shaded the front yard and promised a bumper crop of walnuts, and there was a "Big Bird" swing set in the backyard and a great patio, perfect for outdoor birthday parties.

As the days in our new house began to go by, the absence of any knocks on the door by neighborhood kids began to dampen our brief burst of enthusiasm at embracing our new home and its garden treasures, and our kids began to really miss their friends.

Since it was early July, school would not start until September, and the summer loomed long and a little lonely. I, as the "camp counselor," ran what had become our usual summer projects, supervising the making of papier-mâché piñatas in preparation of each boy's July birthday party, uncertain of whom we would find to attend the parties, and taking the kids to the bookstore to purchase new books for summer reading for book reports they would do and turn in to me for money, and devising new math games for pennies. The kids stuck together and began to make up games and scripts for movies, which they hoped would be filmed by their father on the family video camera when rehearsals were complete. I thought, "Well, at least they have each other and are being creative and inclusive of each other. Maybe this is the kind of time that creates fond memories that will forever bind them together as adult brothers and sister." But, a day or two later, I was upstairs putting some laundry away and spotted them from the window. There were my children tenuously walking closely together, three in a row, hand in hand, on the front sidewalk up and down the street, with Robbie holding up a poster board-sized sign with large black letters obviously written by one of his older siblings that read, "Looking for Friends." That just about broke my heart.

There had been no real reception in the neighborhood of the new people who had moved in except by one family who lived diagonally across the street. The two kids were teenagers and very friendly, and had rushed over to meet us on our arrival day. They had followed up the next day by taking the kids and me on a little hike up to the top of one of the "golden hills" nearby and explained the weather patterns to us. No, the hills were not dead grass; they were just brown, "golden" to the native Californians, for the dry season. They would turn green during the rainy season. I thought, "Crap, there is a rainy season?" The good news was that it would be sunny and warm every day from the first of April through Halloween; then, it would rain every day for the next five months, during which time the hills would turn green in time for Christmas. The parents, as friendly as their teenagers, had invited us over to the house, and offered the baby-sitting services of their daughter. Both parents worked, one in San Francisco, and one in Sacramento, and they explained the nature of our new little neighborhood, describing it as a bedroom community for each of the cities located about forty miles on either side of us, where it was much more expensive to own property.

Everybody had six-foot privacy fences around the backs and sides of their homes. All the parents seemed to work, and it was impossible to tell where children might be located. The neighborhood seemed very quiet and closed. The kids and I decided that we would simply knock on everyone's door until we met some kids. Surely, there had to be some kids here. We visited every house on our block one afternoon, knocking on the front doors or ringing the doorbells; finally, one door was answered, and the residents turned out to be a retired couple who lived behind us. In response to finding us on their front porch, and to my greeting, "Hi, we are your new neighbors. We just wanted to come by and introduce ourselves. I think we live just behind you," the woman asked the kids if they ever played any ball out back. Mark and Robbie said that they liked to play basketball inside our garage, where we had a smaller than regulation net. Lisa volunteered that they played "chase the ball" with Augie, using a tennis ball out back. The woman sternly quipped, "Well, we have a Japanese Koi pond in our backyard. You better be sure that no tennis balls ever come over that fence! A stray tennis ball could kill one of my fish if it landed in the pond. So you keep those balls to yourself!" I smiled and said, "It was nice meeting you," and we turned around and began walking home, actually much happier than we had been about most people not being home to answer the door.

Back at home, munching on some fresh-from-the-oven chocolate-chip cookies, we speculated that maybe kids were gone for the summer, away at camp or visiting relatives or on vacation, and that they would all be coming back by the end of the summer before school started. The kids pitched the idea of getting a kitten. Kids know when their parents are vulnerable and most amenable to ideas, and since everybody except Augie thought this to be a good idea, we rescued a couple of littermate kittens from the mall pet store. After a great deal of discussion, the kids decided to name the black male, who had not a single spot of any other color on him except for his pink nose, Luke. Guess what they named the pretty little gray tabby female with the strikingly large pale green eyes; Leia, of course. Although Leia would always be a princess, Luke would grow into more of a Darth Vader than a Luke Skywalker, but you only know so much when you bring adorable kittens home.

Shortly after our brief foray around the neighborhood looking for friends, Mammaw and Pop Pop came to visit us, which was a real treat for the kids. We asked the thirteen-year-old young lady from the family across the street we had met on the first day to babysit while we went out to dinner. We only planned to be gone for about two hours. She was happy to do it, and the kids were happy to have another "kid" around for the evening, and we went out to a nice dinner, returned as planned, paid her, put the kids to bed, and then sat down to talk in the family room located in the back of the house. All of a sudden, our conversation was interrupted by a very loud crack followed by the sound of shattering glass, sounding like it came from the front of the house. It almost sounded like a gunshot. I rushed into the living room with Mammaw and Pop Pop close behind not knowing whether or not to crouch, while Mark flew to the front door and flung it open, barking dog in guard mode at his side, just in time to see the lights from a car speeding away around a curve in the street. It was, otherwise, completely dark outside, and we didn't see any damage or source of the "gunshot" sound at first, but when I pulled the drapes back in the living room to inspect the large picture window, there was a gaping hole in the glass and half of a brick lying inside the room behind the couch that sat in front of the window.

We were awe-struck into silence, mouths gaping. We had lived there for little more than two weeks. Who would do such a thing to us? Who lived there before us? Had the last occupants created an enemy? Was hurling bricks just a random pastime for somebody? Who or what was strong enough to propel a brick through an insulated glass, double-paned picture window? The young babysitter was a strikingly beautiful young lady who looked several years older than her tender true age, and her parents seemed to be very protective and strict with her. Perhaps she was plagued by older young hoodlums who were mad because she wouldn't allow any of them to enter our house while babysitting? We called the police, and we called the babysitters' parents, because we had not been home for more than forty-five minutes when the incident took place, and we feared for the girl's safety and felt that her parents should know. The babysitter's parents and older brother all came over and were as horrified as we were. The police had nothing to go on, since we could give no description of the car. All we had was a brick half. We considered ourselves lucky that the insulated heavy drapes had been pulled closed, and that we were not sitting in that room when it occurred, but we were left with a very unsettled feeling.

Two days later, I finally met another neighbor. When she asked me how things were going so far, I haltingly said pretty well, and after momentary consideration, I relayed the brick story to her, hoping for some little tidbit that might explain the strange occurrence. What I got was this tidbit:

"Think about who you have been associating with."
"What? We hardly know anybody, and we have barely been here for two weeks."
"I know."
"Who are you talking about?"
Silence.
"You mean the air force?"
Shrug.
"Somebody has something against the military?"

I couldn't fathom what she could possibly be talking about, and I could tell that she was considering what to tell me, almost weighing her words. Finally, after a long silent pause in our conversation, to my lingering furrowed brow of bewilderment, she said, "We are not home very often, but let us know if you need anything." Then, in more hushed tones, she leaned in closer and almost hissed "This area has a very active clan."

With that, she had turned on her heel and walked back inside her house. As I stood there no less bewildered, I thought, Clan? What is she talking about? The neighbors are clannish? Clan. Not like, clan with a "K"? No, it can't be. This is California, where people are "laid back," which until recently, I had always supposed meant easy-going and friendly. "And, it's 1986, for Pete's sake," Was my very white neighbor, literally porcelain in her skin color, really telling me that we were targeted by the freakin' Klan because our first friend in the neighborhood was a black family? Man, this was a strange land so far. We had the wicked witch of the west with her Koi pond living behind our privacy fence in the back, and the KKK living behind the privacy fence nearby. I was beginning to think that I didn't really want to know who else lived inside all the rest of the neighborhood stockades, and I was contemplating an automatic tennis ball machine for one of our back upstairs bedrooms aimed in the direction of a certain Koi pond.

In contrast to these first two weeks of continued perplexing astonishment at home, Mark found himself surrounded by rock-solid people at David Grant in the universally familiar medical environment in which he had grown comfortable over the years. He and his partners were already board certified in oncology, and all were planning to take the hematology boards in November. Unlike fellowship, and just as he had expected, there was no time to study at work at all because they were booked back-to-back with clinic patients all day. The military only staffed oncologists at their largest regional medical centers, designated as tertiary care centers, and since Travis was one of the few air force tertiary care centers in the United States, cancer patients and patients with serious hematological problems were flown in from all over the western region. They included active duty personnel and their dependents, as well as retired military folks and their spouses. Once again, he would have the opportunity to see all types of rare cancers and blood disorders, and his Walter Reed training would serve him well.

The oncologists were responsible for all of the inpatients on the cancer ward as well as for their busy outpatient clinics. The clinics were located in a separate area of the hospital utilized only for outpatients, and each oncologist had his own miniscule office, which also served as his miniscule exam room. Housing a small grey metal desk, a desk chair, an exam table, and one extra chair, the room was not much bigger than a closet and felt pretty claustrophobic when the door was shut, despite the one small window. At Walter Reed, the outpatient clinic had been located in a totally separate area from where the doctors' offices were, and when they were in the clinic, they just went from exam room to exam room before returning to their offices at the end of the clinic day. His experience at Tyndall had been more like Travis in that each doctor had only one exam room which had also been inside the doctor's office, but the room was much larger and had at least been fitted with a track that held a privacy curtain to create two distinct spaces.

There was no such privacy at the Travis hospital clinic. And, after having had the ability to go from one exam room to another at Walter Reed, Mark discovered the inefficiency of having only one exam room in which to see a whole day's worth of cancer patients. The patient schedule was at the mercy of each patient's ability to dress and undress in a timely fashion and totally dependent on the doctor's ability to usher a patient out of his one and only exam room/office in order to clear it and have it prepped for the next patient. The doctor was constantly having to step out of his office/exam room into the hallway to give the patient privacy to dress and undress, and the doctor had no privacy in the hallway to dictate a note or address questions from his nursing staff about other chemotherapy patients, since the hallway held a line-up of chairs filled with waiting patients and family members. Mark's office also had one additional claim on inefficiency: it housed the telephone closet containing the telephone system for the entire hospital, and he was frequently interrupted while seeing patients anytime a phone problem arose. During those times, both patient and doctor had to step out of the exam room into the hallway.

The operation of outpatient clinics housed within the hospital was pretty much a bare bones kind of situation. Mark's office/

exam room had probably been originally designed as a supply closet, but the air force made do with what it had to serve the population for which it was responsible. The actual chemotherapy room was down the hall from the exam area and consisted of one room with many chemotherapy chairs. Understaffed but compassionate nurses administered chemotherapy to as many patients as they could serve at one time, and patients who experienced intense nausea from their treatments vomited in front of all the other chemotherapy patients in the room. In 1986, the wonderful anti-emetics that were being developed by the pharmaceutical industry were not yet on the market, and intense nausea was very common. The nurses also tried to assess patient status and address patient questions which justifiably arose during the course of treatment, but many questions regarding potentially serious if not uncomfortable side effects were probably never asked by the patients due to their intimate and personal nature and the forced lack of privacy. Who wants to ask about chemotherapy induced vaginal dryness or constipation in front of a bunch of mixed-gender strangers? They just opted to wait until their next doctor's appointment, which was once per chemotherapy cycle, a standard within the practice of oncology.

Although David Grant was not as large or as well appointed as Walter Reed, it was a teaching hospital for the air force and did have a family practice residency program. So, even though the oncologists had no fellows under them who could make oncology decisions for the inpatients, they had the pleasure of having the family practice house staff present in the hospital at all times, and they carried out the orders from the oncologists on a daily and nightly basis. The oncologists' hospital roles were largely those of consultants, who shared call with each other on a rotating basis, but who rarely had to go back to the hospital once they went home for the day, and on most days they left the hospital and their clinics at a reasonable hour, except when there was some special air force training exercise going on.

Unlike Walter Reed, where Mark was excluded from the army training exercises, he had no such exclusion from routine air force training exercises at an air force facility. He had to participate on Friday fatigue days (which simply meant wearing his camouflage uniform to the hospital/clinic instead of his usual air force blues), and occasional "camp-outs" on the premises, when the doctors would pretend to eat field rations, but somehow manage to send out a large order for pizza delivery and go home at midnight. Red Flag, which was only required once per year, was a strict military training camp-out held for a long weekend at an undisclosed "remote" area, during which there was no contact from family to officer or officer to family unless there was an emergency, and then contact only via Red Cross. On mock chemical disaster day, because Mark was a hematologist as well as an oncologist, he was required to see patients all day in his chemical weapons/radiation protective gear, mask included, which made him look to his patients like he was a Ghostbuster. In any radioactive emergency situation, hematologists would play a key role in caring for those exposed to radiation, due to the types of illnesses and coagulation problems that would rapidly become critical situations, and the doctors had to be prepared to protect themselves while working in the exposure zone.

During a time of peace, which the United States was then enjoying, these relatively rare exercises offered a glimpse of life as it might be for an air force subspecialty doctor during either a time of war or a time of national or international emergency. Unlike the non-medical corps of the air force, whose daily jobs involved routinely practicing and preparing for non-peaceful times, the doctors were slammed everyday with patients who were their first priority, and they considered patient care to be their real job. Mark was not enthusiastic about any of the other "boy scout" stuff. Fortunately for him, the decision to send the hematologists from Travis to assist in the nuclear power plant disaster at Chernobyl, which had occurred just prior to our active duty assignment at Travis in April, kept being delayed and finally never materialized.

He studied for the hematology boards at home in an office we had set up for him on the first floor in the perfect double-door study that was positioned to the left of the Spanish-tiled foyer. I surprised him with a beautiful large oak roll-top desk with all kinds of cubbies and little drawers for his early August birthday, so that the doctor who was now a real oncologist could trade in his old surplus salvage desk and have a real office in which to work at home. (I bought it with a Master Card; so there were really two surprises, one on his birthday, and one when the charge card statement came.) Just as in Rockville, the kids knew that when daddy was in that office with the doors closed, there were no interruptions, and voices were to be hushed any time they were in the vicinity of the office doors in the foyer. With three young children, two cats, and a dog, it was almost as quiet as one would reasonably expect it to be.

When I took the kids over to the school to register them for the upcoming school year, I thought it would be a good opportunity for them to get excited about their new school and potential new friends. I was flabbergasted when the school secretary told me that there was no room in the school for them. "What does that mean? This is a public school, and we live in this district."

She elaborated, "It is true that you live in the district, and this school is the school your kids would attend if it wasn't already full." I had never heard of such a thing. I thought public schools had to find room for any student who lived in the district. "Where will my kids go to school then?" She replied, "They will be bussed across town to another elementary school." Bussed?

I was beginning to feel like we had landed on the moon. Nothing was what we had expected it to be. When the kids and I drove over to register at that school, I quickly realized that it was in the worst part of town. Compared to our nice neat little neighborhood, strange as it was, this area was full of apartment buildings in varying states of disrepair; rusty, broken, old chain-link fencing; and dogs roaming without leashes. The school itself was very well maintained, and was located right next to the mall, which was itself fairly new. After dutifully registering the kids, I took them to the mall, where much to their delight, there was a Chick-Filet; little things make the sacrifices in life worthwhile. They really didn't care what school they went to as long as it contained kids who might become their friends.

I was rapidly becoming very disenchanted with California. I broke down and cried on the night before the first day of school while I was packing everybody's brown paper bag lunches for the following day. The kids were already in bed. Mark was no more enamored by our civilian life than I was and was equally worried about the kids and the lack of educational opportunity toward which they appeared to be headed, but he tried to console me by saying, "Things will turn out okay," and "We are only here for two years"—all the time feeling guilty, blaming himself for being in the air force and causing disruption and misery to the family.

We decided that night that I would become a very visible volunteer at the school so that I could keep an eye on everything and know first-hand what was happening with our children. That would turn out to be one of the smartest decisions and best preemptive strikes that we ever made. We were to become very well educated in latch-key children whose parents were either in jail, working all night, or in absentia in general. The dry borax from the soap dispensers in the kindergarten classroom would later be described to me by one little student as looking just like "that stuff my daddy puts up his nose."

The professional challenges from a medical standpoint for Mark at David Grant were exactly what he had expected them to be, and being well prepared to undertake them, he performed well. His patients loved him. He quickly earned the professional respect of his physician colleagues, as well as the rest of the medical community that made up the workforce at the medical center. His favorite time at work was being within the four walls of the exam room by himself with his patients. They were all interesting. Some of them were famous. None of them were "crocks." They all had legitimate needs as they battled the cancer demon. He was finally doing what had been written in the stars so long ago, and he was fulfilled by that fact.

The professional challenges that he had not expected and thought that he had left back at Tyndall, had to do with the system.

One of his biggest frustrations was that, once again, the support staff in the oncology clinic was not controlled by the doctors. For instance, the nurses reported to the colonel who was the director of nursing, and she decided where and when the oncology nurses worked. They could be and were pulled to work in whatever ward or clinic she deemed had the greatest need. He thought it was ludicrous to have the well-trained oncology nurses, the only nurses who really knew how to administer chemotherapy, working in another area of the medical center when there were cancer patients who needed their expertise. During times when his nurses got pulled, he would register his concern with the nursing director, but not only did the nurses report directly to her, she held rank on the oncology doctors who were majors, and most of the time, she was unyielding.

The same type of hierarchy existed for the med techs. If nobody was around to assist with a bone marrow biopsy, too bad. He hated this lack of control over how efficiently he could practice, and he hated the inconvenience to his patients and thought that the inefficiencies could be detrimental to the patients. There were problems with drug procurement, times when supplies did not arrive on time, and many of these patients had traveled long distances to get there. He shared my opinion that it was really socialized medicine. The military was providing free cancer care to the military masses, but very inefficiently, and not in the most compassionate or state-of-the-art manner.

In November of that first year in California, I became a patient in the system and felt the effects of less-than-optimal care when state-of-the-art care was available elsewhere. During our previous stint at Walter Reed, I had had surgery on my left leg to repair the cause of phlebitis that had plagued me since my early pregnancy at Tyndall. The vascular surgeon removed three perforators, veins that connect the deep venous system to the peripheral venous system. The surgery had been a huge success, and for the first time in two years, I did not have to wear a lower leg compression stocking on that leg, and I had no phlebitic episodes except for a day or two each month according to my hormonal cycle. But on those days, I had full-blown phlebitis despite the stocking. The doctor had told me that even when I had a phlebitic episode, as long as I was wearing the stocking, I was protected from developing a DVT (deep vein thrombosis), and I took Advil, put up with the pain, and did whatever I had to do.

My GYN doctor had a theory that if my hormonal cycle were more controlled to prevent any hormonal surges at various times of the month (which is what triggered the phlebitis) that perhaps I would not have any monthly problems with my leg. The method of stabilizing my cycle would be to go on low dose birth control pills. My vascular doctor strongly disagreed. He advised me never to go on birth control pills, due to deep vein thrombosis risk. He also advised me to never get pregnant again, as he felt it would be life threatening to me, never to smoke, and never to gain weight, all of which would increase my risk of developing a DVT. I did not intend to do any of the above, but I was in a quandary as to what to do about the birth control pills. The most important medical advice that I was afraid to ignore was the vascular surgeon's prediction that if I got pregnant again, it could kill me. About three months before we were to leave for Travis, I had decided to go along with the GYN doctor's advice and try the birth control pills, both to prevent pregnancy and to experiment with his cycle stabilization theory as a way of preventing the monthly phlebitic episodes. On the first day of each pill cycle, I noticed a slight pressure and mild pain in my lower left calf in the area of the surgical repair, but other than that very minor temporary discomfort, I was perfectly fine with no monthly surges of phlebitis. At my three-month follow-up appointment, the GYN doctor was pleased and prescribed a year's supply of the pills, and off we went to Travis.

One morning in November, just before Mark was to take the hematology boards, which was about six months after I began taking the pills, I awoke to incredible pain and swelling in my left leg. Mark, suspecting a DVT, took me to David Grant immediately, and because the only vascular surgeon at Travis was away, I was seen by a different type of surgeon. He was unfamiliar with the particular Doppler, (test that uses sound waves to detect blood flow through the venous system) utilized by David Grant and was not completely sure how to administer the Doppler test to determine if I had a DVT, which he knew could be a very serious situation if a clot was to break loose in the deep vein system in my leg and travel to my heart or lung, where it could be life threatening. He was very compassionate, and he and the substitute tech did their best to make the determination. In their opinion, the Doppler showed no evidence of a clot, and the surgeon advised me to stop the birth control pills, take aspirin, and stay completely off of my feet, leg elevated, and come back to see the vascular surgeon the following week when he would be back in town.

I could not even stand upright for longer than a minute or two without extraordinary pain and swelling. My leg was as tight as a sausage, so I had no choice but to follow the advice as closely as possible, and once again, I found myself scooting around on my butt to keep my leg horizontal while I performed the necessary household and childcare tasks. When I was finally able to see the vascular surgeon the following week, he told me that I had probably had a deep vein thrombosis, which was resolving on its own, and had me fitted for a full set of panty hose compression stockings. I was instructed to never take birth control pills again. To my question as to why I had to punish both legs with tight, hot stockings when only one was affected, he said that I had better get used to it, because I would be wearing them for at least six months. Six months later, seventy-five percent of the daily pain had resolved while wearing the stockings, and I had my monthly full-blown phlebitis back for two days each month. Without the hose, I was still unable to be upright for more than fifteen minutes without the pain, swelling, and discoloration accumulating. He told me that I would have the daily pain forever and would have to wear the stockings for the rest of my life and that there was nothing else I could do. I was so disappointed, and I asked to be allowed to seek a second opinion, since Mark had discovered that one of the top vascular surgeons in the country who specialized in my particular problem was located in San Francisco. Having formerly had such a great response to the vascular surgery at Walter Reed, both Mark and I wondered why I couldn't have a similar procedure now.

Champus denied me. We made an appointment anyway to be paid out of our own pocket; it was expensive, but it was also money well spent. The vascular surgeon in San Francisco was aghast at the fact that I had been prescribed a full set of compression hose, and aghast at the level of compression, which was too great in his opinion. He also was in disbelief that I had not been admitted to the hospital at the time of my acute episode. He did a Doppler study as well as a more invasive dye study of my leg, and found that I had evidence of a former DVT, and possible damage to my leg from the chronic phlebitis. He did not feel that the damage should be surgically repaired at that time and planned to reevaluate me for surgery in six months. He prescribed a half compression stocking for only my one affected leg with less compression than I had been wearing, and after three days in that stocking, I was a new person. I got my life back and was pain free and good as new, except for the cosmetic problem of having to wear the half-stocking, which was far less in my mind when compared to the cosmetic problem of wearing the full set on both legs. I still had my phlebitis episodes each month for a day or two in tandem with my hormonal cycle, but I was pain free for every other day of the month, and that situation was so much more livable than the daily pain and discomfort I had been enduring.

Six months later, when I went back to the San Francisco doctor to be reevaluated for a surgical procedure that might get me out of having to wear the half-stocking, his finding was that I really had irreparable damage inside the veins the entire length of my left leg due to the chronic phlebitis. I was disappointed, but considering what I had formerly been told, and what life had been like inside that full set of very tight compression hose, I still felt that the half-stocking and one or two days of phlebitis per month was very livable. He agreed with my former vascular surgeon from Walter Reed that as long as I wore my stocking, my leg was protected from developing a clot even during my phlebitic days, and on those days, I once again took my Advil and went about the business of living, and I felt extremely fortunate.

The question remains, however, what the situation would have been if way back at Tyndall, I had not had to wait four-and-a-half months for the original compression stockings? My experience with the compression hose back then was that I was able to stay up and function all day as soon as I got them. Might they have saved me from any lasting effects of phlebitis if I had gotten them right away when I first presented at only six weeks pregnant? I would never have had to wait for such an inordinate amount of time for that prescription if it had been ordered outside of the military system. With the competitive nature of suppliers and distributors outside of a regulated system, if one didn't come through in a timely fashion, the supplier would have lost my doctor's business, and another distributor would have been asked to step up to the plate. Of course, had I known how important that first set of compression hose was, I would have paid for them myself outside of the military system. Nobody told me. I just slogged along in the status quo of a system designed to take care of masses of people, not individuals.

That very personal glimpse into the world of socialized medicine completed the experience I had already had with my young children going through their ailments and vaccinations, and I joined Mark in his dissatisfaction of the military medical system. We began counting the days to our release into the civilian world. At least in the United States, the military was the only socialized system of medicine, and we now knew that it was the entire military and not just Tyndall, or Travis, or Walter Reed. A socialized system was not the way Mark intended to practice medicine, and not the way I intended for our family to be patients.

In the spring, Mark found out that he had passed the hematology boards, and our location talks began again. This time, there was much more to our location talks than geography. We discussed standards of medical practice. Knowing medicine was one thing. What were his requirements of the system to practicing it? What was the overall goal? What did one need to be the best doctor one could be? What were the specific needs for a first-class oncology practice? We had no questions in our minds that we would find what he was seeking in the world of private practice, where the doctor was the boss and could therefore look out for the total welfare of his patients, both medically and administratively.

The summer of our last year in the air force began, and the countdown was underway in earnest. At first, we were totally focused on finding an oncology practice on the east coast, mid-Atlantic being the most suitable region, with the Maryland-Virginia-DC area being the best. In the meantime, Mark sought out oncology practice ads in his journals. (Nobody was online yet in 1987.) He made contact with a few practices and mailed off his CV. The opportunities were boundless. It was simply a matter of where did an oncologist want to practice.

Because we were focused on the east coast, and because we wanted to take full advantage of our time in California by seeing some of the sights we had not seen, I traded in the white Honda for a Chevy Van with all the trimmings. The Honda had become mine as soon as we moved into our new house in California, since Mark had once again become a sports car owner. This time it was a black Honda CRX. It was a fun little car, but not a real replacement for the TR6. I let the kids come with me to pick out the van, and we had a blast. The van was burgundy with a luggage rack on top, seven passenger seats, a cocktail table drink holder in the back on the center aisle, an ice chest behind the driver seat, and best of all. . .a TV with a VHS tape player bolted to the ceiling just behind the driver seat. I knew we were going to get good use out of that TV on the cross-country trip that, in less than a year, would transport us back to the east coast from whence we came.

We immediately adopted it as our Redskins van, configured a seven-year payment plan, and drove it off the lot sixty minutes later. It was the perfect color for displaying Redskin paraphernalia, unpopular as it was in Fairfield where everybody was a 49ers fan. We used it to take the kids to Lake Tahoe that Thanksgiving, where we stayed in a log cabin and went hiking and pretended to be pilgrims hunting for our dinner on Thanksgiving Day. Tahoe was experiencing a very rare late autumn without a single snowfall that year, but on awaking early Friday morning, we were delighted by the fact that the lake and the surrounding forest had been transformed overnight into a magical white fairyland. We had not seen snow for a while, and we loved it. California did have some treasures, and we were slowly awakening to the reasons why people loved the state.

In December, the 49ers defied all the bakeries where 49er champion cakes were being pre-displayed, and all the shops with the 49er champion shirts also pre-displayed, and lost to. . .the Redskins. The next month, Super Bowl XXII found Mark and me in San Diego in the Chargers' stadium rooting for our home team against the Broncos, while Mammaw and Pop Pop stayed at our house, took care of the kids, and tried to keep our family's youngest rabid Redskin fan, Little Mark, reasonably calm. We got to witness the best second quarter of football ever played, and Doug Williams became Little Mark's new hero. We had chosen not to take my van down to the game because we wanted to drive down the Pacific Coast Highway. If anybody is ever comfortable on that road, with the unguarded hairpin curves on cliffs that descend at a 90-plus degree angle one thousand feet below to where the sea crashes into them, you could say that we were reasonably comfortable in the little CRX. The sight was breathtaking, and at a roadside pull-off area, I just had to lean over the edge to see the water crashing into the cliffs. I will never forget it. . .and never do it again.

California was beginning to wear on us like new jeans that have been washed just enough to begin to feel comfortable. Although the school situation was every bit as bad as we had feared, any detrimental effects had been reasonably controlled by my presence, and I was there almost every day. Since I had volunteered to do whatever the three teachers who taught my three kids needed, I was tasked with teaching a gifted fourth grade math class, because there was not one already, and there were a few kids who really needed to advance at a much faster rate than the rest of the class; teaching a gifted second grade reading class, again because there was none; and being a kindergarten aid in Robbie's kindergarten class. Lisa had tested into the magnet gifted school which started with the fifth grade, and she was scheduled to attend it if we were still there in the fall. However, the designation was a state designation, meaning that she would be eligible to attend a gifted school anywhere in California. Little Mark's national test scores remained in the ninety-sixth percentile, exactly where they had been when we left Rockville; so, his only detrimental change seemed to be the vocabulary he had developed on the playground. Robbie was surviving the kindergarten class where they were teaching zero reading skills and attempting to teach the social skills he had already learned in preschool. The kids had all made some pretty good friends through school or church and were relatively happy with their situation. Lisa had gone one step ahead of us all and decided that she was a California girl and vocalized often that she wanted to stay in Fairfield. Although Mark and I would not have considered staying in Fairfield, we were beginning to wonder about the possibility of moving to Sacramento where there was an oncology practice that was recruiting.

One had to admit that the state had a lot to offer. Looking ahead to college for the kids, we knew that California's higher education system was excellent and very inexpensive for state residents—a plus. From a weather standpoint, even though both Mark and I loved and missed four distinct seasons of the year, especially the brilliant autumns of the east coast, we attempted to see the advantages to living in a warm climate and "driving to the snow" as the native California people said, or driving to wine country, or to the national parks to witness seasonal splendor, as opposed to living within it every day as each season slowly and magically waxed and waned around us. Vacaville, which was fifteen miles away from us in the direction of Sacramento enjoyed very warm, predominantly sunny weather with no wind. Fairfield had more of the San Francisco wind and weather. So we decided to interview with the practice in Sacramento, and we did seriously consider it. They were a nice bunch of people, and the school situation seemed much better than what we had in Fairfield, but Mark and I still could not shake the feeling that we might never really morph into true Californians.

Shortly after our interview in Sacramento, we flew to Florida, where Mark's brother, Steve, and his family had agreed to take our kids off of our hands for a week and allow us to do a whirl-wind driving tour of east coast practices where we had scheduled interviews. And that is when Robbie finally learned how to swim. None of us had enjoyed braving the daily wind in Fairfield to go to the rec center pool, since one had to immediately don a sweat suit upon coming out of the water regardless of the brilliant sun. So Robbie, who was almost six, still had not learned to swim.

Aunt Beth and Uncle Steve had a lovely Florida home in Sarasota with the requisite Floridian swimming pool encased in a screen cage on the backyard patio accessed by stepping right outside the family room door. Still traumatized by Little Mark's dunk from a few years before, I was pretty terrified to leave Robbie at their house since everybody, including his two cousins, Megan and Katy, who were both within a few months of his age, could swim. I knew there was bound to be mayhem at times, and was sure Robbie would end up in the pool unbeknownst to anyone. Aunt Beth had said not to worry, she would teach him to swim while we were gone. I did worry, but sure enough, she taught him to swim, and the water wings were dropped from his wardrobe by the time we got back.

We interviewed at several practices that week from Maryland to South Carolina and met wonderful people at all of them. We finally chose Columbia, South Carolina, where they seemed to have the best situation with number of hospitals covered by the practice, number of oncologists, and money, enough money to climb out of our credit card debt once and for all. Mark even knew one of the doctors, and he was a great guy who loved the practice. It was the best monetary offer that we had considering the starting salary, number of years to full partnership, and buy-in to the partnership. But as the time drew closer, we were less and less happy with our choice geographically, and decided to reconsider the Maryland-DC offer, even though it was much less money to start, seemed far busier, and involved seven hospitals scattered in a one-hundred–twenty-mile radius around the Maryland-DC area.

I think that we were so blinded by our desire to go back to DC and recapture all the wonderful things we had left behind and still missed that we neglected to see the rationalization process we were using to get there. When we attempted to relocate back to North Farm in Rockville, which was an ideal location for the demands of the practice, our own house that we had sold less than two years before had appreciated/inflated so much in value that we couldn't afford to buy it back, had it been for sale. And, since it was the smallest of the four or five house styles in North Farm, we couldn't afford any other house there either. To people for whom signs as omens had meant so much, we sure missed some fairly brilliant neon out there. We settled for a house in Columbia, which was forty minutes away and closer to Baltimore than to DC.

So essentially, we traded Columbia, South Carolina for Columbia, Maryland, and we were on our way at last to Mark's first "real" job. He had completed four years of college, four years of medical school, three years of residency, three years of fellowship, and eight years of active duty in the air force. He was thirty-eight years old. It was twenty years after his brain tumor operation, twenty years after he had first heard "Hey Jude," and twenty years after the epiphany in his hospital bed.

**Mark and I with my dad, Norman
P. Hamilton, at his retirement party. 1988**

CHAPTER 18

PRIVATE PRACTICE IN DC

For once, there were no long faces or tears as we climbed into my van to put Fairfield, California, into our rear-view mirrors. We were high on life and looking forward to the scenic seven-day route we had mapped out to include Lake Tahoe, the Great Salt Dessert, Yellowstone, the Grand Tetons, Mount Rushmore, and the Football Hall of Fame. Neither of our boys was leaving any super close friends, and to cajole our firmly declared California girl into not pouting her way across the country, we allowed her to invite her best friend to travel with us and stay for a few weeks in our new home. Christy had never been outside her home state of California. We thought it would be a great opportunity for her, and she and her parents were beside themselves with excitement at the prospect. I was at least as excited as they were because, although I had flown across the country, I had never driven it or really seen it myself. So, on June 10, 1988, at 7:20 a.m., we loaded four kids, two California cats, one old large dog, and two responsible adults into the van. I know exactly at what time on what day we fell prey to this lunacy because I kept a journal, which begins, "Let's see this country!"

I documented all the fabulous scenery, snippets of the more ridiculous conversations, the twelve-step process used to enter and exit the van so that no animals escaped, the time limit on Little Mark's bladder capacity (exactly one-and-a-half hours after having a drink), the encounter my van had with a four-foot metal roadside reflector going eighty miles per hour while Mark was both driving and insisting on reading the map himself, the lack of any bear sightings (disappointing to everybody except Robbie), Augie's conversations with buffalo, and on the seventh day, the fact that I was looking forward to toilet seats that were not dependent on the outcome of the current debate as to where the AIDs virus was possibly carried. The title that my journal acquired was "Vacation. Have you seen the movie?"

One thing that we had firmly decided upon and promised the kids, was that since we were finally done with our obligation to the air force, we would not have to move anymore, and we had finally bought the house that would be our permanent house. Emphasis was on the word permanent, and for some reason we all took comfort in that nine-letter word that actually is completely self-defeating in a world that is nothing short of temporary itself. We all hung our hats on it like we meant it. I don't know if we can still get away with saying we were young, but one of my favorite movie lines is from *Hello Dolly*, when Walter Matthau as Horace Vandergelder crustily quips something about a man being paid to make mistakes until he turns forty. Our new permanent house was a beautiful three-year-old, two-story colonial, federal blue with a garnet red front door and shutters to match. Larger than any of our other houses, it was smartly appointed with hardwood floors, two fireplaces, custom draperies, wallpaper, four bedrooms, and a finished walk-out basement with a huge playroom. The cul-de-sac on which it was located had five other lovely homes, all with friendly families. And, best of all, our good friends the Graves were only forty minutes away, not close enough to be an every day or even every weekend thing, but certainly close enough to be able to plan outings and play dates and occasional sleepovers.

We couldn't really afford the house quite yet, but not having to make two moves in order to obtain the kind of family home we wanted was worth having to stretch once again to make ends meet. The promise of an escalating doctor's salary, the specifics of which were as yet unknown, since Mark did not know how much the partners in his new practice earned, was enough to be perceived as light at the end of the tunnel that would see us through the next two leaner years. Mark had a two-year contract as an employed physician that would lead to a partnership offer at the end of the two years if all went well, and if the two existing partners voted him into the partnership. The buy-in amount to become a partner was yet to be determined. His starting salary was $75,000 for the first year and $85,000 for the second year. The Columbia, South Carolina, offer had been $95,000 for the first year with sizeable escalations the next two years leading to a partnership offer, buy-in terms clearly enumerated, at the end of three years. The cost of housing in South Carolina was such that we could have afforded a small castle on that salary if we had so desired.

Mark had actually signed a contract with the practice in South Carolina following our east coast tour of practices shortly after our return to California, but we had had a gnawing apprehension that we were eventually unable to shake that caused us to change our minds. During our visit to Columbia, SC, we had contacted a realtor to show us the area and the possibilities for housing, as was customary when visiting a prospective medical group. The realtor had shown us wonderful neighborhoods, one of which we actually targeted as our proposed "permanent" location, but later, during the tour of the actual town of Columbia, the realtor—without any hesitation whatsoever—began pointing out where the "black" schools were, and where the "black" churches were, stating, "Your children wouldn't go to that school. That's the 'black' school. Your children would go to that school over there." I couldn't believe what I was hearing, and I was shocked into silence at first, but then I finally asked, "How can there be separate schools based on race? This is the United States of America, and segregation was outlawed a long time ago." He simply and unabashedly said, "It might have been outlawed, but where there's a will, there's a way." Then he pointed to a car which had not stopped at the stop sign at an upcoming intersection with the main road on which we were currently driving and had begun to pull out in front of us, and while laying on the horn, he said, "There's a car load of 'em right now." He then uttered a racial slur, beginning it with their lack of intelligence.

That encounter completely blew my mind and turned me off to the whole state, let alone the town, which may have been an unfair assumption on my part, but I had never before been in the company of anyone who just assumed that my skin color meant that I held such abject bigoted opinions. Despite the fact that any ethnic or religious remarks were strictly forbidden by a realtor—so much so that one could lose his license and his livelihood—these abhorrent remarks just rolled right off his tongue so easily that I felt that his attitude must be shared and accepted by many. And the fact that there really appeared to be a "white" school right across the street from a "black" school gave undeniable credence to my theory. Having lived in Winston-Salem, North Carolina, for a decade, I had become very comfortable in the South. Perhaps the academic atmosphere in which we had lived for so long had sheltered us, or perhaps there really was a difference in the "deep south." At any rate, neither Mark nor I had any intention of raising our children in an atmosphere that could afford them an opportunity of feeling like they might be better than any other person on earth because of the color of their skin. So far, we felt that we had been successful.

That realtor encounter was really the only negative aspect of the oncology practice in Columbia, SC, but it opened up such a huge potential can of worms. The group of doctors and their families showed no evidence of those unacceptable attitudes, and we really liked all the doctors and spouses, and the offer was a great offer. What's more, we really did believe that what we taught at home as parents could overcome anything, and we had demonstrated evidence of that parenting philosophy just by surviving our particular schooling circumstances in Fairfield. We agreed to sign the contract and told our families the good news about Mark's new job and our new prospective relocation to South Carolina. But we were people analyzing the unknown about all the locations and practices at which we had interviewed, searching for a decision that was right for us. In the absence of facts that only the future can provide, omens step in, and as the weeks progressed, we couldn't deny the omen provided by the realtor and gut feeling that we had made the wrong decision. Mark had to make the terrible telephone call to the senior partner of the wonderful oncology group, who thought they had found the new doctor they needed, to tell them that he had changed his mind. Ugh.

There are lots of signs and omens in life; sometimes I think we just choose the ones we want to choose and ignore the ones we want to ignore. Our signs led us back to DC, at least to the practice in the DC area, even if we were living in the outskirts of Baltimore. One of the seven hospitals that Mark's new group of three physicians served was Howard County Hospital, which was located in Columbia, Maryland, only about five minutes from our house, which seemed more than reasonable, even lucky to us. And one of the other partners also lived in Columbia. The other six hospitals were all located in Maryland in the greater DC area.

The practice was organized in such a way that the three physicians equally split call with each other, taking call a week at a time, in other words, every third week. Because all three doctors pitched in to make daily morning rounds during the work-week at all the hospitals, the only time a doctor absolutely had to go to all seven hospitals on a given day was during Saturday and Sunday of his call week. During call week, the doctor on call did not see patients in the office. He merely rode the circuit and took all the new hospital consults. He also took all the night calls for that seven-day period of time. Since it was impossible to be in seven hospitals fanned out in a one-hundred-mile circumference at one time, and only a certain amount of zigging and zagging could feasibly be done while following the chronological order of consults, some of the consults had to be postponed until the following morning when the rounding doctor would pick up the new patient. On the weekends, since the offices were closed, all the daytime calls were added to the existing nighttime calls, and it was not unusual to answer sixty or seventy calls on a given weekend.

The two doctors who were not on call saw outpatients in three offices, none of which was open all five days in the working week. The main office was in Greenbelt, which was open for patients three days per week and located a couple of miles from Doctor's Hospital. The other two offices, one of which was in Laurel, located across the street from the Laurel Hospital, and the other, on the campus of the Washington Adventist Hospital, were each open for one day per week. Two physicians always worked together in the same office and were assisted by the same office staff, who traveled to all three offices. The patients were shared by the physicians, meaning no patient had his or her own primary oncologist in the group. Each patient saw whoever was first available on the appointment days, depending on which doctors were seeing patients in the office that day.

The offices were small, but the number of patients who were seen on a daily basis was large. Office hours were from 8:30 a.m. to 5:00 p.m., with new patient consults allotted thirty to forty-five minutes. Follow-up appointments were slotted for every five to ten minutes, and all treatment patients were seen by the doctor once per week. The average number of patients seen in the office on any given day was about eighty. There was no chemotherapy room with reclining treatment chairs in any of the three offices. Instead, chemotherapy was given right in the exam rooms via pic lines, small catheter intravenous lines that were introduced into the patient's arm by the nurse prior to the first treatment and remained in place covered by a dressing between treatments.

The lead chemotherapy nurse, according to Mark, "was a great lady who rolled with the punches, put the patients and the doctors at ease, and accomplished more work than should have been possible for one person." And she did it all with a great sense of humor. One of her favorite phrases was "pissin' and moanin.'" She would tell hilarious stories about situations involving any one of the doctors, which always included the subject doctor pissin' and moanin' about some problem that she would have to step in and fix. The tales were told during the one-hour lunch periods in the break room, during which time the office was closed and the phones turned off so that everybody could eat together. What a spread they could produce at lunchtime. Whatever else was for lunch, it always involved ice cream at the end of it during all the times when I was there. At first it seemed like a waste of time to Mark, but he soon realized that the extended daily lunch break really fostered the camaraderie and humor that is so important in a practice that ran at the speed of light and daily dealt with complex, life-threatening illness which constantly needed to be met with intelligent medical decision-making and compassion, patient after patient after patient.

The reality of private practice slammed Mark right in the face and made the last two years spent in the air force seem cushy, and the money wasn't any better yet to make up for it, if money could indeed make up for it. Although the gross amount of his first-year salary in private practice was more than the gross amount of his air force salary, the free benefits provided by the air force, such as health care, commissary prices, and geographically based housing allowances, made the two salaries equivalent. DC was a very high-cost area, and the practice was as busy as the beltway. He had been accustomed to seeing fifteen to twenty patients per day at Travis and having only one hospital to cover, with that hospital physically attached to his clinic, as well as the added bonus of the family practice house staff to perform the actual care of the hospital patients. Having to see thirty-five or forty patients per day in the office, after rounding at three or four hospitals spread out in all directions, was a challenging escalation of duties.

Watching the other two doctors operate smoothly, speedily, and effectively, Mark realized that the key to success was efficiency, and he was determined to meet and then exceed the expectation of his two new employers. His goal to be the best oncologist he could be needed to be enlarged to also include making himself indispensable to his new group if he ever wanted to become a partner. In order to accomplish the expanded objective, he simply had to learn to see his patients faster—quality of the visit not being dictated by the quantity of time spent—dictate shorter progress notes, literally speak faster into the tape recorder, and get up earlier.

He began getting up in the morning at 4:30 and leaving the house by 5:00 so that he could round at his designated hospitals—sometimes driving one hundred miles from the first hospital to the last, where there might be multiple consults that were either left over from the day before or had been called in during the night to the doc on call and then transferred to him in the morning—and then try to arrive at the office by 8:30 a.m. to begin seeing his half of the seventy-five or eighty patients scheduled for the day. No matter what he tried, his driving time always seemed to thwart his best laid plans, since the morning rush hour commenced around 6:00 a.m., and he always got waylaid in one or more of the hospitals. As a result, he was often late to the office. It was embarrassing to rush in at 8:45 with the other doctor already seeing his third patient of the day amidst a backlog beginning to gather in the waiting room, meaning he was already beginning his day behind and not carrying his share of the load. One such day, the senior partner quipped between exam rooms, "What time did you get up?" He didn't really want an answer; he was just letting Mark know that he was going to have to find a way to get to the office on time. Stung by the question, and feeling like he was already doing everything possible towards that end, Mark later decided to humble himself and asked him how in the world he was able to get everything done in the hospitals and get to the office on time to start the day. His mentor succinctly stated, "You gotta get up earlier." That remark absolutely fried Mark. He was looking for advice as to how to become more efficient in the hospitals, not an assumption that he couldn't bring himself to roll out of bed in the morning. Forcing himself to temporarily push aside his resentment, he wisely chose not to respond to his partner's barb, and after complaining bitterly to me about the unjust assumption and callous remark, he began getting up at 4:00 in the morning instead of 4:30. Soon, he was arriving on time and seeing his full share of the daily patients, the tricks of efficiency in the office well learned, the trick of rounding at the wide-spread hospitals and arriving to the office in less than four hours still a mystery. But he was doing what he had to do, and he was earning the respect of his partners and the faith of his patients.

The senior partner's wife was the practice manager, the head accountant, and the biller. She was a smart lady who commanded both respect and admiration from her staff in her demeanor and prowess, and Mark liked her very much. What he didn't like was the fact that he didn't seem to be entitled to any practice finances. He had no way to measure productivity and its relationship to the financial viability of the practice, which is just as important to the newly employed physician in assessing his future with the group as it is to the partners in assessing the same thing. He also had no idea of what the partner salaries were; neither partner would say anything more specific than, "Enough. Trust me."

Trust is one of those concepts that requires some concrete evidence in order to distinguish it from faith. Whereas faith can be blind and related much more to a gut feeling, trust is something that is earned, and earned rather slowly over time as you get to know people. Where financial futures are concerned, faith is not enough. Mark is better at trusting people and situations right off the bat than I am, and that might make him a nicer person than me, but this is yet another area where we are each other's barometers and complement each other. In this instance, his barometric pressure was unusually stormier than mine.

Being the provider for his family, and having made the decision to leave the shelter of the air force, Mark needed to know where he was headed, hopefully out of debt and able to afford the "permanent" house and lifestyle in which he had already immersed his family. To him, although he trusted his new partners as well-meaning people, he did not trust them to know what his own financial and lifestyle requirements were. In addition, he felt the need to learn the business aspects of the practice of medicine in order to be able to accurately assess the direction in which he was headed. Business aspects of medicine are not taught in medical school or residency or fellowship or in the military. Doctors are not necessarily good businessmen, but they all like control. Control is an essential part of a doctor's personality, a characteristic with which they have to be comfortable and successfully hone early on in medical school in order to become the people who will be in charge of other's people health and be able to make the all important medical decisions that nobody else knows how to make.

Bound and determined that this practice was going to work out in order to fulfill our "permanent" house promise, I reasoned in discussions with Mark that both of his partners lived in nice houses, were well dressed, sent their kids to private schools, drove nice cars. They must know what they were doing with their medical practice to make it successful. They were, however, undeniably working much harder than we had ever imagined Mark would be working, and the daily driving time and mileage was way beyond the pale. But this was DC, and DC was busy and high cost with expensive attractions, top-of-the-line cultural activities, restaurants, sports, fashion. Whether or not working that hard was worth being able to live in and take full advantage of that area was a personal choice. Whether working that hard to make X number of dollars was worth it, was again personal choice, but what was X? Was it more than enough? Was it barely enough? What was X?

Furthermore, what would the buy-in be? How would it be determined? Would partnership really be a true option, or were his new partners merely interested in eternally employing physicians who made the practice much more money than they were paid, with all of the profits always going to the original partners? Mark had no way to know why they were so closed about the financial particulars of the practice. They wouldn't even give him a ballpark figure as to how much they made. Did they not trust him to keep their information confidential, or did they have something to hide? He became increasingly frustrated and increasingly tired.

We decided that I should also go back to work, to safeguard our financial unknowns. Robbie had entered first grade and was in school all day for the first time, which would allow me much more child-free time. However, I wanted to remain involved in the school system as a volunteer to assess my children's educational situation, and I wanted a career that would afford me that opportunity. Real estate seemed to be the perfect answer, according to Mark. I took classes in Baltimore for two weeks, passed my state exam for my license, and went to work for a large real estate firm, and, for many reasons, I hated it.

The first reason I hated it was because I had to drive to Baltimore for two weeks to take classes that did not adjourn until 5:00 p.m., which meant that for two weeks, I had latchkey children for three hours every afternoon, since the rush hour traffic did not afford me the opportunity to arrive home before 6:30 p.m., much too early to expect Mark to be home. But it was only two weeks. How bad could it be? Well . . .other than my kids not necessarily getting along with Lisa trying to play Miss General to unwilling brothers, we all survived the first week. Dinner wasn't our usual family fare, but again, a temporary inconvenience. The second day of the second week, Columbia experienced an unpredicted snow-storm which was only represented by a few flakes of very light snow in Baltimore. Unbeknownst to me, my children's school decided to send all the kids home right after lunch, two hours early, due to the worsening weather conditions. I guess one was supposed to listen to the radio or be watching TV to know when or if school was suddenly being cancelled, because the parents certainly weren't notified by utilizing any home or emergency telephone numbers that the school had on file. The other thing the school didn't do was monitor well, if at all, which kids got on the correct buses to get home since the bus schedule had to be altered for the entire county. In fact, the school didn't even monitor *if* all the kids got on a bus.

All I know was that at two o'clock I was sitting in my after-noon session of the real estate class struggling to stay awake as my instructor read verbatim from the book I had studied the night before, when my new cell phone, which I had purchased for my new career, rang. Knowing that only my husband, children, and school had my new number, I excused myself from class while tak-ing the call. I was greatly surprised to hear Lisa's voice.

"Mom?"
"Hi honey, what's up?"
"The boys weren't on the bus."
"What bus?"
"The school bus."
"It's only 2 o'clock. You guys didn't have a half day. . .did you?"
"School got cancelled, and they sent everybody home at 1 o'clock."
"What? Why would they do that?"
"Because of the snow."
"What snow?"

"Mom, look out the window; it's snowing really hard."

"Well, where are the boys?"

"I don't know. That's why I am calling you."

"Well, didn't you realize that the boys weren't on the bus?"

"Yes, but all the buses were different than usual. It was confusing."

"Okay. I will call the school and call you back."

"I already called the school."

"You did? What did they say? Did they know what bus they got on?"

"No."

"I am on my way. Call me if you hear anything."

I went flying out the door while calling the school at the same time, leaving my class books on the table. The school said that they had thought I was picking up the boys and that they would start checking all the buses to find out which one my boys might have boarded by mistake. Without the rush hour traffic, I could have made it to the school in about thirty minutes, but as I approached Columbia, the very light dusting of snow that had graced Baltimore became a blinding snow storm and forced me to slow almost to the speed of caution. I was terrified at the thought that my boys might have gotten off the bus in some unfamiliar area. I ran from the school parking lot into the office and breathlessly, with eyes wide with fear, demanded to know where my boys were.

"Well, they evidently didn't get on any bus."

"Then where are they?"

"Maybe they got a ride with another parent?"

"Maybe? How can you not know where they are?"

"Well, they got into the line of kids waiting for parent rides."

"So, you're telling me that my boys are not here, and you don't have a clue as to where they are!?!"

I was panicked, mad, and praying while running like a crazy person back to my van. Right then, Lisa called me and said that one of her friends said that she thought the boys had walked home. "Oh, dear God!" The school had to be a forty-five minute walk at best across some pretty major intersections—*if* you could find your way through the winding maze of neighborhood entrances and cul-de-sacs. I pulled out of the parking lot and began driving slowly and searching for two small figures on the side of the road, deciding to follow the route one would take driving straight home in a car as opposed to the route the bus might take, since I didn't know the whole bus route, and hoped that my first and third graders had some sort of instinct about the direction of their home. I turned onto our home street, feeling desperate with my lack of success and starting to cry, knowing I could never cover all the snowy territory in Columbia where two little boys could get lost, when I saw what appeared to be two little snowmen tramping along about three hundred yards from our house. They were barely recognizable, their jackets, school pants, and bootless shoes solidly caked into one thick, white, frozen mass. Even their eyelashes were coated with snow, and they were so cold, they could barely speak. They had not known what else to do with the confusing instructions given at the school, and they had indeed finally taken matters into their own hands and begun walking home after the last bus had left the school. It was now 3:45. School had closed almost three hours ago. I was elated. I was relieved. I was hopping mad at the school, and having been a stay-at-home, volunteer-at-school, cookie-baking mom for ten years, I hated the new job I didn't even have yet.

Disaster averted but not forgotten, I still didn't have a better solution for controlling my own work schedule during the week, and most of the real work in real estate occurred on the weekends, when most of the potential home buyers were enjoying time off from their own jobs. Since Mark would be home to supervise the kids two weekends out of three, I would be freed up, so to speak, to work. I didn't know yet about the "write it now or lose it" competition in residential real estate that caused the weekends to be unpredictable with bursts of immediate contract demands at all hours of the day and evening, and neither did he.

What we did know was that once again, we were not enamored with the school situation for the kids. Here we were, having moved back to civilization as we knew it, to a county with a good reputation for its public schools—not as good as Montgomery County in which North Farm was located, but certainly with a decent reputation and certainly one which accepted all the kids who lived within the designated district, and our school was the one elementary school singled out of all of Howard County to pioneer the first year of a highly controversial experimental reading program. This program affected only one of our three children, the same one who had survived the California kindergarten class which taught zero reading skills. The experimental program was based on some sort of nonsense whereby the kids didn't have reading books. They just kept journals and wrote down words that they heard in whatever way seemed natural to them. The theory was that by the end of third grade, they would all have bumbled their way to the same reading level they would have achieved via some of the more standard reading programs taught at all the other elementary schools in the county. So by Christmas, Robbie knew how to spell and write the words, "delicious" and "surprise," but he didn't have a clue as to how to spell the words "the" or "those" and didn't recognize them when he came across them in books we read together.

I also didn't like the open classroom format in the school where there were four first grades going on in the same large room which had been separated into pods with carpets and movable bulletin boards. The theory was that all the external stimuli from three other classes being conducted simultaneously forced the individual students to focus on their own group and helped them learn how to filter out unnecessary noise and develop better concentration skills than being in a closed classroom with four walls and a door without any external stimulus during learning times. I don't know when those better concentration skills are supposed to develop, but my theory is that if a student is perhaps more interested in what is possibly going on in the classroom pod next door, he focuses more on the pod next door. Then, there would be the learning disability children, attention deficits and whatnot. What about them?

Not only was I not buying what that school was selling in the first grade, there was also something horribly wrong with the third grade. They were located in an old-fashioned classroom with four walls and a door, but there appeared to be a competition among the boys in the class as to who could lean back the farthest in their chairs and get away with saying the rudest words to the teacher, who appeared to have no control over her class. When discussing this problem with the teacher, she said her hands were tied because she had no administrative backup and that it was against school policy to send a child out of her classroom to the principal's office for discipline. She was also limited in the disciplinary measures she could take within her own classroom. When I followed up with an appointment to discuss this information with the principal, I was enlightened to learn that the teacher was exactly right.

When Lisa came home from school early in the school year and said she no longer wanted to participate in the fifth grade gifted and talented program—which was a program whereby the kids were taken out of class twice per week for an afternoon to work on projects, but were still responsible for all the work they missed in the home classroom as well as all the extra homework they had in connection with the special projects—I asked to sit in on one of the gifted sessions. I thought that perhaps she did not want to leave her new best friend for the afternoon or that she resented the extra homework, but she said she was bored and just wanted to be "a normal kid in a normal class." At my first and last gifted session, the class was being conducted by a very dry instructor who monotoned on about "delineating your criteria in your business plan in such a manner as to be proposed as a plausible solution" to the actual problems that an actual local business group was having. While his advice might have been a nice fit for an MBA class, I understood perfectly why my fifth-grade daughter was bored and disinterested. She was also shy and not inclined to want to give any presentation, let alone a fifth-grade devised business plan, in front of a group of strangers.

It began to appear that even if one lived in the "right" school district in the "permanent" house, the assumptions which had preceded those decisions didn't necessarily follow them intact. On one of my working Saturdays, Mark took matters into his own hands and taught Robbie to read. . .the old fashioned way. He went to a school education store at the mall and bought some Dick, Jane, Spot, and Puff flash cards and taught him to read on the family room floor. Every night thereafter for the next few months, just before Robbie went to bed, he learned pronunciation, spelling, and sight reading while he and his father made sentences. If Mark wasn't home before bedtime for the kids, I stepped in as the substitute teacher.

I volunteered for everything Mark's third grade teacher would allow, and used my time in the classroom to dominate the boys who thought it was okay to be rude to their poor teacher with my commanding presence. I was hoping that my demonstrations of common sense mob control, such as utilizing certain facial expressions and firm speech at an appropriate volume, which proved extremely successful in achieving the necessary alpha status, would rub off on the sweetly soft-spoken teacher. It never did, but nobody cussed at her or flicked pencils across the room while I was present. My teaching perspective was that with or without the admin back up, each one of those kids had at least one parent if not two, and I knew who they were. Never did a five-foot-four, one–hundred-twelve-pound blonde woman command such a presence. Of course, I had a secret weapon at home, which was feeding young Mark pertinent information which I thought would be helpful inducement for respectable behavior from him as well as the other boys in the class.

Lisa was always quiet in school and the boss of all who would listen at home. I granted her wish to be "a normal kid in a normal class," and the biggest problem thereafter had to do with wanting to go home with her new best friend after school. When I found out that her new best friend had no parent at home before 7 p.m. on school days, her new best friend got to come home to our house anytime, and Lisa got to go to her house at no time.

My real estate schedule revolved around school time and husband-at-home time. I worked in the office when I was not volunteering at school. I did all the usual entry-level real estate work that nobody else wants to do: man the phones, sit at empty open houses, and figure out how to market myself. One of my neighbors kept trying to abuse his privilege of living a few houses from the new realtor and insisted on trying to get me to research the going rates of high-priced condos in which he wanted to invest, and then writing absurd low-ball offers on them. Within my first two weeks as a licensed realtor, I wrote one contract for him, which was, of course, a bust, and refused to write about ten other similar contracts for him.

Within four weeks, I wrote an offer on a house for Robbie's teacher, who was a wonderful young person excited about owning her first home. Since there was a competing contract written the same day by another realtor in my office, we met with the listing agent together and presented our contracts at the same time. My customer's offer was the highest one with no financial complications, and I was congratulated early on my success. However, the other agent with the losing contract reached into his interior jacket pocket and removed a different signed contract by the same prospective buyer for a higher price. This behavior was called "shopping a contract," and was grounds for having one's license revoked by the state real estate board. A real estate agent, unless he was a buyer agent, was always working for the seller and had a fiduciary responsibility to get the best price for the seller by extracting the highest possible offer from the buyer and presenting only that contract. He was not allowed to knowingly attempt to get the seller to sign a lower-priced contract if he knew that the buyer was willing to sign a contract with a higher sale price. We all knew what had happened, and we all knew that I wasn't happy about it, and we all knew that any one of us could report the agent, who was being a complete jackass, to the board and put his career in jeopardy. The listing agent called in the managing broker under whom all of our licenses were listed in the Columbia office, told her what had happened, and she called me into her office by myself and politely explained that since the jackass was an agent with a great deal of sales for the company, and I was a novice with no sales for the company, nobody would be reporting the shopped contract to the board.

Although I didn't like their so-called ethics, and I didn't like jackass, and I didn't like what appeared to be the cutthroat nature of the real estate world in general, I didn't like being a loser more. I was determined to get a sale on the books. During my next required phone answering period, I took a call from a woman who said she did not have an agent and was looking for a condo in a certain price range. I asked her for a few more specifics, isolated an area acceptable to her, and then told her that while there was nothing on the market yet, I thought I just might have one getting ready to come on the market that would be perfect for her. She couldn't believe it. She said she had been waiting for something to come on the market for a year. "Might" was the critical word which kept me from being in the fib range of what I told her, since I didn't have any clients at this stage of the game who wanted to list their homes with me. But I did know a neighborhood of very upscale condos that seemed like they would fit her finicky requirements, and my plan was to solicit one of them to list just to sell it to her.

I printed up some of those flyers that state, "I have a buyer interested in your neighborhood," and knowing that most such flyers are trashed, I enhanced my flyer by listing all the specifics the buyer had given me and which I knew existed in certain floor plans in that neighborhood. I was hoping that my ability to enumerate exactly the perfect match between buyer and condo would induce a serious seller to believe that I really did have a serious potential buyer. "If you are thinking of selling your home, and your home fits this description, please call Lynn Ellis." I then loaded up the kids in the van after school, drove to the condo neighborhood, and divided and conquered the entire neighborhood delivering all the flyers to all the mailboxes. And somebody called me. I listed and sold that guy's condo the following Saturday afternoon and smiled at jackass at the Monday weekly sales meeting when the customary announcements of newly listed homes with listing agents and newly sold homes with selling agents were made. I couldn't wait to see the look on his face when he found out that the undaunted pissant had turned a lowly cold call into two commissions. Admittedly, I would have been prouder if the manager had not preceded the announcement of my accomplishment by stating to the eighty or so agents in the meeting, "It gives me great pleasure to announce that in just six weeks, Lynn Ellis has lost her virginity."

Life became very busy for all of us, and despite some of the challenges, the kids and I were settling in and enjoying ourselves. The kids, once again, all had a zillion extracurricular activities from which to choose, saw their old friends from Rockville on some weekends and played with new friends on others. Success did not increase my love for my new career, but I was able to work it around what I considered to be my most important and fulfilling job, which was being a mom who was available for most of her kids' needs, and a mom who had the privilege of being able to participate in their school as well as their extracurricular lives on a daily basis. Unexpectedly, there was one more aspect of my life as a realtor which became very meaningful for me: my job afforded me my first opportunity to have a patient's glimpse into the oncologist to whom I was married, through the eyes of one of the other realtors who became his patient.

She was a good-natured, seasoned real estate agent whose desk was located a few desk areas from mine, and because she knew that I was his wife, she felt comfortable sharing her devastating breast cancer diagnosis with me, how scared she was, how scared her family was. She also shared with me how compassionate my husband was and how lucky I was to be married to someone like him. She told me about his office and her frustrations about not being able to see Dr. Ellis every time because she was so comfortable with him. Despite the fact that she felt lousy on chemotherapy, he filled her with hope, and she didn't feel like just another number in the busy office as the cancer patients streamed in and out. For some reason, she told me, she always felt better about her condition and life in general after her appointments with him.

She was the first of many report cards on my husband as a doctor—this man, whom his children knew only as their father, and whom I expected to be completely channeled on being a husband and father as soon as he hit the driveway. Although I didn't know it at the time, she had carved a new niche on my timeline. From that day forward, not only did I begin to know my husband in his professional capacity, but I began my life with a new responsibility to Mark as well as to his patients, because those who knew us both would look to me for comfort also. Even though I had no medical or counseling background, I was guilty by association of being in possession of both. I think that is when I decided to really hone my listening skills, because without the knowledge of being educated as a physician or as a nurse, there was still an expectation placed on me, and I did have something to give that I perceived was needed. I could listen, and after I listened, I could look patients in the eye and give them the assurance of my faith that Dr. Ellis would take good care of them. As I got to meet more and more of his patients, my assurance became absolute, and my faith became complete.

Despite the fact that Mark was gratified to be achieving rapport with both his patients and his partners, he wasn't quite as enthralled with his new life as the kids and I were with ours. His sixteen-hour workdays consisted of getting up at 4:00 a.m., driving one hundred miles each day, seeing forty to fifty cancer patients, and returning home around 8:00 p.m. The two weeks on either side of the call weekend were strung together to be twelve days in a row prior to having a weekend off to recover. His partners worked just as hard, but unlike him, they seemed to thrive on it. Could the difference be that they were earning what they thought their job was worth? As the new employed physician in the group, Mark expected to be underpaid compared to the value of his job; he expected to pay his dues for the first couple of years, but some light at the end of the tunnel would have been so helpful, some incentive to relieve his sleep deprivation and allow him to know that he was at least being a good provider while he traded work for missed family dinners, homework questions, daily comical dog and cat and kid occurrences, the little worthwhile moments in family life that can only be lived in the very fleeting present.

Into this atmosphere an old air force buddy named Bill, who had left the military to join a private oncology practice in Tidewater, Virginia, began to call. About a month prior to his first phone call, he happened to have been on the receiving end of a patient referred by Mark to his group and had re-established contact then. He loved his group, and he loved his life as an oncologist outside of the air force, and he glowingly spoke about the Tidewater area, the water, the weather, his partners. Mark found that he could not speak quite so enthusiastically about his own situation in DC. When his air force buddy called back in a few weeks, it was to tell Mark that he knew of a local practice that was in need of a partner. They were getting "crushed," and he wondered if Mark would be interested. Although the practice and the lifestyle sounded wonderful, Mark had only been with his present group for six months, and he turned him down.

The next time Bill called, it was not to Mark's office; it was to our house, and Mark was not home yet. So he talked to me. I firmly but politely told him we were not moving again. The practice sounded great, and it was too bad they weren't shopping when we were looking, but we had already made our decision. The next recruitment call Bill made was on one of Mark's call weekends. I referred him to Mark's cell phone, and when he asked Mark how his weekend was going, he replied, "The usual, driving to seven hospitals, some of them twice." Bill retorted, "I'm on call too. Guess where I am? Busch Gardens!" He was quite a marketer, and although Mark turned him down again, the seed had fallen on fertile ground.

We didn't even want to think about moving again, but I couldn't deny the fact that Mark was increasingly frustrated with his current situation. To add to the lack of billing and financial data that was provided him, there was some sort of bad blood situation in the office between the office secretary and one of the two partners, another peculiarity to which Mark was not privy. She seemed to be protected by one partner to the frustration of the other partner, and every once in a while, the wheels would come off the wagon, so to speak. As time went on, she began to attempt to poison Mark's opinion of her nemesis, much to his discomfort.

During this time of turmoil, a few doctors from one of the hospitals came to Mark and told him about a business deal they were considering and asked him if he would like to be a part of it. The deal had nothing to do with any particular practice. It had been conceived by a couple of MBA types, and it had to do with owning shares of diagnostic centers being established in the area. The shares were being sold to several doctors who wanted to participate, and $1,000 was the minimum investment. The answer to that deal was an easy one for us since we didn't have $1,000 anywhere that wasn't long committed before it was received. But one of the doctors offered to lend Mark the $1,000 because it was "just too good an investment to pass up." Now the answer wasn't quite so easy and precipitated a lively discussion between husband and wife. I said no to borrowing any money from a professional friend. I lost. Mark invested the borrowed money.

One thing that was becoming clear to both of us was that medicine outside of the military and outside of the academic world was a business, and we felt ill prepared to face those business challenges. And we felt like understanding them was a necessity. As spring emerged, Mark felt that he had proven himself to his group enough to be trusted with the financial mechanics of the practice, and he made a decision that if he could not be provided with the knowledge that he sought, he was going to have to consider leaving the group. The partners, sensing his seriousness, finally relented enough to allow the business manager to show him how the billing was done. Mark spent a couple of afternoons with her in her office, peppering her with questions about charges, reimbursement, denials, etc. She answered all of his questions about the mechanics, but as soon as one of his questions bordered on the practice expenses versus the practice income, she clammed up. He tried one more time to discuss his frustration with his partners, to no avail, and during the kids' spring break from school, we traveled to Virginia to take a look at yet another practice.

Being favorably impressed with all the circumstances and people related to the prospective practice, Mark made the tough decision that would force another move on his family. Shortly after returning home, he received an offer that clearly enumerated the terms of employment, road to partnership, buy-in, and partnership salary. The partnership salary, which met our hopes and requirements had been further described as "what we pay each other now, which we expect will continue," because when one is in business for oneself, which private practitioners are, one can only make as much money as one can generate. There are no guarantees. There is no parent company.

I think that description was our first inkling of actually understanding that concept, which is a difficult one when you have been paid a check by someone else all of your working life. Even as an employee of a private practice prior to becoming a partner, you are still getting a check from another entity, albeit with your revenue from your own work helping to produce it.

In May, Mark signed the contract. Then, he told the two partner physicians in his current practice, who tried to talk him out of leaving them, telling him he was making a huge mistake, but still offering no financial data to back up their statement. We broke the news to the kids using our new destination's proximity to Busch Gardens to help cushion the blow of our relocation, which this time was not the fault of the air force. It was a difficult sell, but we promised them a day at said theme park in Williamsburg during a house-hunting excursion—that promise being one that had a high probability of being kept. I then performed my last real estate transaction ever as a realtor and listed our "permanent" house. I spent the last few weeks at work marketing it and perusing the multiple listing service in the area of our new destination, where I became intrigued with a picture of an English Tudor that looked like it just might be right for the new Ellis home. Our "permanent" house sold for full price in six weeks.

Mark Jr. still says that we always moved on his birthday. Although our relocations were admittedly approximately on his birthday, the move into our "permanent" house in Columbia, Maryland, had actually been exactly on his eighth birthday. Precisely 364 days later, we moved out and headed to Williamsburg, Virginia, full of hope for the new private practice, dreams of a truly permanent home, and mixed feelings towards the kids' new Catholic school—mixed in that the parents were looking forward to standard educational methods and discipline, while the kids were dreading the uniforms.

Epilogue

HUMANITY OF MEDICINE

Williamsburg was to become home for the next twenty years. The kids would all graduate from the Catholic school chosen on their behalf prior to our relocation, the dreaded uniforms having become commonplace by the end of the first week of school. After two rental houses over the course of eighteen months, the picture of an English Tudor would slowly grow into a reality that we would daily witness as the land was cleared, the footers poured, and each brick cemented into place, and would become as close to a "permanent" house as one ever gets.

The practice would start off with camaraderie, friendship, and trust, but would become complicated as the partners grew in number from four to five to six and beyond. Cancer care itself would change dramatically and rapidly, but if anything over the next twenty years was to change faster than the evolution of cancer treatment, it would be the concept of health care itself. Medicine would increasingly be seen as a business—big business—and it would be the dominance of that business sought by insurance companies, pharmaceutical companies, management companies, and government that would become a mammoth challenge to all doctors as they struggled to maintain control over their medical decisions.

Despite all of the changes that were to occur over the next twenty years, Mark's particular style in his practice of oncology would remain constant and true. He would not only diagnose and treat thousands of cancer patients, he would get to know, really get to know, thousands of cancer patients, and he would remember and marvel at their particulars: their dogs, cats, sports teams, musical tastes, their spirituality, the unique details that made them who they were. Who served in what wars, flew what aircraft, met the

Beatles, cheered with the Redskinettes, survived the Holocaust. In return, thousands of cancer patients would grow to love Dr. Ellis as their doctor and remember his particular interests and be touched by his special gifts. There would be fantastic advancements in the treatments and cures for various types of cancer and some cancers that would remain frustratingly stubborn and seemingly untouchable.

I would be drafted to assist him in creating his own oncology practice in 1993 by serving as the administrative director and adding a whole new dimension to our relationship that neither of us would ever regret. His professional world would become my professional world, and over the next sixteen years, I would experience him as the visionary and have the honor and the privilege and the challenge of the struggle and ultimate success of navigating the politics and the monumental changes in the delivery of health care and developing with him his dreams and goals of the way cancer medicine ought to be practiced.

Together in Williamsburg, against seemingly insurmountable obstacles, we would build the first cancer center in the region to incorporate radiation therapy and medical oncology under one roof. Mark would be the first oncologist in the region to incorporate pet therapy and massage therapy into his practice, eventually achieving his dream practice of integrating not only those therapies, but also music therapy, nutritional counseling, family cancer care education, guided imagery techniques, yoga and others to complement and coincide with the standard chemotherapy therapies—all under one roof. What's more, the complementary therapies would all be provided for free to his patients. As a pioneer, Mark would realize that these services would not be viewed as necessary services to the standard of care and therefore remain ineligible for reimbursement by all insurance companies. As a visionary, these services would come to be viewed by him as necessary for complete care of the cancer patient; together, we would build a program with a health system that would follow his integrative medicine vision. He would win a healthcare hero award and eventually be dubbed the "father of oncology" in our little town.

Mark E. Ellis, MD, was destined to have a brilliant career, and I was destined to be a part of it. We didn't know that, of course, in 1989 upon our arrival in Williamsburg, but together our awakening would continue one day at a time as we journeyed down the road of experience, and Mark would remain cancer free until 2008.

The kids' highschool graduations: Lisa in 1996, Mark Jr. in 1998, and Robert in 2000. All three would go on to graduate from Wake Forest University and establish us as a true Wake Forest family.

Mark and I in front of our old religion classroom at Wake Forest where we met in 1973. Picture was taken on our twenty-fifth wedding anniversary in 2001.

**Mark and I at a Wake football game in 2004.
Photo taken by Mary Beyer.**

Mark and the Wake Forest Deacon at the
ACC football championship game in 2007.

Author's Note

I wrote this book several years ago as a little family treasure, mostly for the kids and potential grandkids, because to know Mark as a young man is to understand that there is a way to face all of life's challenges and to risk oneself enough to turn dreams into goals, and to also understand that the route one takes to achieve those goals is never as direct as it sounds after the fact.

I did contemplate the possibility of publishing *The Humanity of Medicine* at some point in the future, perhaps upon Mark's retirement, as an inspiration to others, but I never expected to be publishing this book posthumously. Mark had such an amazing life, including a career worthy of legacy, that I guess I expected it to keep going. I expected that he would continue to lead himself, the family, and me through our journeys on this beautiful planet we call Earth forever. I did not expect that his forever would come so soon.

In November of 2008, after enjoying forty years cancer free, Mark was diagnosed once again with a new primary malignant melanoma, which was excised with clear margins and no lymph node involvement. A PET/CT done at the time also showed no evidence of disease, and we went on with our lives, albeit with newly restored appreciation for our many blessings and rekindled talk of retirement. In June of 2009, the Mydnight Sonn had a forty-year reunion at our house in Williamsburg, and they sounded even better than they had sounded in high school. Who knew? It was a great weekend for the band members, a highlight in Mark's life, and thank God it happened in June.

In August, Mark fractured his back while jumping on the diving board in preparation for diving into our pool, the simple jarring of the spine due to the impact of his feet on the board being the only trauma to his vertebrae. Not realizing that it was broken, and being determined to tough out whatever injury he had acquired, perhaps a pulled muscle, slight disc slip, whatever, he continued to work for two weeks until he was in so much pain that he was truly physically disabled, at which time he finally had an MRI which showed a nasty fracture that had caused one vertebrae to crush into the vertebrae below it. Initially diagnosed as a "burst fracture" which would take three months to heal, he was forced to take a few weeks off from work to rest and recuperate. After three weeks and increasing pain, he had further diagnostic tests which showed a possible lesion on the bone. A PET/CT confirmed our worst fears and showed widely metastatic cancer with lesions on several vertebrae, and a biopsy of the lesion at the fracture sight proved the cancer to be metastatic melanoma. He began a combined modality treatment plan of chemotherapy and radiation therapy, and shortly thereafter, wrote a farewell letter to his patients.

After forty years of cancer research, metastatic malignant melanoma is still a deadly disease with a very poor survival rate. Although we tried old treatments as well as new treatments, there was no stopping the cancer this time, and after a few months, Mark told me that he knew that nothing short of a miracle would save his life and that his heart told him he had had his miracle forty years earlier. He felt that it was simply his time, and we began to live our lives with that knowledge. One thing that I had learned from my years of working with him was that he was almost never wrong in his prognostic predictions, and although I never stopped praying for a miracle, I trusted his instincts completely. Once again, he was right, and he took his last breath on April 3, 2010.

Knowing that I do not stand alone with my broken heart, I feel compelled to let all who mourn his loss know that just like his life, even his death was amazing. He forged ahead and plowed the ground that we all must tread at some point and by example showed us how to die bravely and with dignity, finding all the silver linings to his final bout with cancer. He took the time to say what he wanted to say to his kids, his family, to me. We transposed one of our retirement plans by taking virtual trips rather than real ones to all the national parks via the Ken Burns DVD series called *The National Parks: America's Best Idea.* We philosophized and conversed about our spirituality and prepared for his passing, and we loved and we laughed and we took care of each other at home. The kids and I were with him when he died and witnessed the miracle of his crossing over into the next life. It wasn't the miracle for which we had prayed, but it was the miracle with which God answered, and since his passing, he has let us know without a doubt that he is not only okay, but happy, filled with purpose, and very much still with us.

Of special note:

On the following pages can be found Mark's farewell letter to his patients, written during his illness, which, I think, is a testimony to his relationship with his patients. I have also included his obituary, which lists several of his career accomplishments. *The Humanity of Medicine, part II, Living The Dream* is under construction.

10-16-09

My Dear Patients,

As you may be aware, I fractured my back in late August of this year, while jumping off a diving board and have been out of work since that time. Although this injury was initially thought to be a simple compression fracture, the symptoms did not improve, and additional scanning with a biopsy proved the injury to be the result of metastatic malignant melanoma. Additional evaluation revealed several other areas of cancer (spine, lung, lymph nodes), for which I am now undergoing treatment with radiation and chemotherapy, under the care of Dr. Laura Kerbin, Dr. Ron Kersh, and Dr. Jim Lesnick.

Unfortunately, this disease and its treatment will prevent me from functioning as your primary oncologist/hematologist for an indefinite period of time. My wonderful and extremely capable colleagues at Peninsula Cancer Institute stand ready to see my patients and continue your care without interruption. So, please let them know whatever you need, and don't delay your medical care due to my absence.

As I have often told you, we are all in this together; the only difference is that I am now in the boat with you as a patient instead of as your doctor. As many of you may know, the prognosis for my illness is not good, but I had the same disease and prognosis over 40 years ago and beat it then. Many of you have also beaten serious illness, and you now serve as examples for me, with your courage, faith and love. Please know that you are never far from my thoughts and prayers.

I promise that I will follow doctors' orders and try to recover as soon as possible, as I once again take the journey of a patient on the long and winding road through cancer.

Stay strong, laugh a lot, and may God bless you.

Mark E. Ellis, MD

Dr. Mark Ellis passed away on April 3, 2010 at home surrounded by his loving family after a long battle with cancer. Mark Edward Ellis was born in Cambridge Massachusetts on August 7, 1950. He received his undergraduate degree in Microbiology at Wake Forest University, where he also met his wife, Lynn. After earning his MD from Bowman Gray School of Medicine at Wake Forest University where he was awarded the CB Deane Memorial Award for Excellence in Clinical Oncology, he completed his Internal Medicine Residency at North Carolina Baptist Hospital in Winston-Salem, NC. He completed his Fellowship in Hematology and Oncology at Walter Reed Army Medical Center in Washington, DC where he earned the Erskine B. Graves Award for outstanding Fellow. While serving his country in the USAF for 8 years, he was awarded the Instructor of the Year as a staff oncologist at David Grant USAF Medical Center at Travis AFB in California.

Making his home in Williamsburg in 1989, he dedicated his life as an oncologist and hematologist to caring for cancer patients in Williamsburg and the surrounding peninsula as well as Gloucester and the Middle Peninsula. He was instrumental in bringing radiation therapy to Williamsburg in 1996 and served as the 1995 Dept of Medicine and 1997 Chief of Medical Staff at Williamsburg Community Hospital. His dedication to the community and to his patients earned him many service awards during his career, among them, the Sharon H. Kohlenberg Healthcare Service Award from the Virginia Breast Cancer Foundation, and the Health Care Hero Award presented by the Williamsburg Community Health Foundation. He served on and chaired numerous Boards during his tenure, including the Williamsburg VA unit of the American Cancer Society Board of Directors, the Virginia Branch of the Leukemia Society Board of Directors, Hospice House and Support Care of Williamsburg Board of Directors, Williamsburg Community Hospital Board of Directors, Williamsburg Community Health Foundation Board of Directors, and the Williamsburg Radiation Therapy Center Board of Directors.

He championed the cause of bringing Doctors' Hospital to Williamsburg, and he was honored to serve as the Chairman of the Advisory Board for Doctors Hospital. Since 2004, he served as the Medical Director for the Riverside Cancer Program. As the Founder and Managing Physician of Riverside's Peninsula Cancer Institute in 2004, he successfully established an oncology practice that achieved his vision of holistic care through an integrative approach to cancer care, incorporating massage therapy, nutritional counseling, music therapy, pet therapy, family services, and patient education with standard chemotherapies and clinical trials. Despite his long list of accomplishments in his career, the favorite part of his practice as described by him over the years was, "the time spent within the four walls of the rooms with my patients."

Outside of the world of medicine, Mark was a member of the Williamsburg United Methodist Church for 21 years and a generous supporter of numerous community organizations. Known as an avid sports fan, especially regarding the Demon Deacons of Wake Forest, he was a very generous supporter of both the university and its athletic programs and could be found on the front row of nearly all the WFU home basketball games and in his sky box at all the home football games. An accomplished musician on the guitar, he loved music, especially the Beatles. Always humbled by the love bestowed upon him by his patients, his staff, and the community, he will long be remembered as a wonderful compassionate doctor, as well as a loving husband and father with a warm sense of humor, and he will be loved and respected forever by his family. He is survived by his wife, Lynn and grown children, Lisa Ellis Rosler, Mark Edward Ellis, Jr., Robert Christopher Ellis, brother Stephen F. Ellis, and parents, Charles and Jeanne Ellis.

A public celebration of his life memorial service will be held at the Williamsburg United Methodist Church located at 500 Jamestown Road in Williamsburg on Friday, April 9, at 11AM.

In lieu of flowers, Mark would be honored if donations were made to:
Cancer Care Services Endowment Fund which supports his vision of integrative cancer care at Riverside's Peninsula Cancer Institute. Checks may be made out to:

Cancer Care Services Endowment Fund and sent to:
The Riverside Health System Foundation
701 Town Center Drive, Suite 1000
Newport News, VA 23606-4286
Attention: Debbie Atkinson

References to Popular Music

"A Good Man Is Hard to Find," music and lyrics written by Eddie Green in 1918.

Beatles catalogue of music including: "Hey Jude," "Here Comes the Sun," "In My Life," "Rocky Raccoon," "Strawberry Fields Forever", music and lyrics by Lennon-McCartney, or Lennon, McCartney, Harrison, recorded by The Beatles, Sony ATV, LLC, Copyright 1984.

"Gloria," music and lyrics by Van Morrison in 1964, recorded by Shadows of Knight in 1966, Copyright 1964.

"House of the Rising Sun," old English folksong, author unknown, recorded by the Animals in 1964. Recording Copyright 1964.

"Hungry Heart," music and lyrics by Bruce Springsteen, recorded by Bruce Springsteen, Bruce Springsteen, Copyright 1980.

"I Can See Clearly Now," music and lyrics by Johnny Nash, Copyright 1972.

"Light My Fire," music and lyrics by the Doors, Copyright 1966.

"The Lion Sleeps Tonight," written in the 1920's by Solomon Linda in South Africa, recorded by the Tokens in 1961. Recording copyright 1961.

"MacArthur Park," music and lyrics by Jimmy Webb, recorded by Richard Harris, Copyright 1968.

"Piano Man," music and lyrics by Billy Joel, recorded by Billy Joel, Columbia Broadcasting System, Inc., Sony BMG Music Entertainment, Copyright 1973.

References to Media

All My Children, television soap opera created by Agnes Nixox, aired on ABC 1970 to 2011, Copyright 1970.

All Over Town, play written by Murray Schisgal, published byDramatists Play Service,Inc., Copyright unpublished 1972, Copyright published 1975.

Annie, musical film directed by John Huston, adaptation of the 1977 Broadway play based on the Little Orphan Annie comic strip by Harold Gray, RCA Columbia Pictures, Home video Copyright 1983.

Auggie Doggie television cartoon, written by Michael Maltese 1959-1961, directed by Hanna Barbera, Hanna Barbera, Copyright 1940.

The Empire Strikes Back, created by George Lucas, directed by Irvin Kershner, Universal Pictures, Copyright 1980.

Ghost, film directed by Jerry Zucker, written by Bruce Joel Rubin, Paramount Pictures, Copyright 1990.

Hello Dolly, musical film directed by Gene Kelly, based on Broadway musical production in 1964 by David Merrick, based on book, *The Merchant of Yonkers* by Thornton Wilder, Twentieth Century Fox, Copyright 1969.

Jaws, film directed by Stephen Spielberg based on the novel *Jaws* by Peter Benchley, Universal Pictures, Copyright 1975.

Mickey and the Beanstalk, animated film directed by Walt Disney based on the English fairytale *Jack and the Beanstalk*, RKO Radio pictures, Copyright 1947.

Norman Rockwell Picture of Doctor and Doll, March 29, 1929 cover of the Saturday Evening Post, Copyright 1929.

Our Gang, Little Rascals, Hal Roach Studios 1927,sold to MGM 1938, Copyright 1938.

Prince Valiant newspaper comic strip, by Hal Foster, King Features Syndicate, Copyright 1937.

Return of the Jedi, created by George Lucas, directed by Richard Marquand, Universal Pictures, Copyright 1983.

"Snoopy," character from *Peanuts,* newspaper comic strip by Charles Schulz, United Feature Syndicate, Copyright 1950.

Star Wars, created and directed by George Lucas, Universal Pictures, Copyright 1977.

Wizard of Oz, film directed by Victor Fleming, based on the novel *The Wonderful Wizard of Oz* written by L. Frank Baum in 1900, MGM, Copyright 1939.

BOOK REFERENCES

Gray Matter. Bowman Gray's annual yearbook. *Gray Matter*, 1975.

Eisenmann, Charles P. *The Better Dog: The Educated Dog.* Eisenmann, 1976.

Eisenmann, Charles P. *Stop, Sit and Think.* Eisenmann, 1975.

Fitzpatrick, Thomas B. "Malignant Melanoma." In *Harrison's Principles of Internal Medicine*, seventh edition, edited by T. R. Harrison, Wintrobe, Thorn, Adams, Braunwald, Isselbacher, Petersdorf, 2026. McGraw-Hill, New York, NY, 1974.

Grant, J.C. Boileau. *Grant's Atlas of Anatomy*, sixth edition. Williams and Wilkens, Baltimore, MD, 1972.

Morris, Jeannie. *Brian Piccolo.* Rand McNally, 1971.

ACKNOWLEDGMENTS

I would like to thank my family readers: Lisa Ellis, Mark Ellis Jr., Robert Ellis, Steve Ellis, and Ann Hamilton for their critique, contributions, ideas, and encouragement.

I would like to thank Tyler Middleton, Esq. for her expert legal advice and friendship, my editors for their expert editorial critique and advice, and the Wickham's Grant Ladies' Book Club of Williamsburg for the early book review and wonderful accolade.

BOOK CLUB QUESTIONS

HUMANITY OF MEDICINE

1. Why is this book titled "The Humanity of Medicine?"
   a. What did Mark mean when he said he was struck by "the humanity of medicine?"
   b. What do you think the author means by the phrase, "humanity of medicine?"
   c. What does "humanity of medicine" mean to you?

2. What kind of book is this book? Is it a simple biography? Is it a love story? Is it a memoir?

3. What characteristics do you see in Mark? Is he likeable as portrayed in the book?

4. What characteristics do you see in Lynn? Is she likeable?

5. What themes can you identify in this book?
   a. Themes in Mark's life: (music, hope, cosmic signs, cancer, roads/paths)
   b. Themes in Mark and Lynn's life together.
   c. Themes in Medicine in general: (changes in standard of care, changes from general practitioners to specialists, research advances in cancer outcomes)

6. Other than specific dates, can you cite examples in the text that give clues as to the decade in which events are unfolding?

7. What obstacles did Mark have to overcome related to his cancer?

a. Were any of those obstacles surprising to you?

8. Were there any obstacles Mark had to overcome not related to his cancer?

9. How does Mark feel about cosmic signs?

10. How does Lynn feel about cosmic signs?

11. Do you believe in cosmic signs?

12. How do Mark and Lynn differ?

13. Can cancer be an epiphany? How unique is having an epiphany that keeps one focused and centered for an entire lifetime?

14. What do the Beatles mean to Mark? What does music in general mean to Mark?

15. Did *Hey Jude* identify an existing theme in Mark's life, or did it give him a theme for his life?

16. Is there any special music that means something to you? Is there a specific piece of music that has added so much meaning to your life that it has become a theme of your life?

17. How does Mark view himself according to this book?

18. How does Lynn view him?

19. Can you see any changes in Mark evolving throughout his journey?

20. How does Lynn view herself according to the book?

21. How does Mark view her?

22. How does she change during the journey?

23. Is there any social commentary regarding medicine in general?

24. How is the military system of the delivery of healthcare viewed by Mark in the book? Lynn? Why? Do you agree?

25. Do you think Mark or Lynn viewed socialized medicine as a bad thing or a good thing?

26. Is any form of spirituality expressed in the book? Can you cite examples?

27. What do you think cured Mark's cancer as a young man? To what do you think Mark attributed his cure?

28. Do you like where and how the author chose to end the book?

29. Why do you think the author ended the book upon the arrival to Williamsburg and dealt with the career years only in epilogue in general terms?

30. Did the ending make you want to know more specifics about his career years?

31. Can one have a brilliant career in a small geographic region? What defines a visionary?

32. Is it necessarily a bad or sad circumstance to die before having or taking the opportunity to retire?

33. Did you get a sense of what it was like to go through medical school, residency, fellowship etc?

34. Did you get a sense of what it is like to live with a "doctor in the house" as a family? To live with a cancer doctor in the house?

35. What is the predominant emotion you as the reader are left feeling after reading the book?

36. Would a young person feel inspired after reading this book?

37. What is the most surprising aspect of this story to you?

38. What is your favorite story in the book?

39. What is the best thing about the book?

40. What is the worst thing about the book?